Between Literature and Science
Poe, Lem, and Explorations in Aesthetics,
Cognitive Science, and Literary Knowledge

In *Between Literature and Science* Peter Swirski examines the true intellectual scope of Edgar Allan Poe and Stanislaw Lem. Using a genuinely interdisciplinary approach he shows that they propose far-reaching hypotheses in aesthetics, epistemology, cognitive science, philosophy of science, literary studies, and pragmatics as well as in cosmology, artificial intelligence, and futurology. Swirski argues that previous studies of their science fiction works, in neglecting these broader philosophical and scientific ambitions, have misrepresented Poe and Lem's artistic achievements.

Through close analysis of *Eureka* and *The Purloined Letter*, Swirski evaluates Poe's epistemological theses in the light of contemporary philosophy of science and presents literary interpretation as a cooperative game played by the author and reader, thereby illuminating how we read fiction. The analysis of Poe's little-studied *Eureka* provides the basis for his discussion of Lem's critique of scientific reductionism and futurological forecasts. Drawing on his own interviews with Lem as well as analysis of his works, Swirski considers the author's scenarios involving computers capable of creative acts and discusses their socio-cultural implications. His analysis leads to bold arguments about the nature of literature and its relation to a broad range of other disciplines.

PETER SWIRSKI is a lecturer in the Department of English at the University of Toronto.

BETWEEN LITERATURE AND SCIENCE

Poe, Lem, and Explorations
in Aesthetics, Cognitive Science,
and Literary Knowledge

Peter Swirski

Liverpool University Press

© McGill-Queen's University Press 2000
ISBN 0-85323-896-0 (cloth)
ISBN 0-85323-906-1 (paper)

Legal deposit second quarter 2000
Bibliothèque nationale du Québec

Printed in Canada on acid-free paper

Published simultaneously in the European Union
by Liverpool University Press

This book has been published with the help of a grant from the
Humanities and Social Sciences Federation of Canada, using funds
provided by the Social Sciences and Humanities Research Council
of Canada.

McGill-Queen's University Press acknowledges the financial support of
the Government of Canada through the Book Publishing Industry
Development Program (BPIDP) for its activities. We also acknowledge the
support of the Canada Council for the Arts for our publishing program.

British Library Cataloguing in Publication Data

A British Library CIP record is available

This book was typeset by Caractéra inc.
in 10/12 Minion.

This book is dedicated to
Gregory, Irini, Ginette, Paisley, Sarah, Peter,
Chris, Craig, Jeff, Jon, Phyllis, Philip, Jerry,
Brad, Raine, Greig, and others

Contents

Introduction

And whatever pains these researches may cost us,
we may think ourselves sufficiently rewarded,
not only in point of profit but of pleasure, if,
by that means, we can make any addition to our
stock of knowledge in subjects of such unspeak-
able importance.

David Hume,
An Inquiry Concerning Human Understanding

BETWEEN LITERATURE AND SCIENCE

It is not results but *methods* that can be trans-
ferred with profit from the sphere of the special
sciences to ... philosophy.

Bertrand Russell

There is a vast chunk of territory in the no-man's-land between fictional
flights of fancy and systematic studies pursued by the sciences. So at least
goes the accepted belief. The Two Cultures are supposed to be alienated from,
if not openly antagonistic towards, each other. On this view, literary scholars,
oblivious of the second law of thermodynamics and other synecdoches of
science, live in the self-contained kingdom of fancy and make-believe. Mean-
while, scientists, ignorant of the other cultural icon, Shakespeare's sonnets,
inhabit the epistemic temple of truth and knowledge into which writers and
critics never stray, unless by accident or folly.

As with every cliché, this one has some truth in it, but, as with every cliché,
the reality is both more complex and more interesting. To begin, the chunk
of territory between literature and science is not so vast as has been maintained by some philosophers of science (e.g., Hempel) or literature (e.g.,

Ingarden). Michel Pierssens is only one among many scholars who have in recent years painstakingly documented that literature "thinks" and "acts" in a manner comparable to other disciplines, the human sciences and philosophy among them.[1] Even more importantly, there are numerous writers of fiction who have regularly ventured into the scientific Holy Land, building epistemic bridges along the way. Their works bear proof of the cognitive value of such "transgressions" and belie the opposition between the literary and the scientific modes of inquiry.[2]

Only narrow ideological and philosophical commitments could have led some scholars to deny literature its cognitive power, with nihilistic claims that "literature in our time [is] essentially impossible" (Jameson 158). There are countless instances in the history of belles lettres, some recorded in Grant McColley's pioneering *Literature and Science* (1940), to prove that literary fictions conduct their own form of inquiry. Their "field-specific" strategy, as we may call it, takes the form of original hypotheses, fictional thought-experiments, and narrative modelling.[3] To anyone who reads literature, rather than what has been written about it in the last thirty years, it is clear that fiction has always faithfully carried out its cognitive function. The nature of this function of knowing the world and bringing it to justice has, of course, evolved over the ages, adapting to the complex and changing times. But despite recent accusations of narrative autarky or outright impotence, writers of fiction have never surrendered their cognitive aspirations, even while pursuing artistic and aesthetic goals.

In "Narrative and Chaos" (1992) Alex Argyros rightly points out that in the contemporary world, literature can play the much-needed roles of a cultural data bank and a narrative modelling laboratory. Literary fictions are, in his words, an inexhaustible source of hypotheses "about the nature of an existing slice of reality or about the potential consequences of certain variations on a model of the world" (667). Whether written to inform, edify, or entertain, literary works harbour a great variety of hypotheses about the world: tacit and overt, particular and general, testable and not, field-specific and interdisciplinary, and so on. And the demonstrable philosophical and social-scientific payoffs of such fictional thought experiments offer a potent incentive to study writers who throw literary bridges over to the scientific mainland. Indeed, as I show in this book, in some cases such bridges have been much stronger, and have existed for much longer, than many of us would suspect.

EDGAR ALLAN POE AND STANISLAW LEM

I am he that aspired to KNOW, and thou?
Elizabeth Barrett Browning

Edgar Allan Poe and Stanislaw Lem are read, written about, and celebrated the world over.[4] Their works have sold dozens of millions of copies, attracting scores of translations. Many have been turned into successful motion pictures, both in Europe and in America. There have been hundreds, if not thousands, of critical books and articles written on Poe and Lem in all the major, and dozens of minor, languages of the world. And yet, this literary recognition has generated remarkably little critical commentary on Poe's and Lem's cognitive ambitions. But is it possible to appreciate their works in full without taking these cognitive ambitions into account? The fact is that in their fictions and nonfictions Poe and Lem debate concrete hypotheses in a number of fields of inquiry, including pragmatics, epistemology, cosmology, philosophy of science, the cognitive sciences, and even futurology.

For example, in one of his most celebrated tales Poe isolates and identifies key strategic mechanisms that lie behind a staggering range of social interactions. His narrative vehicle is deceptively simple: a master detective and a master criminal locked in a labyrinthine contest of wits. In another story Poe pinpoints and illustrates some of the pragmatic factors involved in our interpretations of literary fictions. He accomplishes this by means of a clever and remarkably effective strategy: he renders the achievements of nineteenth-century technology and science in the idiom of an ancient Arabian tale. Elsewhere, in what surely remains his most ambitious endeavour, he undertakes a formal critique of the way philosophers and scientists have pursued inquiry since the ancient Greeks. Ahead of his times, Poe recognizes the shortcomings of traditional epistemology and tries to replace it with a system of a decidedly more poetic and aesthetic flavour. Never one to stop half-way, he fuses this project with an elaborate cosmological hypothesis on the nature, history, and ultimate fate of the entire material and spiritual universe. The agreement among literary and cultural critics that among all nineteenth-century writers Poe was the most interested in and most influenced by science and philosophy is amply confirmed by his writings, which on more than one occasion cross over from imaginative fiction to philosophy.

If Poe's writings may be a suitable literary barometer of the role that science and philosophy played in nineteenth-century society, in the twentieth century this function has been taken over almost single-handedly by Stanislaw Lem. There can be no doubt about the centrality of philosophical and scientific thought in Lem's writings. As a matter of fact, the author of *Solaris, The Invincible, His Master's Voice, A Perfect Vacuum, Imaginary Magnitude, Peace on Earth,* and *Fiasco* (to name only a few of his landmark fictions) stands apart from his contemporaries in his systematic address to the interdisciplinary court of appeal.

Thus, in one of his key works Lem investigates why a crew of scientists equipped with the best military and scientific technology should falter in the

xii Introduction

face of a swarm of miniature inanimate crystals. The author illustrates his thesis about the perils of unchecked reductionism in inquiry by imagining an instrumental Goliath, crippled by a conceptually elusive opponent. In another of his recent fictions we encounter a new generation of super-computers, machines able to create, think, write, and cultivate ideas well beyond the grasp of human minds. Lem's social and cultural predictions centre here around the modern-day Golem – the writing and thinking computer. His futurological scenario is especially intriguing in its literary and meta-literary ramifications, leading back to the question, Can such things ever come to pass? Rigorous and complex enough to sustain genera-tions of commentators, these hypotheses are the closest any best-selling fiction writer has come to giving us a philosophy of the future.[5]

Transcending the limits of belles lettres, Poe and Lem contribute in their works to the time-honoured dialogue between the literary, philosophical, and scientific cultures. A critical approach to either writer that ignores this fact opens itself to the charge of misrepresenting their artistic goals and aspira-tions. Only a genuinely interdisciplinary analysis, sympathetic to the speculative freedom of literary fiction and the analytic rigour of science, offers a way to capture the unique character of their writings. Defining, justifying, and carrying out such an interdisciplinary study is the goal of my book.

In general, my approach is premised on two related epistemological assumptions. The first is that literary fictions can be potent and exciting instruments of knowledge. The second is that this knowledge can be profit-ably evaluated in terms of interdisciplinary criteria.[6] It is one thing, of course, to approach Poe's and Lem's writings as works of art, in which case we should be attuned to the aesthetic attributes within the art-historical contexts in which such works were produced. It is another to read them in the context of current social-scientific theories and models, with an eye to the cognitive payoffs such readings may yield. Discussing, critiquing, and refining many of the hypotheses articulated in Poe's and Lem's writings, this book is intended to be primarily an instance of the latter approach. Interestingly, however, it can be shown that in the case of either writer a critic can simultaneously pursue *both* goals. As I will argue, this is so because the expression of philosophic and scientific content often figures among their successfully realized *artistic* intentions.

POE: A PHILOSOPHER WITH A CAUSE

Procrustes, you will remember, stretched or
chopped down his guests to fit the bed he had
constructed. But perhaps you have not heard the
rest of the story. He measured them up before
they left the next morning, and wrote a learned

paper "On the Uniformity of Stature of Travellers"
for the Anthropological Society of Attica.

Arthur Eddington

My investigation of the two writers' forays into the no-man's-land between
literature and science fills a noticeable hole in Poe and Lem studies. Regret-
tably, literary scholarship makes often only token attempts to address
theories and hypotheses that clearly demand interdisciplinary study. A good
case in point may be the disciplinary preoccupation with Poe's literary
formalism, typically at the expense of the philosophical context in which he
wrote. One result of such a critical orientation has been a remarkable lack
of attention to Poe's cognitive ambitions.

Some of his works are especially ill-suited to fit the disciplinary "this is
only fiction" straitjacket. Among these, the exemplary case must be *Eureka*,
Poe's mesmerizing work in scientific philosophy, which many take to be the
greatest undertaking of his entire career. These days, when not dismissed as
a hoax (e.g., by G.R. Thompson), *Eureka* is used by critics to synthesize all
of Poe's writings (i.e., his prose fiction, poetry, philosophy, and criticism) by
means of the common denominator thought to be found in the essay. This
trend to see Poe's Discovery as just another "Essay on Criticism" – identifiable already in Allen Tate's *Man of Letters in the Modern World* (1955) –
persists in the face of evidence that *Eureka* had been conceived as a serious
epistemological and cosmological project. As a result of such disciplinary
bias, Poe's elaborate treatise in philosophy and cosmology is interpreted
mainly as a cryptic restatement of his poetic principles. These are taken to
shed light on his specific works, general themes, or even on his entire œuvre
– but not on anything else.

Typically, then, Geoffrey Rans's *Edgar Allan Poe* (1965) regards *Eureka* as
little more than the fusion of "Poe's sense of universal harmony and symmetry with his aesthetic" (37). In a similar vein, Louis Broussard's *The
Measure of Poe* (1969) looks for a thematic and conceptual unity in Poe's
writings, based on principles derived from *Eureka*. Broussard views the essay
chiefly as a primer on literary theory since, in his opinion, "what Poe wrote
in *Eureka* he had been saying all along, in his poems and his short stories
and, to some extent, in his criticism also" (49). David Hoffman continues
the trend in *Poe Poe Poe Poe Poe Poe Poe* (1972), openly hailing *Eureka* as
little more than "a master code-breaker to Poe's *œuvre*" (279). Completing
the picture, Mabbott's (1978) fine edition of Poe's collected works does not
include *Eureka* at all, and the recent studies by Symons (1978), Silverman
(1991), or Meyers (1992) add little new to the case. In a summary of this
situation, Ketterer wrote in 1979, "In *Eureka*, published in 1848, Poe claims
to have discovered the secret mechanics of the universe, and many of his
critics believe they have discovered a key to his writings" (255).

To the scholars in question the epistemological and cosmological theories that Poe developed with such meticulous care are of negligible consequence. Not surprisingly, once *Eureka* has been reduced to a symbolic decoder of Poe's other writings, it receives little attention as an independent work. One of my critical aims is to redress this imbalance and throw a fresh light on Poe's literary and extra-literary achievements by interpreting the essay in a manner that follows his creative intentions. In other words, I approach *Eureka* as a systematic collection of hypotheses that culminates its author's ambitious, even if occasionally flawed, philosophical investigations.

Eureka is an intellectual tour de force of a philosopher and a Romantic man of letters who tries to hammer out a not always easy alliance with nineteenth-century science. The first part of the treatise outlines Poe's new epistemology, grounded in poetic intuition, and the second elaborates what was to be an empirically sound cosmogonic theory. Both goals are of great importance, not only to literature but also potentially to philosophy, or even science. Poe's principle of poetic ratiocination is both an original contribution to and a radical reinterpretation of standard epistemological theory. The precocity of Poe's design (overlooked by literary critics) is evident: his turn away from the "received model" of inquiry has been mirrored by recent developments in the philosophy of science. The long-brewing dissatisfaction with the inflexible standards of logical positivism has, in fact, led to a significant retrenching of the field in ways that parallel Poe's early criticisms.

It is at once regrettable and remarkable that among the welter of Poe criticism there are no studies that discuss these striking correspondences. This book is designed to fill this conspicuous gap. In chapter 2 I examine the contemporary revolution in the philosophy of science in light of Poe's epistemological revisions and evaluate the soundness of his criticisms. In chapter 3 I analyze Poe's cosmological hypothesis, clearly one of the few literary attempts ever to theorize systematically on an empirically testable domain. Were *Eureka* to deliver on either of Poe's claims, it would secure its lasting importance not only as a speculative centrepiece of his literary legacy but as an epistemic document of immense originality and value. The fact that Poe did not fully succeed in realizing his vast cognitive ambitions – as I will demonstrate – does not mean that his bold endeavour should remain unexamined and unacknowledged.

Before this full-scale analysis of *Eureka* it will be useful, however, to set the stage with a look at some of Poe's shorter works. For this reason, in chapter 1 I study a couple of Poe's short stories, the justly famous "Purloined Letter" and the unjustly unfamous "Thousand-and-Second Tale of Scheherazade." Both model with striking acuity the type of problems studied by contemporary writers in aesthetics, enhancing Poe's reputation as a critic and philosopher. "The Purloined Letter," for example, is a source of penetrating insights into the nature of gaming and strategic interpersonal interactions. Poe's intuitive grasp of the nuance of these situations also compares favourably with the recent models suggested by speech-act theory.

Drawing on his intuitions, I apply them to a couple of outstanding problems in aesthetics and literary studies. Specifically, in the first half of chapter 1 I will analyze the nature of the literary interpretive process as a cooperative game played by the author and the reader of a literary work. In the second half of chapter 1 I examine the role of pragmatic factors in the interpretation of literary works. Taking a cue from "The Thousand-and-Second Tale of Scheherazade," I look at the variables that come into play when we read fictions, especially the variables pertaining to the problem of truth in fiction. Poe's tale illuminates the impact of pragmatic considerations on interpreting literary works and anticipates some of the contemporary arguments in aesthetics on that subject.

Although much has been written on Poe's works, and especially on "The Purloined Letter," my interdisciplinary approach departs dramatically from previous formalist or deconstructive readings. Most importantly, it contributes to the appreciation of the philosophical aspects of Poe's writings and to the recognition of his overall cognitive aims, and thus to Poe criticism at large. An additional payoff of such interdisciplinary analysis is the strong evidence it provides for upgrading Poe's reputation as a critic and philosopher, notwithstanding the failure of some of his specific arguments. Moreover, my book offers detailed analyses of Poe's marginalized works, *Eureka* and "The Thousand-and-Second Tale of Scheherazade," and recontextualizes the canonical "Purloined Letter," until now effectively purloined by various poststructuralist writers on the subject.[7] Finally, as will become apparent in the course of my discussions, Poe's writings yield theoretic insights and systematic arguments that can guide today's research in profitable directions.

LEM: A PHILOSOPHER OF THE FUTURE

> Lem has had a lifelong interest in the questions
> we raise in this book. His intuitive and literary
> approach perhaps does a better job of convincing
> readers to his views than any hard-nosed scientific
> article or arcanely reasoned philosophical paper
> might do.
>
>   Douglas R. Hofstadter

Much as with Poe, the conspicuous fact about interdisciplinary approaches to Stanislaw Lem is their conspicuous absence. Lem's complex and diverse œuvre has been interpreted in the light of various critical doctrines: psychoanalytic, structuralist, deconstructive, Marxist, and so on. However, as one

of the more thoughtful scholars observed in a special 1986 Lem issue of
Science-Fiction Studies, the time has come for critics "to adapt their
approaches to his concepts, which are rather alien to most formally and polit-
ically-minded literary theorists." A little further on, Istvan Csicsery-Ronay Jr
explicitly urged literary scholars to work with "ideas compatible with (perhaps even 'approved by') Lem's own ideas and frames of reference" (236).[8]

Notwithstanding this timely appeal, few Anglo-American scholars have as
yet taken advantage of Lem's interdisciplinary ideas and frames of reference.[9]
In fact, the adage about the two cultures captures the marked differences in
approach to Lem's works, indexed by the section of academia in which they
are pursued. Among philosophers and (social) scientists his writings are
hotly debated and studied as potential groundwork for research programs.
To take only one example, the interest in Lem's *Golem XIV* (1981) has already
led to a special workshop at INSTRAT, an interdisciplinary symposium held
under the auspices of the Free University of Berlin.[10] The debates over *Golem*
and Lem's cyber-evolutionary hypotheses have involved philosophers, sociologists, and linguists, as well as computer and cognitive scientists.

The situation is quite different in literary studies, which has more or less
chosen to pass over the interdisciplinary content in Lem's writings. One is,
of course, led to wonder why this should be so, and a partial answer is
suggested by Michael Kandel's witty "Lem in Review (June 2238)." The
reviewer does not conceal the fact that Lem's conceptual frames of reference
are staggering in their proportions. It would take a polymath equal to Lem
himself to engage critically his hypotheses and scenarios, which range over
cybernetics, the theory of automata, information and game theories, prob-
abilistics, linguistics, literary studies, aesthetics, philosophy of science,
computer science, molecular biology, genetics, cosmology, and so forth. This
embarras de richesses may partly explain why so few literary scholars to date
have penetrated these conceptual frameworks in a systematic way.

Lem has openly affirmed on numerous occasions that he regards many of
his works simply as "models of certain situations – alternatively, as situations
that are models of the problems most interesting to me" (249). One of his
most unequivocal testimonials to the importance of cognition in literature
came up during our interview in 1994.[11] Comparing "interdisciplinary inquiries from the borderline of philosophy of science and literature" with typically
literary studies, the writer concluded, "The former approach is certainly
more fruitful" (117). If in my previous analyses of Lem's works I focused on
such cognitive claims, it was because they lie at the *artistic* centre of his
creativity.[12] The present book builds on this approach by opening up an
interdisciplinary dialogue with Lem and his hypotheses.

For this reason, in chapter 4 I examine *The Invincible* (1964), a novel from
the middle of Lem's "golden phase." This short, action-packed, and
immensely readable book serves Lem as a narrative model of reductionist

bias in inquiry. My investigation of his theses will build on the preceding discussion of Poe's *Eureka*, and especially the critique of logical positivism developed in chapter 2. Lem's concerns are underwritten by a similar kind of distrust of positivistic standards of inquiry. Grounded in deductive logic and thus presumed valid for all contexts and situations, positivist tenets falter in the face of a categorically novel phenomenon modelled in *The Invincible* – cybernetic evolution. Although these conclusions and their subject have profound ramifications for the humanities in general and literary studies in particular, one would look in vain for a debate on these issues in contemporary scholarship. Chapter 4 plays thus a double role: it is a first-time literary and interdisciplinary analysis of a key work in Lem's opus, and an introduction to the quiet revolution that has been sweeping epistemology in recent years.

Chapter 5 takes as its point of departure one of Lem's most recent and provocative meta-fictions, "A History of Bitic Literature" (1984).[13] Here I take a detailed look at Lem's bold futurological scenario, which forecasts computers capable of creative behaviour, and notably of writing fiction. I begin with a critique of Lem's key concept of authorship in the context of the computer and follow with an analysis of a host of attendant issues, such as computer thinking, learning, and autonomy. All these subjects lead in one way or another to the notorious Turing test, suggested in 1950 by the British mathematician Alan M. Turing as a means of resolving whether a computing machine can think. Today, almost half a century later and despite staggering strides in the computer sciences, the test is still the focus of intense debate and controversy. For these reasons chapter 5 includes a careful analysis of Turing's proposals, as well as some postulates of my own regarding the efficacy and implementation of the test.

Chapter 6 is devoted to the quasi-futurological scenario outlined in "A History of Bitic Literature," particularly to the sociocultural implications of the envisioned computer revolution. I trace with special interest the potential reaction of the academic community, and especially of departments of literature, to the fact that machines may one day assume at least some of the creative functions that today still belong exclusively to human beings. My discussion closes with a look at present-day computing trends and forecasts to assess whether the future according to Lem, featuring "computhors" and "biterature," can indeed become reality.

THE NEW INTERDISCIPLINARITY

Despite the current excitement about it,
interdisciplinarity is not new in criticism;
it appears in the oldest critical texts we possess.
                                             Richard Levin

This book is a product of my conviction that a cognitive, research-oriented approach is not only a legitimate but often a preferred interpretive strategy vis-à-vis a significant number of literary fictions. The growing interest in crossing disciplinary borders in search of a better perspective from which to appreciate works of literature makes undertakings like the present one even more timely. This is far from claiming, of course, that such an approach is, or ought to be, the only one in any critic's repertoire. As I have argued elsewhere, goals of literary scholarship are many, and as such must inevitably be reflected in the plurality of critical tools and methods.[14] It goes without saying that an interdisciplinary approach is only one among many interpretive strategies open to students and professors of literature. It is, however, an important and – insofar as one can generalize on its status in the present critical environment – a neglected one.

It is regrettable that many of today's critical and scholarly writings suffer from a lack of genuinely interdisciplinary methodology, attuned to the best in social scientific and philosophical research. It is even more regrettable that few studies have lucidly and persuasively articulated the theoretical premises behind such a research orientation. Pursuing interdisciplinary research in a way that could contribute *both* to literary studies and to the research programs outside it is a difficult task, but one fraught with potential rewards. Fortunately, as documented in the recent (1996) PMLA forum, the questions and challenges surrounding interdisciplinarity across the literary-critical spectrum are slowly finding a receptive ear in the profession.

Appearing at a crossroads in the history of literary studies as a *research* discipline, the present book tries to set such a rigorous example for its disciplinary and interdisciplinary future. It integrates literary theory and practice with the best and most recent research in aesthetics, pragmatics, philosophy of science, and philosophy of mind and uses this framework to make significant contributions to Poe and Lem criticism. The detailed analyses of some of the most acclaimed and ambitious works by these writers are a source of concrete hypotheses in literary theory, philosophy of literature, pragmatics, and the cognitive sciences. More generally, this book is designed to introduce readers, students, and scholars of literature to an interdisciplinary body of knowledge that extends to many of the topics with which they are normally concerned. I hope that it will compel all of us to take a closer look at this rich storehouse of ideas that we call literature through the prism of knowledge in which all disciplinary colours blend into one.

Between Literature and Science

CHAPTER ONE

The Pragmatic Side of Aesthetics

> They [pragmatic writers] only ask what we mean
> by truth, and they find the answer more intricate
> than previous philosophers, with their relatively
> simple minds, had suspected.
>> William James, *Pragmatism and Truth*

Some of Poe's most interesting philosophical insights are in the fields of pragmatics and aesthetics. As a professional editor, critic, and reviewer, Poe was attuned to the pragmatic side of literary transactions. It was likely this experience that helped him write so successfully on matters involving strategy and interdependence in "The Purloined Letter." Although the pragmatic context is equally interesting in "The Thousand-and-Second Tale of Scheherazade," there his emphasis shifts towards more typically literary, aesthetic, and interpretive concerns. The story is Poe's primer on the pragmatics of interpretation, making an appreciable contribution to the understanding of the problem of "truth in fiction."

THE SERIOUS BUSINESS OF PLAYING GAMES

> Decision theory, like any other theory, considers
> models of situations rather than situations in
> all their complexities and ramifications.
>> Anatol Rapoport

"The Purloined Letter" opens in the Paris apartment of C. Auguste Dupin, a detective and eccentric, in whose library the narrator and Dupin meet Monsieur G., the prefect of the municipal *gendarmerie*. The Paris police are working on a singular case, for the solution to which G. hopes to enlist Dupin's powers of ratiocination. The matter concerns a theft of an incriminating letter from the boudoir of the queen. The individual who purloined it is known; in fact, his spectacular move was executed in the presence, and with the implicit consent, of the lady. The evil genius is Minister D– who, anticipating that the Queen would not cry "Thief" for fear of drawing attention to the contents of the letter, brazenly exploits the situation.

Informed of the police's failure to find the letter despite repeated searches of the thief's quarters, Dupin forms a hypothesis about its location. He reasons correctly that D–, anticipating the search of his premises, will try to "hide" the letter in the most conspicuous place. Under a minor pretext he pays a visit to the minister's apartment and indeed spots the stolen note in the letter rack. The detective arranges for another visit and, using a cleverly orchestrated ruse, purloins the letter himself. In its place he leaves a facsimile that, in its cryptic way, reveals to D– the identity of the person who has foiled his sinister plans.

"The Purloined Letter" is a source of some penetrating observations about a battle of intellects between a brilliant criminal and a brilliant detective. Poe captures the nature of this interaction in a way that naturally extends to a large class of contexts that have nothing to do with crime, or even conflict. In order to appreciate his skill and accuracy in modelling this type of situation, we need to compare it to the body of knowledge developed precisely to study human interactions. This interdisciplinary domain is the theory of games, better known today as game theory.[1]

What, in a nutshell, is game theory? It is a theory of decision making in circumstances involving more than a single agent. To better understand what is distinctive about it, we can begin with its close relative, decision theory. Decision theory, true to its name, is a mathematical theory for making best (optimal) choices. What is characteristic about it is that the outcome of the agent's decisions does not depend in any way on anybody else. The complete range of the decision maker's possible options, executed actions, and eventual results is determined entirely by his preferences and by states of nature.

In a sample situation you may be asked to divide a piece of cheesecake between yourself and another agent. Given your actual preferences – you love cheesecake and dislike the other person, who may happen to be your pesky younger brother – decision theory helps you map out the best course of rational action to secure the desired result (cut a bigger piece for yourself). So far this may seem simple, even trivial. Yet this type of reasoning becomes much more intractable when dealing with real life situations. People's preferences are often more complex and interdependent than in our example, their range of options is significantly greater, and their knowledge of the variables involved much less complete.

There is, however, another, categorically different source of complexity that overshadows all the others. Not coincidentally, it is also the single most important difference between decision theory and game theory. Consider again our piece of cheesecake. Given that your preferences are still the same, how would you divide it, knowing that your younger brother will choose the first piece? No matter how you feel about it, there seems to be only one rational course of action left: cut the cake into equal parts. Since your preference for cheesecake has not changed, obviously there must be a new and powerful factor at play in your considerations.

What is different then?

Only one thing: now you have to consider not only your own preferences and actions but also those of another agent who loves cheesecake as much as you do. If you simply followed your own preferences and cut one piece bigger than the other, it would no doubt end up in the hands and in the mouth of your pesky opponent in this game. Therefore, trying to get the best for yourself and at the same time to limit your brother's share, you will divide the cake evenly. In this way you will ensure the maximum gain for yourself and the minimum for him, given that your interests are diametrically opposed.[2]

FIGHTS, GAMES, AND DEBATES

Like chess players, world leaders in conflict
situations make carefully considered moves and
countermoves. But the outcomes are not always
what the players or onlookers expect; in particular,
it is sometimes hard to understand why players
choose conflict over cooperation.

Steven Brams

Let me restate the main points of the previous section in a slightly more precise manner. Game theory is a mathematical theory of strategy that aims to optimize the decision-making process in situations where the results of each agent's actions are, at least to some degree, interdependent. One may even say that game theory is a theory of making interdependent decisions.

The agents, or players, involved in a strategic encounter need not be individuals, so long as the similarity of their goals and preferences makes it possible to treat them as such. To get the analysis going, game theorists imagine rational players who seek better outcomes according to their preferences in view of the anticipated rational choices of other players in the game. A strategy describes a complete plan of action for a player for all possible contingencies that may arise during the course of the game. The actions executed by players, called *moves*, are taken independently, in the sense that the players are assumed not to be able to coordinate their decisions beforehand. However, as I said before, in another sense the player's decisions are *interdependent*, since each arrives at his decision given his anticipation of what the other(s) will do.

The spectrum of games in which we engage constantly throughout our lives stretches from total cooperation, on the one extreme, to total conflict, on the other, with the vast majority somewhere between the two.[3] The title of Anatol Rapoport's 1960 book, *Fights, Games and Debates*, uses properly evocative terms to describe the essence of these situations. For Rapoport, fights are zerosum situations where the players' interests are diametrically opposite. In debates their interests are identical, leaving only the task of finding the proper course of coordinating the players' moves. Games cover everything in between, from parlour games, political lobbying, atomic warfare planning, or constructing a fair voting system to choosing a mate, advertising movies, or even – as we will see – reading works of literature.

The more one realizes the interdisciplinary potential of game theory, the more one must appreciate it as much more than just another mathematical theory. One of its most attractive attributes is the ease with which it lends itself to applications across a staggering range of disciplines and contexts. Game theoretic models and strategies have been successfully applied in psychology, criminology, agriculture, political science, economics, sociology, military studies, advertising, jurisprudence, legislature, sports, biology, behavioural science, international relations, conflict resolution, accounting, and management, to name a few areas. This is why, in *Nuts and Bolts for the Social Sciences* (1989), Jon Elster describes game theory not as "a theory in the ordinary sense, but [as] the natural, indispensable framework for understanding human interaction" (28).

Seeing that game theory has proven its worth in so many disciplines, can it be employed in literary studies? On balance the answer must be positive. Although still uncommon, there have been several fruitful applications of game theory in the interpretation of literary fictions. Taking cue from Steven Brams's pioneering *Biblical Games*, the theory has been used to model and analyze fictional agents' actions, as well as the motives for and outcomes of these actions.[4] Clearly, game theory can be of great help in identifying purposeful connections between agents' actions and their intentional attitudes (beliefs, desires). It can help account for the strategic choices open to agents by exploring the links between their motives and actions and the plot. It can also address interpretive questions, such as whether the ordinary calculations of characters in fiction can explain at least some of their behaviour. As such, it may even assist in determining the optimum range of reception strategies for a given work.

On the other hand, attempts to extend game theory to literary pragmatics have been quite scarce.[5] Yet, as a theory of strategic interdependence, game theory should be of great value in the analysis of the reading process, viewed as a game between the author and the reader. It is important to note that in this context, "game" need not denote any form of playful or even deceptive behaviour. Clearly, not just Poe and the elaborate games (hoaxes) he often played with his contemporary audiences, but the interaction between *all* authors and *all* readers is open to this type of analysis. One reason to seek a precise game theoretic model of the reading process is the hope that it will lead to a deeper understanding of the complex variables that come into play. Before we can formulate such a model, we must, however, elaborate the nature of the process, especially the interdependence of the principal players. And here Poe turns out to be of considerable help.

A MODEL OF RECIPROCAL DEPENDENCE

> The more featureless and commonplace a crime
> is, the more difficult it is to bring home.
> > Arthur Conan Doyle

One of Poe's most popular fictions, "The Purloined Letter" provides a brilliant example of a two-person game characterized by a reciprocal awareness of the other party – essentially the situation in the reading process. One reason why Poe's tale is so interesting is that it foregrounds the analytical structure of the underlying conflict at the expense of the social and psychological background (what in game theory is sometimes referred to as the framing environment). Far from being a realistic narrative, with the psychological depth and veracity of its psychosocial framing, "The Purloined Letter" is a model of an intriguing interactive situation, stripped down to its narrative essentials.

Acclaimed for his portrayals of the darker reaches of the human psyche, here Poe sets out to analyze the essence of a reciprocal guessing game. This emphasis on the deep structure of the conflict gives the story its sparse analytic appearance. One would look in vain in "The Purloined Letter" for the psychological or pathological complexity of a Roderick Usher or even for an action-driven plot like that of *Arthur Gordon Pym*. Instead, the reader is presented with a parsimonious, logical structure of a game of cops and robbers.

The cast of dramatis personae is limited to four generic types: the arch-villain, the assiduous but inept officer of the law, the master detective, and the faithful sidekick.[6] Equally unrealistically, the central incident in which the crime is perpetrated is a result of a chain of credulity-defying coincidences. Not only is the queen reading an incriminating letter precisely at the moment when the king pays her an unannounced visit, not only is she unable to conceal the letter, not only does the king fail to catch anything amiss, not only does the malefactor D– elect to visit the royal boudoir at this opportune instance, not only does he immediately notice the envelope and recognize the handwriting, not only does he happen to be in possession of another look-alike letter, but, conceiving his Machiavellian plan on the spot, he executes it without a hitch, by switching the letters.

It is remarkable how even this brief scene offers a strong indication of how the interests and strategies of the players are interrelated and mutually anticipatory. In order to steal the letter from under the queen's very nose, D– must be relatively sure that he will not be apprehended (one could even say, app*red*handed) in the act. This knowledge can only be a result of his clever reasoning *about the queen's point of view*. It involves a careful analysis of her choices and their respective outcomes: (1) stop the thief, but reveal the contents of the fateful letter, and (2) consent to the theft but preserve the anonymity of the contents of the letter. The minister, having weighed the queen's likely preferences about these outcomes, makes the first move, revealing his strategy and committing himself to the course of action.

However, perhaps he is not risking that much, since the similarity of the letters effectively limits the queen's options. Were she to cry foul, seeking to punish the minister at the cost of compromising herself, the diabolical D– could always ascribe his behaviour to a guileless error. The queen's range of replies to D–'s opening move in this game of perfect (and possibly complete) information is thus severely restricted. In games of perfect information the players know the moves of the other players at each stage in the game. In games of complete information the players know each other's preferences, as well as the rules of play. In Poe's artful scenario, both players know exactly what is going on in the royal boudoir and can effectively reason what course of action (or in the queen's case, inaction) is open to the other. The lady dares not call attention to the theft, anticipating humiliation at no cost to D–. The minister, reproducing the queen's train of thought, anticipates her passivity and thus emboldened, proceeds to exploit it.

What makes the story so illuminating, in light both of game theory and of literary pragmatics, is the interdependence of both players' gaming behaviour. By interdependence (or reciprocity) I mean not only the need to consider the other player's moves but also the need to anticipate the other player's anticipation of one's own moves as well. In other words, reciprocal dependence turns the tables not just on the other player but on oneself as well. In "The Purloined Letter" Poe expresses it in terms of "the robber's knowledge of the loser's knowledge of the robber" (977).[7] Poe's awareness of the importance of the concept is evident: in the text, the formula is first stated by his narrator, only to be restated verbatim by Dupin two paragraphs later. In another example, when the prefect G. describes the ease with which he gains access to the malefactor's house and person, one begins to suspect that D– must have anticipated G.'s moves and was in fact playing into his hands. Dupin, who, by dint of his position in the detective game, needs to anticipate the minister's moves, understands this at once. He describes D– as "not altogether a fool" who "must have anticipated these waylayings, as a matter of course" (979).

This statement confirms the reciprocal relation between D– and Dupin, symbolically highlighted by the similarity of their D-displaying names (which echoes another famous Poe story, "William Wilson"). In order to outwit his opponent, Dupin must preempt his moves, by staying ahead of the antici-pated anticipation of his own (although, in the minister's eyes, his opponent is the Parisian *gendarmerie*). Thus Dupin properly interprets the prefect's apparent success: D– "could not have failed to anticipate – and events have proved that he did not fail to anticipate – the waylayings to which he was subjected," just as he "must have foreseen ... the secret investigations of his premises" (988).

RECOGNIZING INTENDED INTENTIONS

> Reciprocation among distantly related or unrelated
> individuals is the key to human society.
>   Edward O. Wilson

Modelling a strategically original game (in effect, creating one), Poe unerr-ingly focuses on the key elements of its underlying structure. As a matter of fact, "The Purloined Letter" introduces three different games: the zerosum "letter" game of perfect information between the Queen and Minister D–; the interpolated zerosum game of guessing marbles;[8] and the detective game involving D– and his august opponent, Dupin. The last one is not a game of perfect or complete information. The rules of the interaction, involving the available strategies, moves, and outcomes, are not known to the same degree by both participants. In fact, Dupin's concluding remarks reveal that D– is not even aware that the detective is his nemesis.

Games of imperfect information are important to us, since literary inter-pretation, in which the author and the reader are relatively free to adopt and adapt rules and conventions, is an example of such a game. Of even greater importance, however, is the final paragraph of the story, in which Poe reveals his intuitive grasp of the strategic nuance of such a game. Describing the content of the note that the detective leaves for the villain, Poe subtly shifts the interaction between Dupin and D– towards partial cooperation. Although in the text the change is almost imperceptible, there is nothing subtle about the dramatic change from the strictly competitive "letter" game. Poe's astuteness as a writer shows in grasping and accentuating the funda-mental difference between zerosum fights and non-zerosum games with an element of cooperation.

It is, of course, possible for the author and the reader to end up in an uncooperative game. The players' motives may be mixed or even, in extreme cases, competitive (e.g., due to envy, ignorance, deception, ludic consider-ations, or even, in the case of kitsch, a superior aesthetic perspective). When that happens, the reader/critic will ignore the textual and extratextual clues intended by the author – who makes the opening move in the game – to induce cooperation.[9] But by and large this kind of context must be considered atypical. Authors and readers are much more likely to interact in a manner that, while not always purely cooperative, is nevertheless cooperative to a significant degree.[10] (The first stage of this cooperation typically depends on grasping the story content; I will return to this problem during the discussion of truth in fiction).

What kind of process does Dupin go through while deciding on the contents of the note for D–? The detective clearly desires D– to "get the message," as it were. The process of choosing the precise text – analogous to a similar process in a writer of fiction – is again likely to be the result of a reciprocal anticipation. Note that Dupin's intentions are quite complex at this point. For one, he seems to wish not to disclose his identity outright, but he wants to convey enough information for the minister to guess it. At the same time, although it does not seem "altogether right to leave the interior blank – that would have been insulting" (993), Dupin does in fact want to signal his superiority to his enemy. Last but not least, he wishes to accomplish all of the above while making an oblique reference to "an evil turn" (993) that D– had done him in Vienna.

Intending his message to express all this, Dupin must also take into account its anticipated reading by the minister. Describing the detective's intentions for settling on his specific text, Poe depicts intentions that are intended to be recognized as having been intended to be recognized. This gives "The Purloined Letter" its remarkable strategic and pragmatic acuity.

SPEECH-ACT THEORY MEETS GAME THEORY

> When you follow two separate chains of thought,
> Watson, you will find some point of intersection
> which should approximate truth.
>   Arthur Conan Doyle

So far, I have formulated a number of not very systematic insights into the interactions between players involved in a reciprocal game, where the moves of one side are at least partly inflected by the anticipated moves of the other. I will now situate these intuitions in a broader context of communicative exchange. In my analysis of illocutionary acts and intentions I rely on the account given by Bach and Harnish, which, generally, incorporates the findings of other philosophers, notably Strawson and Searle (although their versions differ in specifics).

All speech-act theorists broadly agree on the type of intention involved in any distinctly illocutionary and communicative act. It was first described by Paul Grice in "Meaning," an influential paper from 1957.[11] Grice characterizes it as a reflexive intention, essentially of the type encountered during the discussion of reciprocity in "The Purloined Letter." In brief, a reflexive intention is one intended to be recognized as having been intended to be recognized. Thus an act of linguistic, and by extension literary, communication is taken to be successful if the "attitude the speaker expresses is identified by the hearer by means of recognizing the reflexive intention to express it" (Bach and Harnish xv).

This formulation is easily adaptable to the reading process. The author's intention to communicate with the reader by means of the literary work is identifiable by the latter as reflexive – intended to be recognized as intended to be recognized. When identifying the contents and attitudes conveyed by means of the work, both participants make use of Mutual Contextual Beliefs (MCBS). In literary works, one of the most central of these is genre, but there are other, even more fundamental ones (e.g., truth disclosure within the story, or linguistic and modelling uniformity). MCBS are thus a crucial constituent of the reflexive inferences made by both the author and the reader. Bach and Harnish explain: "We call such items of information 'beliefs' rather than 'knowledge' because they need not be true in order to figure in the speaker's intention and the hearer's inference. We call them 'contextual' because they are both relevant to and activated by the context of the utterance (or by the utterance itself). And we call them 'mutual' because s and H not only both have them, they believe they both have them and believe the other to believe they both have them" (5).[12]

Of course the reflexive intention is not sufficient by itself to lead to acceptance of a proposition, i.e., to instill a belief commensurate with the meaning and force of the utterance. Beliefs, intentions, or actions are not generated merely by recognizing the intention to generate them. Thus, even if the author intends the reader to approach his work in a specific way and the reader recognizes this intention as one that he is supposed to recognize, he can still choose to ignore it (recall our ignorant, spiteful, ludic, or refined critic from the previous section).

The interaction between the author and the reader is just one in a variety of communicative acts, all governed by mutual beliefs. For our purposes, the most important aspects of the interpretive process considered as a communicative act are

1 the interdependence and its reflexive recognition by the participants,
2 the presence and activation of mutually shared beliefs (e.g., the genre),
3 the reader's assumption of reflexive intentionality on the part of the author in approaching the exchange.

The above is not to say that every tactical move on the writer's part (word choice, punctuation, symbolism, and so on) must be regarded as explicitly intentional. However, considering the structure of the interactive process, the knowledge of its explicit and implicit conventions, and the reflexive awareness of this knowledge, the assumption of intentionality is the only one that makes sense in the situation. As Bach and Harnish put it, "Awareness of the situation invokes the rules; recognition of the rules activates the expectations" (95).

Naturally, in fiction, much as in the rest of our lives, we do not always speak literally. In literary works this problem is often compounded by the attendant symbolism across the entire private/public spectrum. Here again, we can rely on the intentionalist principle (point 3 above) to understand the type of relation between the author and the reader. The content of a literary work is regulated by the text, as well as by the reader's reflexive recognition that the work is the product of an intentional strategy adopted by the author for a specific literary game. Broadly speaking, we can say that the reader computes the author's intentions – the intended meaning or effect in the story – on the basis of the text and their MCBS.

The "game" of literary interpretation is readily expressed as a variant on the Gricean communicative model. The reader uses the work to infer what the author reflexively intended the reader to infer in this cooperative game. A strong confirmation that this model depicts the situation correctly comes from game theory.[13] In fact, the correspondence between speech-act theory and the kind of strategic analyses favoured by game theorists is nothing short of remarkable. Compare how Thomas Schelling describes the strategy involved in a tacit coordinative process, in this case involving two people who have lost each other in a busy store: "One does not simply predict where the other will go, since the other will go where he predicts the first to go, which is wherever the first predicts the second to predict the first to go, and so ad infinitum. What is necessary is to coordinate prediction, to read the same message in the common situation, to identity the one course of action that the expectations of each can converge on. They must 'mutually recognize' some unique signal that coordinates their expectations of each other" (54). We can expect reflexively intentional signals to play an important, albeit not always fully conscious, role in the reading process, as part of the overall strategy of communication.

ECONOMIC AND LITERARY BARGAINING

> The arguments often heard that because of the
> human element, of psychological factors, etc., or
> because there is – allegedly – no measurement
> of important factors, mathematics will find no
> application, can be dismissed as utterly mistaken.
> John von Neumann and Oscar Morgenstern

So far, using Poe's intuitions and their game theoretic analogues, I have analyzed the literary game as a type of cooperative exchange governed by rules and conventions tacitly embraced by both players. The process is tacit, since the players do not negotiate their terms directly. I will now systematize these insights by outlining a precise strategic model of a literary game. I propose that the interaction between the author and the reader can be expressed as a variant of a nonfinite, two-person, non-zerosum, one-sided, tacit bargaining process of incomplete and imperfect information.[14]

Although the tacit bargaining model was originally developed in economics, it illustrates surprisingly well the distinctive aspects of our encounters with works of literature. Among them are

1 a mutual reflexive interdependence of players;
2 a fixed order of play (author first);
3 the one-sidedness of the communicative process, from the author to the reader;
4 the possibility of limited pre-play communication, owing to the author's publishing record or advertising;
5 an inability to make side-payments or binding agreements (on the other hand, it may be interesting to investigate situations involving sequels, or books intended to form a series – Dickens, Conan Doyle, or Asimov may be some obvious examples – where, it could be argued, the author does enter into a tacit form of agreement with the reader, who is subsequently "rewarded" with the continuation of a desired book or series. The desired commodity for the author would, in this case, be reader loyalty);
6 the typical absence of cyclical iteration of a particular game;
7 the possibility of constructing metagames reflecting a feedback link with the past history of the game (e.g., the reception of the work);
8 some means of inducing cooperative behaviour in the second (by the order of play) player;
9 the possibility of applying various models of arbitration schemes to the work of literary critics, especially in cases where the cooperative game degenerates into a partially competitive one.

As I argued above, the reading process in its paradigmatic form is not a zerosum game (a game of total conflict). The preferred interpretive outcome on the part of either player does not necessarily entail a corresponding loss on the part of the other.[15] Take Poe and his preferred outcome in the literary game called "The Purloined Letter." Although my interdisciplinary reading departs in some ways from the author's reflexive intentions, it surely adds to, rather than detracts from, the story's overall value. In general, game theory and relevant experimental results indicate that the more cooperative the game, the more significant the ability to communicate. Schelling's 1960 classic, *The Strategy of Conflict*, quoted above, explains precisely how salient points in a game may be used reflexively by players to coordinate their strategies. The diverse literary conventions – from the general, like genre,

down to specific rhetorical or symbolic devices – can become useful signalling mechanisms demarcating the flexible rules of a given literary game.

As mentioned before, this process is not algorithmic, and it can fail when
the author's reflexive intentions are not reciprocated by the reader. A game
theoretic framework could help us analyze how the cooperative game changes
in such cases. It could also provide analytic models for some, perhaps even
all, variations of the degrees and types of cooperation between the author
and the reader. At present, research into text comprehension and interpretation is still conducted mostly from the functionalist standpoint. It focuses on
the identity and role of textual elements at the expense of the interactive
(gaming) elements in the interpretive process. The proposed inclusion of the
author's reflexive intentions as an integral part of text comprehension and
interpretation would seem thus to be a step in the right direction.

Not all significant variables are, of course, included in our model. The two
most prominent ones may be the lack of public disclosure of results after the
game and the personalities of the players. This methodological fact is simply a
mirror of subtle and complex reality. Despite our best efforts, the vibrant and
colourful world around us is rarely open to a complete analytical reduction.

THE PRAGMATIC REALITY OF FANTASY

> Pragmatism: 1. the quality or condition of being
> pragmatic. 2. an instance of this. 3. in philosophy,
> a system which tests the validity of all concepts by
> their practical results.
>
> *Webster's Dictionary*

The author-reader model of reflexive interdependence will be of great value
to us in considering the problem of implicit story content. Known in philosophy as the problem of truth in fiction, it is a matter of reading competence that allows readers to flesh out literary story lines.[16] Obviously, when
interpreting stories, readers never limit themselves only to what is explicit
in the text. Instead, using a sophisticated array of inferential tactics, they
routinely fill in what in Wolfgang Iser refers to in *The Act of Reading* (1978)
as textual gaps.[17] These gaps require sometimes quite specific knowledge if
the reader is to make coherent sense of a work of fiction.

What reader, for example, would doubt that in "The Purloined Letter"
Dupin has exactly five fingers on each hand? Yet one would look in vain for
any explicit textual statement to that effect. On the other hand, a normal
reader would not infer that, by smoking a pipe, Dupin increases his chances
of getting lung cancer, even though nothing in the text contradicts such a
conclusion. Which background assumptions readers use in retrieving the
contents of fiction and what role the author's intentions plays in this process

are the questions I try to answer in the rest of this chapter. Drawing on the points argued heretofore, I intend to show that a successful account of truth in fiction will rely on the author's reflexive intentions, making it a kind of equilibrium outcome for a given literary game.

Let us begin with a look at Poe's "Thousand-and-Second Tale of Scheherazade," which brings out the importance of pragmatic considerations in our contacts with fiction. Poe is clearly aware of problems surrounding the interpretation of truth in fiction. In fact, the entire story is premised on the recognition of the diverse pragmatic factors that may influence interpretation. It would be an exaggeration to claim that "Scheherazade" provides a specific answer to the problem, but Poe's brilliant manipulation of the conventions of realism and fantasy points towards a plausible solution.

Embedded in a mocking framework of the Arabian Nights, "Scheherazade" is a meta-fictional account of Sinbad's marvellous journey through the natural and scientific wonders of nineteenth-century 'Cockneigh'-land. This introduction to the story proper is contained in an even larger frame, in which the narrator recounts the results of his research on an obscure Oriental text, *Tellmenow Isitsöornot* (or, Tell-me-now Is-it-so-or-not?). He claims to have discovered the true, even if apocryphal, account of what had happened to Scheherazade on the thousand-and-second night. The narrator therefore re-tells the story allegedly narrated by the queen, in a style that lampoons the Arabian epic.

In his story-within-a-story-within-a-story, Sinbad, the intrepid wayfarer of antiquity, embarks on the mother of all voyages. This time his destination is estranged not only geographically but temporally as well, for Sinbad's trip ends up being an anachronistic romp through the wonders of Poe's nineteenth-century world. Picked up by a passing steamship and befriended by one of the "men-animals" who run it, this early Gulliver masters their language and joins them on a round-the-world cruise. Along the way Sinbad records with a keen but innocent eye the marvels of nature known in Poe's times, as well as the multiple triumphs of Western science and technology.

Poe stuns and amuses his readers by filtering these common facts through the sensibility of an anachronistic observer, estranging the ostensibly banal industrial reality into a tale of mind-boggling wonder. At critical moments, however, he punctures the flow of the story with allusions to purely fantastic (from our point of view) objects, such as a giant sky-blue cow. In this self-reflexive manner, Poe illustrates the conventional nature of literary interpretive strategies, displaying a refined grasp of the philosophy behind pragmatics. (I return to the subject of self-reflexivity in fiction in chapter 4). The scarce critical commentary has generally identified "Scheherazade" as a minor satire of the crass materialism of mid-nineteenth century industrial America or as a parody of sensational pop-journalism.[18] For our purposes, however, it is more important as a perceptive study of the pragmatic factors

behind literary conventions and, in particular, the conventions of realism
and fantasy.

In the motto, befitting a tale that inverts reality and fantasy, Poe cautions,
"Truth is stranger than fiction" (1151). He is clearly aware of the conventions
the author can reflexively expect his readers to adopt in the interpretation
of a given fiction. A good example is his mocking allusion to Sale's Koran
(1165), whereby orthodox believers like the sultan of the story believe in a
continent supported by the aforementioned giant sky-blue cow. Such an
interpretation has precious little to do with scientific veracity and everything
to do with the beliefs held in the fictional community of the sultan and the
Koran writer. As Robert Hough puts it, for Poe "verisimilitude had not to
do with the artist's veracity but with the reader's faith in it" (xxii). Stretching
the conventions of literary fantasy and realism, Poe cheerfully proposes that
believability and not factual soundness may be their determining factor.

Following the motto, the story opens with a review of the research that
has led the narrator to the account of Sindbad's voyage. Yet this paragraph-
long sentence is so silly, so convoluted, and so at odds with the ostensible
purpose of documenting the search that it completely undercuts the veracity
of these sources. Poe's flip tone confirms his grasp of the conventionality
behind what is interpreted as factual (i.e., nonfictional) and fantastic in
literary fictions. Signalling the tension between truth and fiction in the motto
and sabotaging the seriousness of his own "scholarly" discourse, Poe sets the
stage for the inquiry into what rules we employ to determine what is true
in fiction. Sindbad's voyage through the reality-as-fantasy of nineteenth-
century America parallels the reader's voyage through the literary conventions of realism and fantasy.

BELIEFS RELEVANT TO A GIVEN FICTION

It is as absurd to argue men, as to torture them,
into believing.
                              Cardinal Newman

In the second narrative frame Queen Scheherazade entertains her husband
with a tale involving, among other things, a blue rat and a pink clockwork
horse with green wings, wound up with an indigo key. Yet, as peculiar and
incredible as these details are, the sultan accepts them as true. Clearly the
criteria that determine for the fairy tale monarch the plausibility of a tale
are different from those that we would employ for that purpose. In fact, they
are symmetrically reversed: what is fantastic for us, creatures of the real
world, is real to inhabitants of fairy tale, and vice versa. By means of this
ingenious symmetry, Poe estranges the real wonders of nature and technology

into fairy tale miracles. The mutual beliefs of the teller of and listener to the story are thus the determinant factors of what would, prima facie, seem an empirical or even ontological question.

Instead of a clear and unambiguous depiction of his material, Poe goes for the sensational by exaggerating the fantastic appearance of his subject *both* to the sultan of the tale and to the contemporary reader. He carefully selects facts and artifacts with singular properties and uses a number of rhetorical tropes to increase the impression of futuristic novelty. In one hyperbole he describes ash from a volcanic explosion to be so dense that at one hundred and fifty miles away it is "impossible to see the whitest object" (1161), however closely held to the eye. With no warning, the next passage adopts the viewpoint of a Lilliputian, describing "monstrous animals with horns resembling scythes" that inhabit "vast caverns in the soil" (1162). It takes the unsuspecting reader a while to realize the relative size-shift in the description and recognize in the rapacious giant a tiny lion-ant.

Likewise, Poe's oblique allusions to facts of science have lost none of their force for the contemporary reader. At one point Sindbad describes the local atmosphere to be "so dense as to sustain iron or steel, just as our own does feathers" (1161). Poe refers in this roundabout way to *powdered* steel, which, indeed, can float in atmospheric air. Without foreknowledge of this fact, the reader, contemplating this seemingly outrageous statement in light of something like the Reality Principle (see below), is bound to deny its truth. Realizing Poe's narrative ruse, he is shocked into a new perspective on things, which estrangement is supposed to produce.

The effectiveness of Poe's technique is amplified by the descriptive tone. Far from being surprised or enthralled, the narrator is thoroughly at home with exotic formations of nature and science. She reports them with patient nonchalance, so at odds with her husband's excitable incredulity. Poe carries this prosaic, brave-new-worldly tone into Scheherazade's report of yet another miracle. This time it is an entire continent supported on the back of a "sky-blue cow that had no fewer than four hundred horns" (1165). What is the sultan's reaction to this apparent "fact"? Consistent with his previous acceptance of blue rats and pink horses, Scheherazade's husband finds the imaginary cow entirely more believable than the empirical reality of Poe's times. Evidently, writes Jerome D. Denuccio, the efficacy of the "facts" described by the queen hinges "not upon their inherent truth or falsity, but upon their credibility" (367).

By means of this "ontological" transformation Poe alerts the reader to some important pragmatic-interpretive principles. For one, he shows that the knowledge of conventional beliefs *relevant to a given fiction* is indispensable to its proper understanding and interpretation. Second, he suggests that such background knowledge may take precedence over nominal facts of science. By illustrating that we cannot read fictions without taking the pragmatic stance, Poe points in this way to some important aspects of readers' expertise in story content "retrieval." In what follows I will clarify and reinforce his points in a systematic account of truth in fiction.

POSSIBLE AND FICTIONAL WORLDS

> Do there exist many worlds, or is there but a
> single world? This is one of the most noble and
> exalted questions in the study of Nature.
>   Albertus Magnus

The account of what happens in the story is a crucial first step in any contact with a work of fiction. We must know, after all, what we interpret in order to interpret it. Although few literary scholars seem to realize it, a rigorous account of truth in fiction is a necessary prerequisite for any theory of interpretation. The distinction between these two levels of reading, often confused by critics, is important inasmuch as the theory of truth in fiction aims at the level of story content and not at a higher level of interpretation (e.g., symbolic, archetypal, cultural, etc.). Every reader and critic of fiction begins his or her deliberations by figuring out what happens in the story or, in other words, what is true in it. Few, however, are aware of the work in aesthetics that tries to analyze this process.

To begin, much like in nonfiction, a proper understanding of story content must obey some basic causal constraints. Any claims about the influence of Conan Doyle's Sherlock Holmes (1892) on Poe's Dupin (1845) must be judged anachronistic and unacceptable. Still, this puts only the broadest restrictions on admissible inferences. A successful theory must specify in more detail the ways in which we fill in textual gaps that require background knowledge.[19]

Propositions can be true in the story, and true *simpliciter* (i.e., true in our world, or simply true). The whole point of "Scheherazade," for example, is that the natural and scientific wonders described by Poe really exist. It is thus true in his fiction and true in our world that (in the Mammoth Cave of Kentucky) there are "immense rivers as black as ebony, swarming with fish that had no eyes" (1161) or that one can make "a deep darkness out of two brilliant lights" (1168) using light-wave superposition. However, propositions can also be true in the story and simply not true. It is true in Poe's fiction that Scheherazade recounts Sinbad's adventures, but not true that either character ever existed in reality.

Truth is thus one thing, and truth in fiction another. They can, but need not, correspond to each other. Distinct as they are, however, there have been attempts to relate truth and fictional truth to each other. The most common has been through the appeal to the so-called fictional worlds, believed to be coincidental with possible worlds (as understood in possible worlds semantics).[20] Although a fictional proposition need not be true in our world, it could be true in a possible world, it is held. However, the equation of fictional "worlds" and possible ones fails for the following reasons:

1 Unlike fictional worlds, possible worlds are always *in principle* determinate with respect to truth. Take the number of crewmen on Sinbad's ship. Although it must be determinate, neither the text nor any form of background knowledge can even in principle determine the exact value of "a vast number" (1157).
2 Possible worlds are consistent; nothing logically impossible can be true in them. Not so in fictional worlds. Stanislaw Lem invokes superluminal paradoxes in "The Seventh Voyage" (in *The Star Diaries* [first ed. 1957]), and chronomotion entails all kinds of logical inconsistencies (see the final section of this chapter).
3 It is epistemically and psychologically impossible that readers do, or even could, reconstruct complete possible worlds from works of fiction.
4 There is no one-to-one correspondence between possible and fictional worlds. In fact, any fictional world is consistent with an infinity of possible worlds. The entire contents of "Scheherazade" are compatible with possible worlds in which Sinbad owned a flying carpet at the age of five and those in which he did not, in which Martians invaded the Earth a day after Orson Welles's broadcast and did not, in which Frank Zappa released *Sheik Yerbouti* in 1979 and did not, and so on, ad infinitum.

IS TRUTH IN FICTION A COUNTERFACTUAL?

> We need scarcely add that the contemplation in
> natural science of a wider domain than the actual
> leads to a far better understanding of the actual.
>   Arthur Eddington

We must forget the idea that a fictional world is a possible world. But what about truth in various possible worlds, all consistent with a single story-world? David Lewis has approached the conditions for truth in fiction in terms of such counterfactual situations. He has proposed that what is true in fiction can be treated as if it was uttered in the world of the story as known fact.[21] To get to this possible story-world, Lewis considers a plurality of possible worlds (which he calls s-worlds) associated with a story. Note that the intersection of all s-worlds associated with a single story corresponds to what is explicit in the text. As a consequence, it makes no sense to equate fictional truth with what is true in all s-worlds, since that would make it identical with the text. Thus we reject analysis 0: the idea that truth in fiction is delimited strictly by what is explicit in the text.

In "Truth in Fiction" (1983) Lewis submits two proposals for selection of relevant background beliefs to be used in fleshing out story contents. Unfortunately both have drawbacks. The first proposal (analysis 1) is what in *Mimesis as Make-Believe* (1990) Kendall Walton calls the Reality Principle. It states that what is true in the story is as close as the text allows to the real world of the reader. Clearly this rule is too broad, and generates various irrelevant results. When reading and trying to understand fictions, we do not invoke *all* and *only* inferences based on the Reality Principle. Let us consider "Scheherazade" again. Is it true in the story that Homer Simpson "mooned for rebuttal" in his debating class? Nothing in the text disputes it, yet the proposition is unquestionably anachronistic and aesthetically irrelevant.

Lewis's second proposal (analysis 2) is the Mutual Belief Principle. It specifies appropriate beliefs for fleshing out story contents as those conventionally believed in the author's community. The principle rules out the Homer Simpson counterexample but runs into another problem. In Poe's vignette "The Oval Portrait" we are to assume that the artist's effort to transfer his wife's lively beauty onto the canvas drains her life spirit until, upon the completion of the work, she dies. The doctrine of mimetic art depleting life from people was not mutually believed in Poe's times, nor is it part of the present-day reader's world knowledge, yet it is necessary to make sense of this story.[22]

In general, what is distinctive about Lewis's account, i.e., his treatment of truth in fiction along the lines of truth in possible worlds, is also the source of its problems. Among others, it forces him to assume that "Truth in a given fiction is closed under implication" (264), which roughly means that all possible implications are true in a given story. Yet, as I noted during the discussion of possible worlds, one of their most unlikely features was the need for readers to make *all* inferences that could be made for a given world. In psychological terms it seems extremely suspect that anything like such a total inference-making process could ever take place. Moreover, as we have seen, a fictional "world" is compatible with any number of possible worlds. Last of all, Lewis's account side-steps the issue of inconsistent fictions, which, by definition, cannot be accommodated in any (logically) possible world.

HYPOTHETICAL INTENTIONALISM

> You're searching, Joe
> for things that don't exist.
> Robert Frost

To describe what is true in fiction, and thus to formulate the first part of a theory of literary interpretation, we need to go beyond Lewis's analyses and look for a principle that will derive only true and only relevant inferences. Before I present my own recommendations, let us consider an important proposal by Gregory Currie. Aware of the problems with Lewis's account, in *The Nature of Fiction* (1990) Currie takes a novel approach by grounding fictional truth in the persona of the fictional author, whom he defines as "that fictional character whom we take to be telling us the story as known fact" (76). Fictional truth is then offered as the joint product of the text and the belief system of the fictional author.

Unfortunately for Currie's account, his central concept of the fictional author is insufficiently elaborated, unnecessary, and irremediably circular. According to Currie we cull the belief system of the fictional author from the text: "as we read we learn more about his beliefs" (76). We thus use the text to get to the fictional author's beliefs, so that, in a vicious circle, we can use his beliefs to interpret the text. The postulate also fails, as Alex Byrne points out in "Truth in Fiction," in the face of "mindless" fictions, i.e., stories without an apparent narrator.[23] What is more, it is again implausible, to say the least, that readers could ever reconstruct a complete belief system of the fictional author, no matter how lengthy the work. Neither does Currie's treatment of inconsistent fictions resolve all relevant cases (see the next section).

In addition, as a consequence of his appeal to the fictional author, Currie pays insufficient attention to genre as part of relevant background beliefs that reflexively regulate interpretation. Let us not forget that fictions belong to genres because authors intend for readers to recognize elements of genre as being employed in order to be recognized as such. Knowledge of genres belongs, however, to the strategy of the real author, of which the fictional author, a heuristic construct, can have no knowledge. Yet genre considerations can seriously affect the contents of literary works. The expectations of verisimilitude and coherence in James's "Turn of the Screw" or, in a less canonical example, W. W. Jacobs's "Monkey's Paw" dramatically alter their content, in accordance with a realistic or fantastic interpretation.

Although Currie is a realist about intentional attitudes in all other respects, he is led to hypothetical intentionalism with regard to story meaning.[24] After all, few real authors could tell their fictions as a known fact, as his counterfactual treatment of truth in fiction demands. On the other hand, Currie cannot simply dispense with the fictional author altogether. Consider the interpretive puzzle of the Flash Stockman, brought up by Lewis. The stockman is an unreliable narrator who believes every boast he makes, while leaving no doubt in the reader's mind that things are just the opposite. What *is* true in this fiction? Clearly that the stockman is a boastful wretch whose verbal antics are not to be taken at face value. But this point of view is clearly not the narrator's, leading Currie, who cannot refer to the real author, to fall back on the fictional one.

Even if we pass over the problems with the fictional author, Currie still needs to stipulate the conditions for competent inferences about story content. Knowing this, he contemplates a proposal operationally similar to Lewis's analysis 2: the right kind of background for a correct interpretation of what is true in a story is formed by the mutual beliefs in the author's community, so long as they are not explicitly contravened by the text. On this view, retrieving what is true in a given fiction, we should follow what was conventionally (in another version, only predominantly) believed in the real author's community and deviate only when the text explicitly contradicts these beliefs.

Note that, although similar, Lewis's and Currie's proposals are in fact categorically distinct. The former involves a possible world, whereas the other relies on a fallible, incomplete, and potentially inconsistent system of beliefs. This is in itself an important improvement. It replaces the dubious demands of inferential completeness, which plagued Lewis's account, with a much more realistic view of actual readers' actual reading strategies. This allows Currie partly to solve the problem of generating true but irrelevant "truths" about fiction.

Still, there are good reasons to reject the mutual belief principle, quite apart from the drawbacks discussed before. Currie himself allows that the deviation from conventional beliefs may be subject to a kind of inferential "domino effect." For example, when a sky-blue cow is explicitly introduced in "Scheherazade," it may be reasonable to conclude that other imaginary entities, such as unicorns, could be included in the story, even though the text makes no mention of them.

I think there is, however, an even subtler reason for rejecting this strategy. In Jacobs's "Monkey's Paw" (1902), an aging couple comes into possession of a magic amulet said to grant three wishes. Immediately they wish for two hundred pounds, which they indeed get the next day, but in the form of compensation for their son who dies in a work accident. Bereaved, they wish for his return, and in the dead of night someone starts breaking into their house. Petrified with terror, the old man uses the third wish to send the intruder away. Clearly, there is not a single supernatural event per se in the story, so the simple retrieval strategy might follow the conventional beliefs of the author's time: to wit, that there are no ghosts, no resurrections, no magic, and so on. But such an interpretation totally contradicts the story, which derives its power and coherence exactly from the implication that there may in fact be a supernatural dimension to our existence.

Having raised questions about the mutual belief principle, Currie frankly admits that he has "no rules to substitute for this one." Instead, he closes the matter with a wishful pronouncement: "I take it there would be considerable agreement in practice about how such inferences as this ought to proceed" (both on 80). The truth is, however, that there never was, and perhaps never will be, any such agreement in critical practice. Moreover, no one ever doubted that readers and critics know how to make appropriate inferences; the sole point of this debate is to fashion a rigorous and compelling model of this process.

THE TRUTH BEHIND TRUTH IN FICTION

> It is a terrible thing for a man to find out
> suddenly that all his life he has been speaking
> nothing but the truth.
>
> Oscar Wilde

I submit that a shift away from Currie's hypothetical intentionalism to real intentionalism can resolve the outstanding problems. We must be careful at this point not to confuse an account of the real author's complex intentions with the old-style intentionalist fallacy and its claims that the meaning of a work is uniquely determined by the author. Clearly, even though artists often communicate their intentions directly in prefaces, interviews, letters, and so forth, the main body of interpretive evidence will always be the text itself. There are several reasons for this. To begin, artistic intentions can change during the writing of a work. Second, complex intentions are difficult to articulate concisely, and presumably the finished work is already the best expression of its author's executive design. Moreover, out of opportunism, forgetfulness, or simply lack of explicit awareness, the author's account can be inaccurate.

On my account truth in fiction derives from (1) what is explicitly stated in or directly warranted by the text, as interpreted standardly in the language(s) in which it is written; (2) a reflexive recognition of the author's successfully executed goals and intentional attitudes *relevant to a given fiction*. The focus on the author's executive intentions, i.e., those that *actually went into the execution of the work*, rules out true but irrelevant inferences. Here is how Paisley Livingston and Alfred Mele characterize a reflexive correlation of the author's executive, and the reader's retrieval, strategies. The author of a work had a reasonable and effective communicative intention for a given proposition if he "had the intention and had good and sufficient reason to believe that the proposition would be imagined and accepted for the purpose of the fiction, on the basis of available evidence, by members of the target audience" (10).[25]

A potential difficulty in intention attribution may be a lack of evidence. Quite simply, in some real-life situations the author's intentions may be inaccessible to the reader outside of the evidence offered by the text itself. However, there is nothing in my proposals to imply that literary authors' intentions will always be perfectly accessible, homogenous, or even cooperative. It is certainly not true that for every work one can determine the author's intentions with incontestable accuracy. This fact yields, however, no ground to *epistemological* arguments against intention attribution. Moreover, theoretical objections of this type are refuted in practice by the successful reconstructive work of historians, archeologists, cryptographers, and, indeed, literary scholars themselves.

The appeal to actual intentions does not yet settle all questions, since works can contain meanings (e.g., puns, irony, allusions) that did not figure in their authors' executive intentions. A complete version of real intentionalism also has to allow for failed intentions, in cases when the evidence shows that the author tried to express a proposition P, and the actual result means *not P*. The intentionalist approach to interpretation does not mean that we interpret the work as meaning P, but it makes it possible to distinguish between P and *not P*, which is of consequence. To resolve such potential problems of unintended meaning, Robert Stecker suggests in "The Role of Intention" that a good place to start may be with the "linguistic, cultural, and artistic [conventions] in place at the time a work is created. It is very plausible that much unintended meaning can be accounted for by the working of such conventions. For example, it is plausible that it is part of the meaning of a work that it puns on a certain word in virtue of linguistic conventions about word meaning and artistic conventions that puns are artistically significant features of works in the genre in question" (485–6).

My theses resolve the objections raised to Currie's theses in the following ways:

1 The circular concept of the fictional author yields to a determinate reality of the real author's executive intentions.
2 Since we are dealing with a real-life person, there is no more need to generate complete belief systems; the relevant background beliefs are now limited to those associated with the author's executive reflexive intentions.
3 A significant part of the real author and the reader's mutual contextual beliefs is the knowledge of genres, used reflexively by the author to signal a relevant context for interpretation.
4 In cases of explicit incoherence, we can interpret the contradiction in terms of the author's executive intentions.

The main difficulty here concerns entailments from inconsistent fictions, which, if derived in standard fashion, would in some cases render a story meaningless, given that *ex contradictio quodlibet*. Since this issue is the litmus test for any account of truth in fiction, we need to look at it in more detail.

I KNOW IT'S CRAZY, BUT IT'S TRUE

How often have I said to you that when you have
eliminated the impossible, whatever remains,
however improbable, must be the truth?

Arthur Conan Doyle

On Currie's view a reader would adopt any interpretation rather than conclude that the author means what he says when writing an inconsistent fiction. The issue here is explicit incoherence, as, for example, in time travel stories, rather than a less troublesome inconsistency, which may arise out of simple forgetfulness.

A good example of the latter may be the position of Watson's Afghan war wound in the Sherlock Holmes stories, originally discussed by Lewis. My approach, based on the fallible and not necessarily complete system of the real-life author's reflexive intentions, offers a sensible way of dealing with such inadvertent inconsistencies. If most of the evidence indicates that the wound is in one place rather than the other, the reader should go along with the greater number (one mistake being more likely than many). If the numbers are roughly equal and the issue cannot be settled by an appeal to the author's intentions, there is no determinate answer. It is then true that the wound is in either place, but not true that it is in one or the other. Thus unintended contradictions are not to be considered fictionally true. This checks with what Currie argues in *The Nature of Fiction* (87).

The problem arises in cases like Stanislaw Lem's "The Seventh Voyage," where the author is not equivocating, misunderstanding his words, or metaphorizing. On the contrary, Lem's exploration of time-travel inconsistencies could hardly be more explicit. In the story, trapped in gravitational vortices, the protagonist Tichy is chrono-duplicated in all stages of his life and made to interact with his own multiple selves, trying to sort out the temporal and causal entanglements of their (his?) chrono-multiplication. Although incoherence in a possible world entails total collapse, this clearly need not be so in fiction. Lem deals with inconsistencies in the following way: he narrates *individual scenes* in a logically consistent way and avoids their globally self-contradictory entailments. For example, although the Tuesday Tichy knows by virtue of being his own older chrono-twin that the Monday Tichy will not help him repair the rocket, he still tries to persuade the latter to change his mind, as if it were indeed possible.

The above pattern is common to most time-travel fiction, from Wells's prototypical *Time Machine* to contemporary blockbusters like *The Terminator*. Although at the deeper level all such stories are irredeemably incoherent, the reader/viewer is meant to suspend judgment with regard to the global implications for the story. This is psychologically plausible, since readers do not and could not trace all implications of all textual propositions anyway. After all, even when we try our best, we often fall prey to deductive corruption, memory lapse, or mental partitioning. Thus, from explicit inconsistencies it need not immediately follow that anything goes for what is true in a given fiction.

If Lem's short story is anything to go by, the correct interpretive method is to allow standard logic within the text, but, once again, only to the extent warranted by the author's reflexive intentions. When such narrative "bubbles" overlap, the reader must acknowledge the global incoherence of the story, without, however, transferring it to individual propositions. Significantly, such narrative games are not always employed for purely ludic purposes. The author's use of an explicit contradiction can be motivated by higher literary goals (rarely seen among primitive sci-fi chronomotion) that outweigh the price levied by the logic department. These higher goals may be thus a good guide to the extent of entailments relevant to the story. I thus agree wholeheartedly with David Davies's conclusion in "Fictional Truth and Fictional Authors" that "the issues of 'truth *in* fiction' and 'truth *through* fiction' are *not* as distinct as some would have us believe" (53).

Since some of my conclusions echo David Lewis's "Postscript to 'Truth in Fiction,'" we can look briefly at the objections that Currie raises with regard to Lewis's account. Clearly the second and third objection are solved by my transfer of the relevant interpretive strategy from a complete and coherent possible world *à la* Lewis to a fallible and not necessarily coherent set of beliefs of the actual author. We are left then with the first argument: "it is not clear that every inconsistent story will have consistent segments from which we could obtain a recognizable narrative" (69). My proposal offers a clear solution: the range of valid implications is determined by the real author's executive intentions, which are independent of the feasibility of segmentation. Of course, there is nothing amiss with segmentation, and in many contexts the appropriate strategy may indeed involve partition of the text into self-contained sections that will follow the standard logic of entailment.

What does all this tell us about the contents of "The Seventh Voyage"? It is true in the story that time travel is possible, but not true that any arbitrary proposition follows. It is true that the past is fixed and determined and that the fictional characters are aware of the fact; indeed some of them use it as an argument not to repair the rocket (if I fix it today, then how come tomorrow me would need to ask me to fix it today?). But it is not true that this knowledge should be the focus in the understanding of the characters' behaviour and beliefs. Instead, these are (by Lem) and should be (by the reader) approached as in a standardly consistent game. As a matter of fact, the hilarity and finesse of Lem's spoof on sf clichés stems precisely from the murderous logic with which he develops the implications of this inherently illogical situation.

CHAPTER TWO

Towards a New Epistemology

> *Eureka* is less important as science than as a cos-
> mological structure based on aesthetic principles.
> As such, it develops Poe's epistemological philo-
> sophy and makes strangely compelling reading.
> David Ketterer, *The Rationale of Deception in Poe*

Eureka has been variously described as a testimony to the waning of Poe's
mental powers in the last years of his life, or as his highest intellectual and
artistic achievement. Although neither extreme is totally defensible, the truth
is certainly closer to the latter. In the essay Poe attempts to make a contribution to matters of great importance to literary scholars, philosophers, and
scientists alike. He begins by developing a theory of knowledge that is to
revolutionize all thinking, in part by replacing the traditional model of
inquiry. Poe's attempt ranks as one of the most ambitious and far-reaching
endeavours of his career. Without doubt, it is also one of the most ambitious
and far-reaching projects ever attempted in philosophy.

PHILOSOPHY AND FICTION

> And he [Archimedes] is so overjoyed at the
> discovery that he jumps up and runs home naked,
> shouting Eureka, Eureka.
> Eduard Jan Dijksterhuis

An interpretation of *Eureka* as a work of philosophy may be of particular
interest to those literary scholars who prefer to see it mainly as a work of
fiction.[1] In chapter 1 I showed how the knowledge of the author's reflexive
intentions may contribute to the understanding of the contents of a work. In
Poe's case the available textual and biographical evidence strongly indicates
that *Eureka* was conceived at least in part as a serious philosophical study.

The essay was unveiled as a public lecture at the Society Library in New York, with a protocol that usually accompanies serious, nonfictional discourse. Poe made his intentions equally clear in his correspondence: "my subject shall *not be literary* at all". Upon completing the essay, he assured George W. Eveleth, "What I have propounded will (in good time) revolutionize the world of Physical and Metaphysical Science." In May 1848, preparing *Eureka* for publication, he wrote to Jane E. Locke of his "duties that just now *will not* be neglected or even postponed – the proofreading of a work of scientific detail in which a trivial error would involve me in very serious embarrassment" (all in Ostrom, 2: 359, 362, 366). And in the preface to the work itself he calls it a revelation that "*is true*: – therefore it cannot die: – or if by any means it be trodden down so that it die, it will 'rise again to the Life Everlasting'" (209).[2]

This is not to deny that on occasion, demurring that *Eureka* be judged as a Poem, Poe appears somewhat less assertive.[3] Some critics have indeed taken these disclaimers at face value; according them they play a central role in explaining his creative intentions. However, as Ketterer reminds us in *The Rationale of Deception in Poe* (1979), Poe is "a much more complicated, duplicitous, and conscious artist than was previously supposed" (xii). In his mesmeric tales, for instance, Poe seems to have been motivated in different degrees by the intentions of writing fiction and advancing original nonfictional hypotheses, as well as doing both in a way that would permit either interpretation.[4] The possible presence of such complex intentions in his other writings imposes some limits on what can reasonably be asserted about *Eureka*.

Poe was fond of hailing *Eureka* as a culmination of his creative life. He considered its physical and metaphysical implications so profound that nothing could sway him from trusting their completeness and accuracy. He even wrote to Maria Clemm with a typical touch of melodrama: "I have no desire to live since I have done 'Eureka.' I could accomplish nothing more" (Ostrom, 2: 452). This affected Romantic pose must be squared, however, with the evidence of a more mundane etiology, indicating that *Eureka* had been composed as a means to raise capital for the establishment of Poe's own literary magazine, the *Stylus*.[5] Obviously, these aims are not mutually exclusive. On the other hand, their incongruity should alert us to the presence of complex pragmatic games in which Poe engaged during his career.

What does it tell us about *Eureka*? Is Poe's essay a work of fiction, a discursive treatise that structurally and stylistically it so much resembles, or both? Any plausible answer must rely at least to some degree on the author's reflexive intentions – those he could expect different audiences to recognize and accept in order to interpret *Eureka*. These seem to have been quite heterogenous, in tune with Poe's recognition of different social circles to which his work might appeal. A good indication of this selectiveness is the preface, where he commends *Eureka* as a *literary* work only to "the few who love me and whom I love" (209) – certainly not the East Coast reading public at large. It seems reasonable, then, to allow that the composition of the essay involved a complex mix of goals: philosophical and fictional, cognitive and aesthetic, as well as crassly pragmatic and social.

Poe's serious philosophical and scientific intentions should not be a surprise. The myth of his negative view of science is, like many myths about him, just a myth. Harold Beaver is only one among several critics who point out that even in the notorious "Sonnet – To Science," Poe speaks out not against science but against "the triumph of mechanical reason" (xiv). This interpretation squares aptly with Poe's documented admiration for science, evident in fictions like "The Thousand-and-Second Tale of Scheherazade" or articles like "A Chapter on Science and Art." In the latter Poe reviews many scientific inventions with a favourable eye and even recommends establishment of a scientific foundation in Washington. Any lingering doubts about his views are surely dispelled in "Marginalia," where, in no ambiguous terms, Poe declares a poem about Saturn a paltry thing next to the breathtaking scientific facts about the planet![6]

This is a dramatic statement from the writer whom some critics like to see as a prophet of antiscientism. And where the juvenile sonnet writer only bemoans the loss of imagination, the mature artist sets out to rectify it with his own theory of inquiry. Poe seeks a poetic modus vivendi in the age of science, which, full of imagination-boggling marvels of its own, threatens in his eyes the need for intuition and imagination. The honour of reversing the process deplored in "To Science" and of reinstating the imagination in *both* poets and scientists is given to his ambitious work of philosophy, *Eureka*.

INTUITION: FOR BETTER OR FOR WORSE?

Though this be madness, yet there is method in't.
William Shakespeare

One of the central reasons for our continued interest in *Eureka* lies in its attempted interdisciplinary cross-over. Armed with a hybrid of intuition and ratiocination, Poe sets out to construct an epistemological bridge between the imagination of poetry, the logic of philosophy, and the empiricism of science. He inaugurates this grand methodological defense of intuition with a fictitious "letter" from the future. In this epistolary mini-essay, reprinted in 1849 as part of "Mellonta Tauta," Poe develops his new epistemology, which he will later use to support his cosmological theory. He opens with a critique of the two methods that have traditionally led inquiry: (deductive) logic and (inductive) empiricism. In their place he outlines a theory rooted in the poetic leap of imagination, symbolized in the methodological oxymoron of intuitive ratiocination. Poe declares that the true philosopher should devote himself to theoretical synthesis, and in the rest of the essay he puts his program to work.

As John Limon writes in *The Place of Fiction in the Time of Science*, mid-nineteenth century American philosophy of science was pedestrian, notably in its misconstrual of science as a generalization from facts only. In contrast, science itself was an almost endless source of revolutionary discoveries and of a dazzling variety of imaginative hypotheses.[7] Poe contends that only when "the [empirical] minutiae vanish altogether" (212–13), can the imagination come into its own by means of the intuitive leap. Inasmuch as he attacks science with a primitive nineteenth-century model of inquiry in mind, his censure seems to wield some clout. Yet, trying to save the imagination from the dullness of scientific philosophy, he ends up sounding as if science itself was dull. The illegitimacy of this extension seriously mars his critique.

Although, as Margaret Allerton has documented in *Origins of Poe's Critical Theory*, Poe frequently borrowed ideas from the philosophical works of his time, it is not clear how much philosophy he actually knew. What *is* clear is that if it was only as much as he knew of logic, it was not much at all. His technical grasp of logic was apparently limited to John Stuart Mill's *System of Logic* (1843), a source not only of his distinction between deductive and inductive systems but probably also of his outdated epistemology. If Vincent Buranelli is right that for a "definition of inductive logic Mill, followed by Poe, goes to Francis Bacon" (1977, 48), it would explain Poe's view of science as animated purely by the Linnaean spirit of gathering and classifying disjointed facts.

In this view Poe is, however, completely unjustified. Although Bacon did attempt to order empirical inquiry by emphasizing the collection of data over the intractable process of theory formation, the former has never been the sole aim of any form of scientific research, past or present. It may be not amiss to quote at least one clear articulation of where Poe goes wrong. No less a thinker than Albert Einstein, whose theories some literary critics hailed as a vindication of *Eureka*, summed up the historical importance of intuition in his "Principles of Research" [1934]: "There is no logical path to ... laws; only intuition, resting on sympathetic understanding of experience, can reach them" (22).

Intuition, whether poetic or scientific, is undoubtedly a crucial element in the process of hypothesis formation. But can it supply the necessary and sufficient methodological framework for proving/falsifying new theories? The answer must be negative. The litmus test of any new hypothesis is the check with the world it tries to describe. As far as anyone can tell, this check can be justified only using the means and methods of science. This is an important point, since Poe's theses about intuition are reached through the exercise of that same intuition, begging the question of the rationale for adopting them.[8] Realizing that he owes his central hypotheses to intuition, in their defence he repeatedly relies on deductive analysis and empirical facts. Ketterer is thus right to conclude that Poe "is not creating a distinct third category if intuition is a matter of the combination or fusion of reason and imagination" (1979, 259). Already at the outset, then, Poe's views on intuition seem more like a Romantic defense of the poetic vision than any ground-breaking and systematic outline of a new epistemology.

Still, it is important to distinguish his reasons for trying to rewrite the epistemological canon from his success in the execution of this project. In *Eureka* Poe sets out to legitimize other fields of inquiry alongside the natural-scientific as sources of knowledge and to provide an epistemological framework within which all fields (scientific, philosophic, and poetic) can conduct their programs. The virtue of his goals is, in this case, categorically separate from his success in defending them. If we should come to feel that some of his supporting arguments may be ill-defended or even wildly incoherent, this need not decide the value of the goals of his vision. In fact, I will argue that Poe's theses are sufficiently similar to the model of inquiry that emerges from the recent work in philosophy of science to partially vindicate his program.

POETIC INTUITION, OR EPISTEMOLOGY IN PROGRESS

> Truth is not that which is demonstrable, but that
> which is ineluctable.
>   Antoine de Saint-Exupéry

Poe begins by setting intuition apart from the axiomatic and empirical – or, in his satire, the Aristotelian and Baconian – methods of inquiry. He accuses them jointly of systematic discrimination and dogmatism. Something like Poe's argument will indeed reappear in contemporary critiques of the so-called covering-law model of inquiry, suggesting that he had a good grasp of the principles of unified inquiry. Yet his specific line of attack unravels in the heat of his rhetorical ardour. For ages, proclaims Poe, no man "dared utter a truth, for which he felt himself indebted to his soul alone" (214). Any theory intuited in this way must perforce lie outside the realm of empirical, or even logical, confirmation. In the very next line he adds, however, that it did not matter "whether the truth was even demonstrably such" (214).

Poe opens himself to the charge of incoherence by embracing both of these mutually exclusive propositions:

1 The imaginative leap is indebted to the soul alone, and not to a demonstration by empirical and/or logical means; hence its value/veracity is
   independent of such means.
2 The imaginative leap can be supported by axiomatic or empirical means,
   which makes its value/veracity indebted to the method used.

In other words, unless the veracity of the intuitive leap is to rest forever on
its creator's conviction of its truth, sooner or later the theory must face a
test of its tenets and thus become indebted to more than his soul alone.

   As a matter of fact, Poe's conviction of the everlasting veracity of his
ratiocinations is based on such an external evaluative criterion. This standard
is consistency, synonymous for him with "absolute and unquestionable
Truth" (219). However, a series of blatant errors casts doubt on his competence to follow this truth. On the first page of his discussion Poe spells out
his foremost charge against deductive logic: "there is, in this world at least,
no such thing as demonstration" (211). Yet shortly thereafter he completely
overturns it by asserting that past intuitive leaps were rejected by the logical
and empirical dogmatists, even though they were "demonstrably" true (214).
This glaring self-contradiction is typical of Poe's readiness to forswear long-
term argumentative soundness for a quick return on rhetorical emphasis.
Once again, his strength will lie in the general methodological principles he
adopts in his endeavour, rather than in the particular arguments or proofs
that are to cement his theses.

   Although consistency is made to be a sine qua non in Poe's ratiocinations,
apart from two occasions where he equates it with truth, there is little else
in *Eureka* on this fundamental principle. Only in the last pages does he
return to it, when he accuses Madler of inconsistent application of analogy
in the latter's theory of galactic gravitation. Insisting that "it is no more
proper that we should abide by analogy" in the formulation than in the
development of a theory (294), Poe blames Madler for shelving analogy the
moment it becomes a burden to the latter's argument. He is apparently
unconcerned that *Eureka* is replete with evidence of his own whimsical
attitude to consistency.

   There are other examples of such a polemical double standard. At one
point Poe shores up his argument by appealing to the principles of dynamics.
Yet a little further on he declares that his critics' use of the laws of dynamics
is an "unwarranted assumption ... at an epoch when no 'principles' in
anything exist" (251). This sounds even less convincing in the context of his
next avowal: "*Each law of Nature is dependent at all points upon all other laws*"
(264). Poe declares by fiat when laws are operative or not and when principles
of science may or may not be used in defence of an argument, while placing
himself (against his own proclamations) above the need for consistency.

A VICTIM OF HIS OWN MAKING

> There is nothing in this world constant but
> inconstancy.
>> Jonathan Swift

Of course, dramatic inconsistency need not yet signify a dearth of original thought. Emerson, for example, tries to make virtue out of necessity and in "Self-Reliance" welcomes contradiction with open arms, scolding foolish consistency as the hobgoblin of small minds. However, the Emersonian steamship displaces little philosophical water. Taken seriously, his "principle" of inconsistency loses coherence as soon as its strictures are turned upon itself, making adherence to it only inconsistently inconsistent, i.e., at least partly consistent.

More importantly, Poe defines himself in a conspicuous and elaborate contrast to Emerson and what he used to snub as the latter's Frogpondian Transcendentalism. In *Eureka* he names consistency a sovereign criterion in judging the results of any form of ratiocination, so much so that he equates "absolute truth" with "perfect consistency" (219). This in itself is an error, since outrageous falsehoods can be no less coherent than truths. Poe's pretences to consistency are sabotaged, however, by his irrepressible penchant for staging argumentative victories over the imagined methodological foes. Some of his self-contradictions are especially flagrant. In one case he begins by twice asserting that there is "*no such thing*" as an axiom or a demonstration (211, 216). Yet when defending his use of the laws of radiation, he states flatly that to demand why these laws are true "would be to demand why the axioms are true upon which their demonstration is based" (241).

It is hard to believe that Poe, who seems to have put so much painstaking effort into his treatise, should have been ignorant of what is obvious to any attentive reader. This incongruity is compounded by his admission to Jane E. Locke that he intended *Eureka* to be unassailable in the rigour of its arguments. One plausible explanation for this incongruity is suggested by Clarence Wylie in "Mathematical Allusions in Poe" (1946). He sees Poe's protracted attack on logic in the opening "letter" section of *Eureka* as a strategic artifice designed to preempt "logical objections [to his own argument] by holding logic up to preliminary ridicule" (234). This explanation seems all the more convincing in that, as I have shown, Poe readily forswears logic and consistency when he senses an opportunity for an argumentative victory.

The discrepancy between the writer's purported intention and the finished work could hardly be greater. Poe, the professor of absolute consistency, becomes a victim of his own making every time he contradicts himself. Of course, in moments like that, it is always possible to turn the tables around and dispute the serious intent of the letter from the *Mare Tenebrarum*. Indeed, perhaps persuaded by the satirical tone, some critics fall back on Poe's protest that he is not to be taken in the "character of Truth Teller" (210). This they interpret as his surrender of claims to the seriousness of his propositions, turning him, in effect, into another Emerson.

This strikes me as a gross misreading of the essay. One of Poe's identifiable goals is exactly *not to* separate *Eureka* from other areas of inquiry but to bring it side by side with the methods and findings of science and logic. Poe contrives to defend the poetic realm by putting it on par with other areas of knowledge and uniting all in a grand Truth-seeking enterprise. In other words, his goal is to *unify* inquiry, no matter in what field-specific methodology it might manifest itself. Poe's epistemological slogan can be reconstructed as "unity without uniformity," and he offers many arguments in support of this view. One of the most explicit must be his description of the poetic intuition as a series of "*de*ductions or *in*ductions of which the processes were so shadowy as to have escaped his consciousness" (220).

Poe's conviction of the unity of science seems to be reflected and substantiated in its ensuing application to his "legitimate thesis, *The Universe*" (221). The cosmological hypothesis points back to the unifying theory of knowledge by proposing as its central principle that "In the Original Unity of the First Thing lies the Secondary Cause of all things" (211). For all the above reasons it seems unfair, not to say incorrect, to attribute to Poe any dualistic views on the nature of knowledge (see below for a more detailed discussion of dualism). *Eureka* is neither to abolish philosophy and science nor to erect the Great Wall of China around poetic, or what we would call today, humanistic inquiry. Instead it is to ameliorate the empirical and deductive methods by infusing them with poetic intuition.

It seems wrong therefore to claim that Poe's reference to *Eureka* as a Poem grants it a special status, incompatible with systematic philosophical ambitions. By calling it a poem, in an essay that throws poetry into the same epistemological pot with philosophy and science, Poe merely stresses its field-specific – i.e., literary – attributes. The stylistic, figurative, and rhetorical features of *Eureka* are, indeed, greatly interesting in the context of Poe's theoretical efforts (for a more detailed analysis, see chapter 3). But reliance on field-specific means of inquiry is common to *all* disciplines and cannot validate separatist arguments for literature's alleged epistemological sovereignty.

I conclude that even if Poe's selective invitation to read *Eureka* as a poetic suggestion is to be taken at face value, it does not contest its status as a genuine essay in philosophy. The literary line of defense of *Eureka* can thus hardly be extended to the argumentative tactics employed to defend its "truths." Once the method is proven to be flawed, the reasons for sanctioning its findings become invalid – even if, by sheer luck, it produces a true result.

THE PROGRESS OF THE EMPIRICAL SNAIL

> The trouble with facts is that there are so many of
> them.
>
> Samuel McChord Crothers

Poe's critique is not confined to logic and its axioms but extends to that alleged "Vulture! whose wings are dull realities!" – empirical science. Poe's objection to the school of Bacon is what he saw as excessive preoccupation with the atoms of factual data, to the neglect of "those ultimate and only legitimate facts, called Law" (215). The established literary critical wisdom – no doubt influenced by Poe's indignant tone – is that he rejected empiricism lock, stock, and barrel. Joan Dayan is typical in ascribing to Poe the view that neither "the fact-finders ... nor the speculators ... can bring us closer to *certainty* or real knowledge" (30).

Although widespread, such opinion is plainly inaccurate, since, even during his attack, Poe is demonstrably aware of the strengths of the Baconian way. The nature of empirical research *does not* affect for him its ability to establish the truth about the world. Its only weakness is slowness, since it does not yield "the maximum amount of truth, even in any long series of ages" (215). The alleged flaw of empiricism is thus not, as Dayan concludes, an inability to discover truth, but its snail-like pace produced by inordinate attention to details. Moreover, although Poe never forgives empiricists for what he sees as their repression of imagination, he acknowledges "*absolute* certainty in the snail progress" (215) to be a methodological point in their favour.[9]

Still, what about the view of empirical science as a dull-winged Vulture? It takes no specialized knowledge to conclude that a mere collection of facts is not science, nor ever has been. Even the Chaldean astronomers of antiquity, who first recorded the apparent motions of heavenly bodies on the firmament, were no mere scientific accountants. The very fact that, by collating and studying their data, they predicted phenomena like lunar phases or eclipses, indicates an active and creative approach to their findings.

The evidence that contradicts Poe's portrayal of science as a plodding exercise in mere fact-gathering is abundant. It is hard to imagine that this intelligent man – an amateur Egyptologist who should have known that the agriculture of the ancient Nile delta was regulated by the ancients' knowledge of astronomy – was ignorant of it. What is more likely is that Poe fought a holy Romantic jihad with the inevitably mechanical and materialistic models of the world. It would be a matter of principle to portray scientific inquiry as dull and predictable and contrast it to the inspired musings of the Romantic poet. It may also help explain why Poe should ignore the fact that the "dull" mechanistic determinism of mid-nineteenth-century science had at its root Newton's laws of motion, perhaps the greatest testimony to the power of scientific imagination.

Poe's twin components of an intuitive leap of imagination – consistency and certainty – clearly fail as reliable guides to the truth. Still, amid multiple instances of self-contradiction, Poe continues to affirm that *"perfect consistency can be nothing but an absolute truth"* (219). It thus seems fair to inquire into the character of this absolute truth to which he refers. Is it logical in nature, perfect and inviolable in its internal design, but not necessarily representing the real world? Or is absolute truth to be found in correspondence to the known empirical facts about Poe's grand thesis, the material Universe?

The underlying dichotomy is aptly illustrated by the so-called Coconut puzzle, a famous mathematical problem involving complicated rules for allotment of coconuts to five people and a monkey after a shipwreck.[10] There is in fact an infinite number of solutions to the problem, but the puzzle asks for the smallest number of coconuts, which turns out to be 15,621. After the problem was posed, however, Paul Dirac came up with another solution: −4 coconuts! Mathematically, both solutions are equal, and, since the latter number is smaller, it should be preferred as the answer to the problem.

Dirac's clever mathematical interpretation of the rules of the puzzle illustrates the nature of speculations not checked by empirical accuracy. Since there are no negative coconuts in our universe, his solution, despite logical consistency with the rules of the puzzle, is false. In other words, unlike self-consistent axioms, *empirical* hypotheses must defer to our best knowledge about the world. The ultimate test of Poe's absolute truths about the universe must be their check with its known physical aspects. Unfortunately, we must add the confusion between the nature of logical systems and empirical research to the list of Poe's errors.

GRINDING HIS AXIOMATIC AXE

The poet only asks to get his head into the heavens.
It is the logician who seeks to get the heavens into
his head. And it is his head that splits.
                                        Gilbert Keith Chesterton

There is no doubt that by insisting on the inherent unaccountability of the imaginative leap, Poe may have intuited something significant about the nonroutine aspects of inquiry. Had he confined himself to that point, he would have been accurate in emphasizing the special role that intuition and imagination plays in our thinking.[11] His persistent questioning of the adequacy of purely logical criteria in evaluating explanations also presages the contemporary dissatisfaction with the so-called deductive-nomological model of knowledge (I return to this subject in the final two sections of this chapter).[12] Indeed, many of Poe's theses point towards the recognition of the nondeductive, or, as we would call it, pragmatic factors in the justification of knowledge. His grasp of the importance of pragmatic factors is all the more impressive in that *Eureka* was written decades before the birth of philosophical pragmatics.

Yet Poe's inspired intuitions swim in a sea of fallacious reasoning, perhaps best seen in his confusion between axiomatic and empirical truth. In any analytic system taken in isolation from empirical data, there is no manner whatsoever to establish its truth other than by the internal consistency of its axioms. Poe is thus completely misguided when he hectors that "*no such things as axioms ever existed or can possibly exist*" (216). This nonsense could only be uttered by someone who does not appreciate the arbitrary nature of axiomatic formulations.

There are at least two problems with Poe's conception of axioms. First, quoting a few false axiomatic statements is in his mind equivalent to showing that all axioms must be invalid. Characteristically, even here he makes an error typical of his rhetorical fervour, including propositions such as "there cannot be antipodes" (216), which have never been axioms at all. Second, he fails to draw proper conclusions from an otherwise correct observation that not all axioms ever used by science pass the experimental test. When axioms are proven empirically wrong, it does not undermine their internal logic or the theorems derived from them. Moreover, once axiomatic self-evidence is put to question, it allows for a proliferation of logical systems not necessarily compatible with each other, yet perfectly self-consistent. Poe overlooks this possibility and repudiates all axioms, no matter how self-evident. In their place he offers intuition as a source of truth, ignoring the fact that without any systematic backing the intuitive leap must ultimately rest on the kind of self-evidence that he had ridiculed in axioms. It is symptomatic of Poe that, while rejecting axioms wholesale, he uses their polemical authority whenever it suits his goals, as during the discussion of the laws of radiation (241).

Poe paints science and logic as ossified and regressive, claiming that any intuitive leap of imagination is immediately stifled if it falls "neither under the category Hog [i.e., Bacon], nor under the category Aries [Aristotle]" (215). What criteria, then, should one adopt in order to decide the value of a poetic leap? It turns out that it is difficult to give an answer in Poe's own terms. It cannot be self-evidence, which did not save axioms from his axe. Neither is it consistency, which, as we saw, does not guarantee the uniqueness of truth. Nor can it be empirical soundness, since correspondence to factual data need not decide the case for Poe's theorist.

The more one studies *Eureka*, the clearer it becomes that there is no surefire way to evaluate the findings of the intuitive leap. Beyond the reach of axiomatic soundness or empirical evidence, it is grounded only in a personal conviction of its truth. Unfortunately for Poe and his Grand Epistemological

Design, science has a low view of any such principle. In "Studies in the Logic of Confirmation," Carl Hempel expressly repudiates it: "a feeling of conviction ... is often deceptive and can certainly serve neither as a necessary nor as a sufficient condition for the soundness of a given assertion" (1965, 10). Moreover, Poe's treatment of intuition begs an important question. How will subjective self-evidence, no matter how keenly experienced, hold against another poetic leap, equally self-evident to its proponent but incompatible with the first?

Unable to prove his point, Poe resorts to a familiar tactic: sophistry. His target is classical logic and one of its cornerstones – the principle of non-contradiction. Poe argues that it is impossible for the following two theses to be simultaneously true:

1 "contradictions cannot *both* be true";
2 "*in no case*, is ability or inability to conceive [a proposition], to be taken as a criterion of axiomatic truth" (both on 218).

Juxtaposing 1 and 2, Poe concludes that logic – which he personifies in John Stuart Mill – must be at fault.

The cause of Poe's misunderstanding is his apparent belief that Mill accepted the principle of non-contradiction only because he could not conceive of its negative. There are, of course, classic proofs to show that a system that asserts of P and *not* P in the same sense and at the same time is empty (it is, in fact, trivial, owing to the infinity of true and false propositions in it). Moreover, Poe is again confused in what he is setting out to achieve. Adopting 1 and 2, all he can hope to show is that 2 does not *have to* be true, not that it *must* be untrue. Finally, the logical anarchy implicit in the suspension of this axiom raises the spectre of total intellectual chaos, with devastating implications for Poe's – or anybody's – research agenda.

KEPLER'S LEAP TO THE STARS

After glimpsing the regularity behind the world,
Kepler and Copernicus were motivated primarily
by the desire to uncover more of it, not to interpret
it or use it to support an extra-scientific
philosophy.

John Barrow

Although the problems of inquiry and its systematic analysis are central to *Eureka* as a whole, they play a particularly important role at the very end of the epistemological "letter." Ironically, what was to be Poe's clinching evidence for the dismissal of science as devoid of imagination is yet another triumph of rhetoric over impartial judgment.

His case against the errors of empiricism is built around Kepler's discovery of the planetary motions (in passing, he also mentions the work of Laplace, as well as Champollion's deciphering of the hieroglyphs). Poe lionizes Kepler, since, in his mind, only true thinkers like him could liberate science from the fact-finding ground moles. Again Poe turns empirical research into an unimaginative, treadmill exercise performed by phalanxes of little men scurrying around in search of more and more raw data. No matter how evocative it may have been to some of his readers, this picture is simply false. Having set up his straw dummy, Poe overlooks a host of basic functions performed by routine science, all of them known in his time:

- directional: diverting research to areas where unsolved problems exist;
- denotational: setting the parameters and specifics of investigated problems;
- verificational: determining the empirical values and accuracy of theoretical predictions;
- transformational: refining problems and concepts into simpler forms;
- relational: studying secondary and related problems in the wake of a successful (in)validation of the theory under test.

One thing is clear: confined to theorizing only, science would perforce not be what and where it is today. Although in some disciplines, such as particle physics, theories often race ahead of experiment, their unchecked proliferation is commonly regarded as a less than ideal state.[13] If science was interested only in quantitative expansion, while rejecting theoreticians with what Poe calls "supreme contempt" (220), it would indeed be a mad enterprise. Moreover, were we to take Poe's picture at face value, it is inconceivable that Kepler and Champollion should ever have been inducted into the Science Hall of Fame. Put simply, either science rebuffs theorists and it did reject Kepler and his work, or it does not and it did not reject Kepler and his work. Since only the second alternative is true, it refutes Poe's major premise.

To close the book on Poe's glorification of Kepler as a supreme theorist who guessed empirical truths solely by dint of his imagination, let us examine the pertinent facts of the scientist's life. There is hardly any doubt that the formulation of Kepler's laws must have involved at some point a creative or associative leap of imagination. But, dwelling on this singular moment, Poe ignores a number of facts from Kepler's life that contest, if not altogether contradict, him. Let us remember Poe's necessary and sufficient conditions for the accuracy of the intuitive leap: one's personal conviction of its truth and internal consistency. What is, then, the historical context?

In 1597, prior to the formulation of his laws, Kepler published a small volume entitled *Mysterium Cosmographicum* (*The Mystery of the Universe*). This work introduced a perfectly consistent theory of planetary motions based on the five Pythagorean solids, a theory of whose veracity Kepler was apparently as certain as if "an oracle had spoken to him from heaven" (Caspar 1959, 63). According to Poe's criteria, Kepler's leap of imagination should have been necessarily correct. Yet it was not, and the issue for the scientist was decided by a confrontation between his predictions and empirical data. Kepler, this inspired genius whose work Poe hailed as a supreme example of the superfluity of ground-mole empiricism, deferred to the facts and abandoned this particular line of reasoning.

Equally important, it is likely that Kepler would never have found his laws had he not been able to avail himself of the astronomical data compiled by Tycho Brahe. Aware of the discrepancies between the Ptolemaic and Copernican theories and observed facts, Brahe formed a kind of prototypal research establishment and embarked on a ground-mole fact-finding mission of the type despised by Poe. If it is true that Brahe could not have accomplished Kepler's work, it is equally true that without Brahe's meticulous observations "Kepler could have never found his planet laws" (Caspar 97). What is more, Brahe's data did not just play the role of a fact store but were indispensable as a source of *inspiration* for Kepler's work. Guided by his patron's findings that the orbit of Mars was by far the most anomalous of the orbits of all the planets, Kepler used the Martian data as a cornerstone for his research. Inspiration or not, Kepler would probably not have discovered much had he studied any other planet but Mars, since the orbits of the other planets are much less elliptical.[14]

It is evident that, in contrast to Poe's assertions, intuitive conviction, no matter how feverishly experienced at the birth of a theory, is not a reliable criterion of its soundness. Having drawn the wrong conclusions from Kepler's research, Poe would have been even more disconcerted to learn the results of modern-day ground-moles' empirical findings. As Jean Kovalevsky puts it, it turns out that Kepler's laws – the cornerstone of Poe's argument – "are of no value [today] in representing the real movements in the solar system" (608).

UNITED WE STAND, DIVIDED WE FALL

> Sometimes truth comes riding into history on the back of error.
>
> Reinhold Niebuhr

Having examined Poe's new epistemology, one is forced to conclude that his specific theses are largely ambiguous and their supporting arguments unconvincing, if not altogether incoherent. What was to be a methodical treatment of logic and science becomes a paradigm of confusion and error. Poe was an inspired and bold thinker, but his pretensions to epistemological rigour do not pass muster. In the spirit of Bertrand Russell's remarks about the profitable transfer of methods rather than explicit findings from the special sciences to other fields, Poe's lasting merit has thus more to do with his general methodological approach than with most of his specific arguments.

One of his most valuable contributions is a clear answer to the epistemological dualists who uphold the need for a separation of disciplinary research-goals and practices. Poe is aware that the explanatory standards favoured outside the natural sciences diverge from those cultivated by philosophers of science and tries to furnish a plausible alternative to any such reductivist theory of inquiry. In this conception Poe is superior to many of his twentieth-century successors. His ideal is to bring the study of human affairs into the circle of the sciences. The desire to bring all disciplines together, instead of perpetuating the myth about their incompatibility, needs to be acknowledged as Poe's enduring philosophical triumph.

The methodological and epistemological dualists can also learn a great deal from Poe's general argumentative strategy. Believing that his intuitive principle can improve on empirical and philosophical means, Poe takes the proper methodological course to try to establish that this is indeed the case. Instead of protecting his theory by some disciplinary version of Frost's adage about how good fences make good neighbours, Poe invites criticisms from the very methods he contests. His maturity as a thinker is again evident not so much in his specific arguments but, more significantly, in openness to interdisciplinary analysis, comparison, and critique. Poe is aware that any theory of knowledge that aims to dethrone the reigning monarch must first present itself at the epistemological court for an audience, where it must show that it can rule the realm at least as well as King Empiricus and Queen Logica. One difference between Poe and Emerson is that the latter never shows up for the audience, while the author of *Eureka* displays his wares in full view of the court.

That Poe's grand project has lost little of its power even for a modern-day philosopher is apparent in Willard Van Orman Quine's admission: "As a young man I was fascinated by a literary piece that certainly was a factor in my becoming interested in philosophy: Edgar Allan Poe's *Eureka*" (in Barradori 38). It is true that few goals can compare with Poe's attempt to redescribe the canonized pattern of inquiry and to systemize the unsystematic – the inspired leap of imagination. Poe tries to give us a New Epistemology tailored for the dawn of the new era of interdisciplinary union of Art, Philosophy, and Science and staggers even today with the sweep and boldness of his ambition.

One way to vindicate the spirit of Poe's epistemological program may be to compare it to the recent developments in philosophy of science. In the remainder of this chapter I will thus develop his keen intuitions about the unity of inquiry and the pragmatic turn in epistemological theory. In this undertaking I am indebted to two studies that, from their respective social-scientific and natural-scientific perspectives, fashion a Poe-like model of inquiry, united in its field-specific variety.

In *Literary Knowledge* (1988) Paisley Livingston defends an epistemological model that contests the much-touted, but superficial, methodological divisions proposed by dualists of various stripes. Much of my task here is to show the incoherence of these Neo-Kantian arguments for separating humanistic inquiry from the type of knowledge sought and valorized by the sciences. For a clear articulation of a positive alternative to such unmitigated dualism I turn to Richard Miller's *Fact and Method* (1988). Although ostensibly a book on philosophy of science, his model of inquiry has wide-ranging implications not only for the natural sciences but for the social sciences as well.[15] Scholars in the humanities in general, and literary studies in particular, should also take heed of Miller's theses. One of his central moves is to establish a unified interdisciplinary framework that gives the social disciplines the much-sought methodological legitimacy, without undermining their field-specific identity.

NOTHING NEW ABOUT NEO-KANTIANISM

> ... the Department of Mathematics requires
> nothing but money for paper, pencils and waste
> paper baskets and the Department of Philosophy
> is better still. It doesn't even ask for waste paper
> baskets.
>
> Anonymous University President

In his trenchant survey of the contemporary theories of inquiry, Livingston applies the tag Neo-Kantian to a composite doctrine that has played the leading role in the humanist wing of academia. Whether adopting Kant, Rickert, Wittgenstein, Ingarden, or Habermas as its central text, its main tenet remains essentially the same. It holds that the quest for knowledge is conducted by two separate and autonomous enterprises, the goals of which are fundamentally different and, for the most part, independent of each other. Their alleged difference is encoded in the labels for the two types of inquiry: idiography and nomothesis. The humanities' allegedly subjective involvement with cultural values and with the exploration of nonrecurrent facets of human existence is contrasted with the natural sciences's preference for objectivity and facts, typically leading to law-like predictions.[16]

The Neo-Kantian argument is used to underwrite any number of parochially disciplinary approaches to humanistic study. It must not, however, be considered in isolation from a deeper epistemological anxiety about unified inquiry. For many scholars scientific interdisciplinarity is indistinguishable from positivism, which they rightly see as an unacceptable model for unified science. As a result, they end up throwing the baby out with the bathwater, dismissing the former when, on reflection, all they want to reject is the latter. Confident that both the classical and probabilistic models worked out by positivists are untenable in a number of legitimate areas of humanist research, Neo-Kantians reject the idea of a fundamentally unified science, of which positivism is after all only one (albeit an immensely influential) model.

In an important sense, humanist scholars are right to insist that positivism has failed to articulate a robust theory of knowledge that could describe and legitimize different fields of inquiry. They are also right to emphasize the importance of field-specific methods and solutions on which various disciplines fall back in evaluating their explanatory accounts. But there are many persuasive reasons for rejecting both the spirit and the letter of the Neo-Kantian dichotomy. The following is a synopsis of some of the central ones.

1 The dualist framework does not command a central, or even privileged, position in the modern research environment. In fact, it was formulated in the first place to shore up the already dwindling prestige of humanities in the nineteenth-century university. If anything, the imbalance in favour of science over the humanities has become even more pronounced since. Routine hierarchical decisions (i.e., honorary or budgetary) are a clear testimony to the institutional partiality towards the nomothetic approach to knowledge and inquiry. The Neo-Kantian pretensions to equal epistemic rights must thus be judged in terms of the prevalent scientific mode of cognition, which is anything but conciliatory towards the autonomous theory of knowledge.[17]

2 One strategy to buttress the humanities is to attack the other side of the dichotomy by denying that the scientific method can produce knowledge that is objective, reliable, cumulative, and so forth. Typically, all diverse strands of poststructuralist "thought" indict science as a contingent and relativized amalgam of socially constructed worldviews, which is supposed to render rational arguments undecidable in terms of their truth value. Clearly such views are incoherent. Their claims are advanced within the framework of epistemic rationality, even as they uphold the idea that epistemic norms are no longer applicable.[18]

3 More important, the extraordinary epistemic, economic, and political successes of the scientific enterprise are a fact that no amount of academic skepticism can undermine. All such skepticism can ever accomplish is to raise doubts about certain logical foundations of science, a policy that does not even begin to address the systematic superiority of the nomothetic

type of inquiry. Bluntly put, the dualist dogma is neither a broadly supported nor an adequate framework to judge the epistemological and socioinstitutional consequences of the coexistence of the humanities and the sciences.[19]

4 According to Neo-Kantians, research in the humanities is based on idiography and cultural hermeneutics. This methodological description does not, however, stand up to scrutiny. Literary studies are a good counterexample, for neither its professed research goals nor actual methods vindicate the official line. Literary scholars do not deal exclusively with particulars, nor can the dualistic ideology account for the nomothetic pressures that have repeatedly been brought to bear on the critical domain, both from within and without. The proud pseudo-scientism of, for example, literary formalists, structuralists, or semioticians, is simply not compatible with the theory of autonomous knowledge enshrined in the dualist doctrine.[20]

5 Finally, the Neo-Kantian framework does not command a meta-perspective from which to arbitrate between claims to epistemic legitimacy. Claims that the scientific method cannot be effectively applied to mutable and fuzzy cultural entities like meaning or value are incoherent and lead straight back to the position they try to reject. If cultural entities are beyond the reach of the scientific method, then it should be possible to give a general proof or demonstration of it. Yet by definition this alternative is denied, considering that the methods of science are banned from operating on cultural entities. It shows that Neo-Kantians cannot coherently establish doubt about the likelihood of success in unifying inquiry. Moreover it is not clear how dualists can coherently assert anything about concepts like value or meaning after having banished such general terms from descriptions of socio-cultural reality.[21]

BETWEEN A ROCK AND A HARD PLACE

If the purpose of scientific methodology is to
prescribe or expound a system of enquiry or even
a code of practice for scientific behaviour, then
scientists seem able to get on very well without it.

Peter Medawar

Unification of inquiry is not a matter of imposing a positivist philosophy of science onto the social sciences and humanities. Nor is it a matter of espousing some vicious form of reductionism or of forming a single uniform body of knowledge. Its goals are at once more modest and more ambitious. In Livingston's words, unification is about "the possibility that some of the most basic principles of natural scientific research, as well as some of the physical and life sciences' specific findings, must play a fundamental role in any genuine human science" (*Literary Knowledge*, 148). These principles find an articulate expression in Richard Miller's *Fact and Method*.

Broadly speaking, positivism rests on the assumption that the foundational scientific notions, such as explanation or confirmation, obey apragmatic logical rules. Such rules are thought to be invariant for all sciences and historical periods; it is enough to know the content of the propositions in question to apply them effectively. Thus the first question of scientific methodology – When does a set of hypotheses, if true, *explain* why something happened? – is thought to be resolved purely by reference to whether the hypotheses and the given event statement are of a proper logical form. For the positivist they must consist of a general empirical law and independent statements of initial conditions that jointly entail the particular event. The second question – When does a body of data *confirm* a given hypothesis? – is also thought to be handled by general a priori rules describing proper types of entailment that connect hypotheses with data.

Over the years a large body of contrary evidence has forced even Hempel, the acknowledged dean of positivism, to revise his opinions.[22] Yet at the same time positivism continues to dominate scientific practice and theory. These days, its insufficiently flexible categories and theories of deductive logic are augmented with the theory of probability and counterfactual analysis. All the same, as a variety of by now canonical examples proves, the positivist covering-law model – so called after the requirement that an empirical general law must always underlie, or cover, an explanation – fails as an account of the theory and practice of science across disciplines.

This puts many nonpartisans in a quandary, since the demise of positivism leaves them too close for comfort to antirealists, who also repudiate Hempel's model of scientific inquiry (especially its account of confirmation). For a typical antirealist, theoretical validity is always relative to a framework of beliefs that, combined with skepticism about a shared framework of scientific inquiry, leads to methodological relativism. For this reason the controversy over the validity and extent of positivism has been pronounced in the social sciences (and, by extension, in the humanities), where theories are more likely to be judged on methodological grounds.

One can broadly identify three ways in which different groups have responded to this situation. First, quite a few social scientists continue to adhere to positivism even in the face of its evident shortcomings. And as long as positivistic subsumption under general laws looms as the Holy Grail of scientific explanation, the search for such laws is defended as the only legitimate goal of scientific research. As such, even patent failures of so many research programs oriented in this way do not discourage its proponents. Even in the face of contrary evidence from the trenches, they do not question the overall battle plan but merely shift troops over to a new location. In

Miller's example, "when social anthropologists discovered that their field work yielded few interesting general laws involving relatively concrete phenomena ... they did not abandon the pursuit of general laws. Many responded by seeking such general relationships among more abstract structural characteristics, such as 'binary opposition.' Many economists elaborate the internal logic of some general model, serenely accepting that their work makes no appreciable contribution to explaining specific episodes of inflation or unemployment, or specific international economic relations" (28).

The above tactics are defended by an appeal to the positivist criteria of explanation and their demand for general laws, which in turn entail working with general models as the most promising strategy for accomplishing this goal. One unattractive feature of such a stance is that it rejects out of hand as pseudo-explanations what, for most people, seem valuable and plausible hypotheses. This is because they are not covered by a general empirical law and thus fail the covering-law model's standard. Many social scientists and scholars in the humanities are justifiably skeptical of having their theories branded "good enough for certain purposes, but strictly and logically speaking inadequate" (26). On the other hand, moving away from positivism in order to avoid such unfounded criticism, many end up professing some form of neo-Kantian dualism. This second type of response, coupled with a frequent denial of scientific realism, has fertilized the proliferation of hermeneutics in the social sciences, together with a feeling of immunity from a genuinely critical discourse.

The third faction is the moderate middle-of-the-road, which finds affinity neither with positivist restrictions on the scope and legitimacy of inquiry nor with the relativist and/or dualist alternatives. It is perfectly coherent, after all, to reject the overly inflexible rules of the covering-law theory of knowledge while continuing to work with the core concepts of the scientific method. Richard Miller's pragmatic and causal model of the scientific method is thus not only an attractive but, on reflection, almost an inevitable alternative to the scientists and scholars of this group.

THE FACT AND METHOD OF UNIFIED INQUIRY

> Though leaves are many, the root is one;
> Through all the lying days of my youth
> I swayed my leaves and flowers in the sun;
> Now I may wither into the truth.
>
> William Butler Yeats

Even before looking at Miller's proposals, we can broadly anticipate the type of theory that could succeed in laying the foundations of unified inquiry. It ought to avoid the positivist myth that scientific explanations and confirmations are a purely logical matter, atemporal and asocial, and thus without pragmatic consequences. Likewise, it ought to shun the Charybdis of constructivist reduction of epistemology to contingent and incompatible frameworks relative to ideological or institutional tribal interests. Finally, it is doubtful that any theory that purports to organize inquiry can do so in isolation from the basic principles and findings of science. All this points towards a realist model of knowledge, grounded in the fallible but self-correcting practice of the scientific disciplines. It relies on a minimal assumption that scientific theories refer at least in part to entities existing independently of our theories and experiments.

Miller's approach meets all of these requirements. In its slogan version, *an explanation is an adequate description of underlying causes that bring about a phenomenon.* Adequacy here is not a matter of logical derivations but of specific standards obtaining in particular scientific fields at particular times. This makes adequacy and explanation – and thus the entire scientific enterprise – "far more contingent, pragmatic and field-specific than positivists allowed, but no less rationally determinable" (6). Causation, for example, is not amenable to general analysis *à la* positivism. Reaching to the world of art, Miller models it after the concept of an artwork, with its diverse but stable core of cases that evolve outwards according to basic principles of science instead of deductive logic. The legitimacy, i.e., explanatory value, of a particular model or theory is thus founded on specific empirical arguments regulating proposed extensions from the core concept.

This pragmatic approach to judging the validity of causal patterns is grounded in the concept of research as a social process ordered around socially accepted procedures. The core concept of causality depends on the social recognition of the core concept, the extension procedure, and intermediate cases. The required causal depth, which precludes explanations from being true but trivial or true but insufficient, is brought out by Miller's analysis of "depth as priority" and "depth as necessity" (86–104). These concepts assure that the causes described are the true underlying mechanisms of change in a given situation (I return to these concepts in chapter 5).

Miller's account of confirmation is likewise causal, comparative, and historical, treating confirmation as a fair causal comparison among rival views. Thus a theory is confirmed if one can plausibly argue that the best available causal analysis of accumulated data and available theories entails the approximate truth of the theory and the falsehood of its current (though not necessarily all hypothetically possible) rivals. Such a dependence on the pragmatic context surrounding the development of any hypothesis turns confirmation into a historical process in a way that squarely contradicts the entrenched tenets of positivism.

This turn away from logical generality to a more contingent, descriptive, and historical approach to knowledge formation has of course wide implications for the social sciences. The most persistent and fervent question in the philosophy of the social sciences has always been whether, as a group, they are fundamentally different from the natural sciences. Any answer to this question must be squared with the fact that the up-and-coming fields, such as economics, linguistics, sociology, psychology, or anthropology, have achieved academic respectability by deliberately emulating the natural scientific paradigm. But only the lingering faith in positivism supports the conclusion that because the social sciences fail to adhere to the covering-law model, they must be more different from the natural sciences than the latter are from each other. In fact, the basic goals and methods of the social sciences are no more different from those of most natural sciences than the basic goals and methods of any single natural science.

No one has ever tried to deny that the social sciences are significantly distinct in their field-specific methods, standards, and interests. But on Miller's account it is difficult to insist that they must differ from the natural sciences in the logical form of their explanations, since the latter display a diversity that outranks even that found among the social sciences. Much as Poe appears to be aware in the epistemological "letter" in *Eureka*, reliance on specific means of inquiry is common to all disciplines, which makes the social sciences very much *like* the natural ones. It is for this reason that Poe puts poetic intuition side by side with the deductive and inductive methods in order to work out a scientific account of universal creation in the second part of *Eureka*.

CHAPTER THREE

An Essay in Cosmology

There is a theory which states that if ever anyone
discovers exactly what the Universe is for and
why it is here, it will instantly disappear and be
replaced by something even more bizarre and
inexplicable.
There is another theory which states that this
already happened.

Douglas Adams,
The Hitch Hiker's Guide to the Galaxy

Cosmology, like astronomy, has for many centuries been almost synonymous
with (natural) philosophy. Beginning with the ancient thinkers, through the
Scholastics, the Neoclassicists and the Romantics, down to the modern times,
theories of the universe have abounded without end. The cosmology proposed by Poe in *Eureka* must be viewed in the context of these earlier, as
well as later, efforts to describe the history and purpose of the Cosmos.
Mindful of science and its critical check on unbridled philosophical speculations, Poe aims to construct a system consistent with the empirical data at
his disposal. His cosmology, perhaps unique in its interdisciplinary reliance
on aesthetics, logic, and empiricism, once more testifies to his philosophical
ambitions, even if not always crowned with full success.

CAN TWO WRONGS MAKE A RIGHT?

All science is cosmology, I believe.
Karl Popper

In this chapter I take a hard look at Poe's cosmological theory of the universal
creation out of unity. Following a summary of the theory's main points, I

examine several of its central elements: Newton's third law of mechanics and Poe's quantitative depiction of the solar system, as well as the role of aesthetic criteria in evaluating empirical theses. Consonant with Poe's allusion to *Eureka* as a Poem, I also discuss his style and specific tropes, showing how he frequently uses his superb rhetorical skills to gloss over more enigmatic, or simply inconsistent, points in his theory. In conclusion I appraise the essay's literary and philosophical contribution.

Before analyzing Poe's cosmological hypothesis, let us recapitulate the errors that hampered his epistemological theory. The main one is incoherence, notwithstanding the writer's protests that *Eureka* is a paradigm of internal harmony and logic. By incoherence I do not mean the opinions imputed to Poe that he largely did not espouse. Although various critics believe that Poe rejected experiment and logic altogether, there is ample evidence that this attitude is more indicative of the tone rather than the content of his actual views. For Poe logic and empirical science are both valid means of getting at the truth about the world. It is only for reasons of efficiency that he regards them with disfavour. His sporadic assertions that "All Experiment proves – all Philosophy admits" (231) his theses, must not therefore be counted as inconsistent.

But there are no mitigating circumstances for many of Poe's overt self-contradictions. In the throes of his italicized righteousness, he can claim that there is "*no such thing*" (211) as demonstration and that "*no such things*" (216) as axioms can exist at all. Yet his own assertions are "so thoroughly demonstrable" (233) that he cannot be bothered to provide even a shred of evidence in their support. This is made even worse by his claims about his mind being "accustomed to the introspective analysis of its own operations" (224). Since this type of error is so common in the first section of *Eureka*, it is natural to question whether Poe can avoid them in his cosmology. At the same time, one can expect another type of defect, mired in the faults of his method: predictive error, i.e., the failure of his speculations to conform to known facts.

The importance of this second type of error is in direct proportion to the question of whether *Eureka* refers to the empirical or the poetic (whatever that could mean) reality. As I argued in the previous chapter, on the whole Poe's tone is consistently factual and assertive. His preface deliberately alludes to Kepler, whose empirical theories were a model of inquiry for Poe. In the same vein, after hedging with the remark that he seeks "but to suggest," Poe affirms his intention "to *convince* through the suggestion" (239). Given the staggering amount of effort that he puts into convincing, one feels justified in taking *Eureka*'s cosmology seriously. After all, let us remember that any conceptual scheme that is in principle falsifiable – that is, one like Poe's – *is* a scientific theory. Is Poe's hypothesis, then, logically consistent and factually accurate? These are the questions I will try to answer below.

E UNO PLURES

Very few people read Newton, because it is
necessary to be learned to understand him.
But everybody talks about him.

Voltaire

The cosmology of *Eureka* opens with a reference to Alexander von Humboldt, one of the eminent scientists of Poe's time. While Humboldt's *Kosmos* (1845) described the physical universe, Poe designs to speak of no less than the "Physical, Metaphysical and Mathematical – of the Material and Spiritual Universe; – of its Essence, its Origin, its Creation, its Present Condition and its Destiny" (211).[1] Here is a general sketch of his theory (the capitalization is all his).

1 Poe opens with his principal cosmological hypothesis: "in the Original Unity of the First Thing lies the Secondary Cause of all Things, with the Germ of their Inevitable Annihilation" (211).

2 After examining the concept of Infinity, he limits his analysis to the Universe of Stars, since he does not wish to "call upon the reader to entertain the impossible conception of an absolute infinity" (225).

3 Poe proposes that God, by dint of his Volition, created one absolute, irrelative particle in a state of Simplicity. As the result of the Divine act, the particle is propagated radially and three-dimensionally through space.

4 With the withdrawal of God's volition, the forces of Action (Gravity, or Attraction) and Reaction (Electromagnetism, or Repulsion) take over. The latter accounts for the expansion of the Universe and the former for its finite size and eventual collapse into matterless, dimensionless Unity.

5 Invoking Newton's Third Law of Mechanics, Poe equates the universal diffusive force with the Material (Body) and the cohesive force with the Spiritual (Soul). He argues that radiation is both necessary and sufficient as a mode of interaction between the diffusive electricity and cohesive gravity.

6 Using Laplace's nebular hypothesis, Poe – within the framework of his cosmology – tries to show that it could account for the creation of the Solar system. He assumes this process of seeking equilibrium between gravitational contraction and electromagnetic repulsion to be typical on the Cosmic scale.[2]

7 Armed with astronomical data, Poe provides a quantitative description of the known Universe, combining space and time in a continuum (spacetime).

8 Four decades before Michelson and Morley's epochal experiment, Poe presciently rejects the idea of a physical ether; instead, he argues for the existence of Spiritual Ether as a source of Thought and Intelligence. Since

matter had been previously assumed to have originated through the Volition of God, Poe sees a direct link between the Creation of the Universe
and the emergence of Life.

9 Poe predicts the eventual catastrophic collapse of all Matter into a primordial, unified state. The process is characterized by "the absorption, by each
individual intelligence, of all other intelligences (that is, of the Universe)
into its own. That God may be in all, each must become God" (309). In
his last words Poe obliquely alludes to a recurring, cyclical Universe.

Poe's cosmology is presented in the longest and perhaps the most original
section of his essay. Unfortunately, it is marred by fundamental mistakes that
put the results of his effort in question. The most serious one, produced
entirely by his ignorance of the science of his day, is his misunderstanding
of Newton's laws of mechanics. This is not an isolated occurrence in Poe's
writings, despite his bombastic assertions about fluent knowledge of the
laws. In "The Purloined Letter," for example, Poe mishandles a matter so
fundamental as Newton's second law, leading Clarence Wylie to question
"how much of it was in any sense intelligible to him" (1946, 230). *Eureka*
supports the picture of an amateurish dilettante, who this time utterly
misinterprets Newton's third law. Roughly speaking, Poe views action and
reaction as temporally consecutive, in contravention of the law, which stip-
ulates that they are simultaneous. Moreover, action entails reaction only in
mechanics, whereas for Poe, "Any deviation from normality involves a tendency to return to it" (248).

Take also Poe's discussion of the diffusion of the primal particle and its
subsequent coalition into unity. Confident in being backed by Newton, the
writer argues that the "*tendency* of the disunited atoms to return into their
normal Unity ... will be without consequence ... until the diffusive energy
... shall leave *it*" (230). The same error returns more apodictically as his
argument gathers steam: "while an act is continued, no reaction, of course,
can take place" (245). At one point, Poe even claims in the same breath that
the "Newtonian Law of Gravity we may, of course, assume as demonstrated"
(270), and that "so long as the [primal] act *lasted*, no reaction, of course,
could commence" (271).

The consequences of Poe's liberty with Newton are in the form of his
assurance that the original diffusion must end in ultimate collapse – i.e., in
a return to the primal state. Poe's misapprehension of the third law leads
him to claim that "to conceive that what had a beginning is to have no end"
is an idea that "cannot *really* be entertained" (231). Of course the same
inability to conceive was previously milked for all its worth in his critique
of classical logic. Poe is thus guilty of another self-contradiction, on top of
his failure to stay abreast of elementary physics.

Another factual error, which runs a close second to Poe's misunderstanding of Newton's laws, is his assertion that electricity is only a repulsive force (231). As with Newton's third law, Poe's statement is all the more egregious since the attractive property of electricity was well known in his times. Even Harold Beaver, otherwise sympathetic to Poe's cosmological undertaking, does not euphemize at this point: Poe is "simply wrong" (405). Negligent of even the most fundamental science, Poe and his theory must already at this point be judged a failure.

A SYNTHESIS OF PHYSICS AND METAPHYSICS

> . . . the greater part of it is nonsense, tricked out
> by a variety of tedious metaphysical conceits, and
> its author can be excused of dishonesty only on
> the grounds that before deceiving others he has
> taken great pains to deceive himself.
>
> Peter Medawar

Considering these fundamental errors, it is no wonder that Poe's everlasting truths fare no better from the perspective of twentieth-century knowledge. In contrast to his assertions, matter was not created *into* space (228), but the entire continuum originated in the same event that created all matter in the universe. Eternal expansion not only *can* be entertained (231) but, in fact, unless the universe contains about ten times more "dark" (i.e., cold) matter in the shape of black holes, massed neutrinos, MACHOS, WIMPS, and other entities, than of visible (hot) matter, it *will* probably expand forever. Infinities are not all the same (255); in fact, the one discussed by Poe is actually of the lowest order. Finally gravity, far from being the strongest of forces (248), is actually the weakest, nor does it act instantaneously throughout the universe (236).[3]

That Poe's specific theses have no scientific value was obvious even to the earliest commentators on *Eureka.* John Henry Hopkins's review from 1848, in a particularly judicious early critique of Poe's essay, concludes that *Eureka* contains "an original, ingenious, profound, and abundant quantity of chaff" (in Walker 285). Writing in 1885, George Woodberry had no illusions that Poe had ever progressed beyond the most elementary physics, mathematics, and astronomy – just enough to "give his confused dogmatism a semblance of a reasoned system" (in Meyers 217).

Still, as other critics are at pains to point out, among the multitude of speculations in *Eureka* one can find a select few that coincide broadly with modern-day scientific theories. Thus, George Nordstedt (1930) juxtaposes *Eureka* with the theories of Einstein; Clayton Hoagland (1939) traces affinities between Poe and Eddington; and Arthur Hobson Quinn (1941) even solicits a response from Eddington himself. Yet even as he concedes that the "correspondence between some of [Poe's] ideas and modern views is interesting," Eddington quickly adds that "any one of independent mind ... is likely to hit the mark sometimes" (555). This deprecating view is seconded by Edmond Bauer: "From the scientific point of view, *Eureka* contains certain assertions, certain theoretical views which may seem to us correct or plausible; it also contains quite a great number of errors and reasoning that are hazy and infantile" (in Bonaparte 740).[4]

Among the more prescient of Poe's intuitions are, of course, his dismissal of cosmic ether and a persistent questioning of the self-evidence of geometric axioms, which occurred just as Lobachevski and Bolyai were formulating the first non-Euclidean geometries. These occasional lucky guesses are, nevertheless, embedded in a bedrock of systematic errors. In his cosmological theory Poe quickly attains "a point where only *Intuition* can aid us" (226) – the same intuition that tells him that his theory must be correct. Today intuition is no longer trusted to provide answers to scientific enigmas. Moreover, some of the cosmological questions raised by Poe can be, and are, put to test in particle accelerators, allowing physicists to test on micro-scale conditions similar to those of the primordial creation. In fact, the award of the 1984 Nobel Prize for physics to Carlo Rubbia's experimental team at the CERN accelerator in Geneva was widely seen as a symbolic recognition of the necessity of experimental check on the theoretical leap.

Faith, professes Poe, "is a matter quite distinct from ... *intellectual* belief" (225). However, on the same page he makes a leap of faith of precisely the kind he warns against. He proposes that the reason why the human mind cannot directly conceive of infinity is because "the Deity has not *designed* it" (215) to do so. Poe's failure to make even a token effort to explain his conviction begs the questions that recur throughout the essay. What authority tells him where the primary volition ends and the secondary scientific causes (gravity, radiation, diffusion, planetary laws) begin? How does he account for his twin assumption of the Godhead whose actions are never supererogatory? Why did not God, in his omnipotence and economy, create the world as it is, without the need for all the secondary causes – the "messy" forces studied by science?

The reason for these omissions and inconsistencies might be the incommensurability of Poe's areas of inquiry. *Eureka* speculates on God and his conception of the universe in the framework of empirical science. The two are, however, by definition separate. In Leszek Kolakowski's apt words, "God is not and cannot be an empirical hypothesis ... if the word 'hypothesis' retains its usual sense" (*Religion* 90). Poe's account of the creation is a good example of how the concessions he needs to make in one area to avoid inconsistency lead him to inconsistency in another. Calling an imbecile anyone who would presume anything about the nature and essence of God, he says, "ignorance of the Deity is an ignorance to which the soul is *everlastingly* condemned" (226). On the next page we read, however, that God's actions are never supererogatory and that the "exercise of the Divine Will will be proportional with that which demands its exertion" (250). Logically, either we know *something* about God, or we don't, and in either case one set of Poe's assumptions negates the other.[5]

A COURSE IN POPULAR ASTRONOMY

The Cosmos is about the smallest hole that a man
can hide his head in.
                            Gilbert Keith Chesterton

The concluding part of Poe's essay (points 6–9 in the summary given earlier in this chapter) is greatly indebted to nineteenth-century science, which provides him with a plethora of factual material to bolster his theses.[6] Poe quotes extensively from Laplace's nebular hypothesis, trying to shore up his purely deductive conclusions. He then gives a quantitative description of the solar system and the galaxy and argues against some contemporary cosmological theories. *Eureka* closes with a brief speculation on the terminal phase of the universe, when, according to Poe, all matter will be united with the Divine Spirit in a vaguely hinted form of spiritual pantheism.[7]

Once again it is abundantly clear that Poe has no need for epistemological relativism. His emphatic distinction between "a labyrinth of Error" and the "most luminous and stupendous temples of Truth" (273) is one of his basic philosophical tenets. For this reason he has no qualms about using science to show his ideas "empirically confirmed at all points" (265). Thus "*facts* of Astronomy" that can bolster his theory are scrupulously accounted for, and the reader is assured that "telescopes ... thoroughly confirm [Poe's theoretical] deductions" (274).

Sadly, this part of *Eureka* is also rife with inconsistencies, errors, and misconceptions. While using every opportunity to buttress his credibility with factual corroboration, Poe simply disregards data that contradicts his theory. It is one thing, for example, to claim that the coalescence of nebulous rings will lead to the formation of planets, although even in Poe's times it was known that an asteroid belt would be more likely. But to cook up ad hoc errata to laws of physics is a proposition of a different order. Yet Poe states that a single ring must have escaped the law – precisely the ring that lies between Mars and Jupiter.

While it is normal to anticipate the results of one's theory, no theoretician worth his salt will bend the rules rather than face the contrary indications of empirical data.[8] Arguing that Madler bends the rules of his argument to account for conclusions reached beforehand, Poe condemns such practice as common to "all *a priori* philosophers" (295). He himself, however, is a fine specimen of their class. His account of planetary formation is full of evidence of his effort to conform the actual state of the Solar system to his hypotheses. "Let us now suppose this mass so far condensed that it occupies *precisely* the … orbit of Neptune" (258), writes Poe, begging the question of why the orbit was conducive to the formation of a planet in the first place. His implied explanation – it happened because Neptune is where it is – is circular and thus no answer at all.

An even better example is Poe's discussion of the asteroid belt, where, according to the then known number of asteroids, he "explains" their presence by positing exactly nine centres of mass in the original ring. After the first printing of *Eureka* one more asteroid was discovered, but an a priori philosopher easily explained it as the product of the tenth centre of gravity. Today we know there are at least fifteen hundred asteroids occupying that region of space, but the number is irrelevant; one can as easily "explain" the presence of nine, as of thousands of bodies, by postulating ad hoc initial conditions. D.J. O'Connor's description of the differences between scientific and nonscientific inquiry provides a fit commentary both on Poe's failed synthesis and on his overall methodological strength: "Scientific explanations are specific and detailed and therefore capable of being confirmed *or refuted* by observable facts. Metaphysical explanations are overly general and con-sistent with any observed state of affairs. No facts count as refuting them, nor, consequently, as confirming them either … The history of human knowledge … has shown decisively that *a priori* dogmatizing gives no lasting results in the search for truth, and that cautious empiricism does in the end give genuine insight into the nature of things" (51, 46). Forcing data into the straitjacket of his theory, Poe behaves like Procrustes, lobbing feet off scien-tific facts whenever required, with little regard for consequences. His refer-ence to empirical findings looks like an a posteriori act of someone who knows well in advance what he wants to prove, and acts accordingly. But the same specificity of his theses, which leaves them open to falsifiability, must again be praised as part of Poe's mature approach to theory-building.

A LA RECHERCHE DU TEMPS PERDU

> Inquiry into final causes is sterile, and, like a
> virgin consecrated to God, produces nothing.
>   Francis Bacon

Poe's inconsistencies can be partly attributed to his desire to account not only for the physical but also the metaphysical universe. *Eureka* is not just about comprehending how but also "comprehending why" (291) the world should manifest itself to us in the way it does. Besides what Aristotle would call efficient causes, then, Poe is interested in formal and/or final universal causes as well. *Eureka* culminates, in fact, his search for the "rational cause" and the "sufficient reason" (291) for the universe as a whole. As such, the problems of final causes, teleology, and determinism deserve our brief attention.

In a letter to Sarah Helen Whitman from 1848 – i.e., at the time of writing *Eureka* – Poe prides himself on being thoroughly "accustomed ... to the Calculus of Probabilities" (Ostrom, 2: 385). The remarks on statistics and probability in his many writings indeed suggest some familiarity with the work of Laplace, Condorcet, Cournot, and Quetelet. What is not so obvious, again, is how much this awareness corresponded to a grasp of the actual theory. In "The Mystery of Marie Roget," for example, Poe comes close to personifying chance, which in itself suggests a misapprehension of the concept. But some of his statements on probability and determinism from *Eureka* ring false even if we grant him a correct understanding of the calculus of probabilities. At stake here is the heart of his cosmology – the role of chance in the universe.

It seems that, along with Laplace's nebular hypothesis, Poe inherited his mentor's ontological determinism. *Eureka* spares no examples of Poe's denial of cosmic accident. In the formation of the solar system, he writes, "of accident in the ordinary sense there was, of course, nothing" (260). Since our system is for Poe analogous to any other in the universe, he concludes that there was nothing accidental in the creation and development of any planetary system. Thus stars "accomplish ... Divine purposes," their density is "the measure in which their purposes *are* accomplished" (291), and matter was created "solely to serve the objects of th[e] spiritual Ether." In fact Poe claims that matter was created "as a Means – not as an End" (305) to the universe.

This picture is reinforced by Poe's views on the mutuality of evolutionary adaptation. The writer marvels at the concordance between the climatic conditions in the arctic, the type of fauna and flora found in that region (he specifically mentions the whale), and their ability to provide the type of nutrients necessary to support human life there. It is difficult to avoid the impression that Poe imagines this nutritional supply-and-demand equilibrium to be the result of an evolutionary master plan. The whales, their habitat, and human dietary habits were all destined to converge at this point in time and space, where they exhibit such perfect reciprocity of adaptation. In other words, the primordial explosion must have carried in itself the seeds of all processes that, in due time, produced the features mentioned by Poe.

The fallacy implicit in Poe's evolutionary determinism is his conviction that the course of the development of the universe was the only one possible, and thus necessary. This thesis bears remarkable semblance to some contemporary arguments advanced by the proponents of the so-called strong anthropic principle (SAP). In its most militant form, reminiscent of the old preformist arguments in biology, the SAP holds that the emergence of Homo sapiens must have been inherent in the big bang. In light of this cosmological principle, the universe becomes a sort of transcendent assembly line for the human species.[9]

Although the SAP has been challenged on many occasions, even if accepted, it is epistemically trivial.[10] Along with humans, an endless number of other species and phenomena came into existence in the course of the path taken by evolution. Whether the entity in question is Homo sapiens, the duck-billed platypus, the SAP, or this very book, there is no argument other than a circular one that could distinguish among them the teleological culmination of an evolutionary master plan. According to such a posteriori reasoning, in principle applicable to anything that actually exists, the universe evolved as much to create the human species, as to produce the platypus or my book – an amusing conclusion, but little more than that.

ARE LITERARY STANDARDS FIELD-SPECIFIC?

> We are unable to obtain a model of the Universe
> without some specifically cosmological assumptions
> which are completely unverifiable.
>
> G.F.R. Ellis

The last part of *Eureka* contains a few conjectures that seem at times to intimate modern scientific ideas. Poe vaguely outlines concepts that, from our perspective, can be interpreted as parallel universes, gravitational collapse, singularity, the universal inflationary "bubble," and even black holes. However, lest we fall into the same trap as the commentators who strive to establish Poe's scientific precocity, let us remember that vague analogies do not prove that their author had anticipated anything of contemporary science. Take black holes, for instance. Nothing in Poe's theory corresponds to stars collapsed beyond Schwarzschild's radius. His nonluminous suns are invisible only because they have not discharged planets for a while. Poe's intuitions are, at best, unsupported guesses that fail him more often than not. Contrary to his intuition – and a vigorous train of ratiocination – the moon is not, nor could it be, self-luminous. Had Poe lived until 1877, he would also have learned that Mars, "proven" by him not to be capable of having any moons, in fact has two.[11]

Under examination, Poe's cosmology reveals multiple errors of fact and interpretation. Worse still, since it was meant in part to legitimize the truth of the intuitive method, it makes the latter look like amateurish philosophy instead of a coherent alternative to the scientific system of inquiry. For if the new epistemology can occasionally intimate some useful ideas, but mostly lead to nonsense, its author's insistence on "Truth as its essentiality" (262) is an act of methodological hara-kiri.

There are, of course, time-honoured scientific principles for separating wrong conjectures from right. Analytic propositions must be free of logical error, and empirical propositions must, in addition, correspond to observed reality. Poe's philosophical endeavour, however noble and grand in design, is neither. What is more, in contravention of his own sound precepts, Poe puts too much faith in disciplinary criteria of epistemic soundness. He declares that "Man cannot long or widely err ... guided by his poetical ... instinct" (300). Hard as it is to believe that poetic intuition works epistemo-logically in the world of art, it is even harder to accept on faith that it may do so outside it.

Although tantalizingly close for Poe, the *field-specific* means and standards of poetry and science differ more than his instinct led him to believe. The twin aesthetic principles of his cosmology – simplicity and symmetry – obtain differently in Art and Science. Unity, pivotal in literary theory and practice since Aristotle, achieves in Poe the rank of a supreme structural rule. When looking for a cosmological principle to reflect his supposition of simplicity, with its aesthetically satisfying circularity and closure, he thus settles for one that has been a cornerstone of his own artistic endeavours.

As a consequence we read in *Eureka* that "*Oneness is a principle abundantly sufficient to account for ... the material Universe*" (227). Astrophysics has, however, a different idea of simplicity that, in short, relies on nothingness (0) and not unity (1).[12] Instead of having originated from a single primordial particle, the universe may be an inflated quantum fluctuation, whose universal attributes (charge, spin, and so forth) do not add up to one but cancel one another out to zero. In a similar vein, even though Poe claims that Laplace's nebular theory is "far too beautiful" (262) not to be true, science has since proven his rash equation of empirical truth and beauty to be false.

The same obtains for the other of Poe's aesthetic assumptions: symmetry. In *Eureka* Poe equates poetry, truth, and symmetry as manifestations of the same intuitive ratiocination. In fact, he holds that "the sense of the symmetrical is an instinct which may be depended on with almost blindfold reliance" (300). Whether it can be in art is, at best, questionable. But be that as it may, symmetry cannot be depended on with almost blindfold reliance elsewhere. This inapplicability goes beyond the difference in the order of complexity, which makes it hard to compare the simplest kinds of symmetry favoured in literary works, analogous to geometric translation and rotation, to the esoteric scientific models known as gauge symmetries.[13] The very principle of symmetry on a cosmic scale was dealt a mortal blow in 1956, when Tsun-Dao Lee and Chen Ning Yang established the universal nonconservation of parity (the breakdown of mirror symmetry on the subatomic level).[14] The conclusion is clear: simplicity and symmetry, Poe's twin theoretical beacons, are not the infallible guides to empirical truth that a simple analogy from his fiction might have suggested to him. Once more, while applying the general methods of science and philosophy with admirable sophistication, Poe errs in his qualitative and quantitative predictions.

THE POWER OF WORDS

> It is no use arguing with a prophet; you can only
> disbelieve him.
>
> Winston Churchill

What kind of knowledge can *Eureka* hope to offer when its new epistemology, as well as specific theses, suffer from fundamental shortcomings? As we have seen, Poe's theory of knowledge guides him to a blundering hypothesis on the evolution of the universe. Yet many critics seem so entranced by Poe's words that they apparently allow it to affect their judgment. A good case in point may be Harold Beaver, whose introduction and notes to the 1976 edition of *Eureka* go a long way towards exposing the treatise's logical and scientific shortcomings. It is a complete surprise, then, to find him still praising it not only for "intellectual coherence," but for the "scientific ... implications [which] – to all who stay the course – remain stupendous" (397)!

Why is it that the same critics who patiently record the deficiencies of Poe's theories, still extol their scientific virtues? How can the author of *Eureka* get away with manifold errors of method, fact, and reasoning? Surely it is impossible that any reader could overlook the essay's flaws, which are just too many and too plain to miss. Yet, as many, though by no means all, critical sources demonstrate, *Eureka* succeeds in sustaining its pretence to systematic knowledge with successive generations of readers.

Following the essay's original publication in 1848, the *New York Evening Express* maintained that *Eureka* had "all the detail and accuracy required in a scientific lecture," while the *New York Daily Tribune* saw in Poe's theories an example of "keenest analysis" (Walker 278, 286). The slightly more oblique *New York Courier and Enquirer* deemed *Eureka* a "nobler effort than any other Mr Poe has yet given to the world" (Beaver 396). Later on it was evident for Paul Valéry that "Poe has extended the application both of the nebular hypothesis and the law of gravity" while laying down the "mathematical foundations" for his cosmogony (110). George Nordstedt tried to verify close parallels between *Eureka* and the relativistic principles of Albert Einstein. Clayton Hoagland, stimulated by Poe's cosmology, tried to relate it to the cosmic theories of De Sitter and Eddington. In 1946 Arthur Hobson Quinn went as far as to solicit opinions from eminent scientists of his day to back up his opinion that *Eureka* makes some "valuable [scientific] suggestions"

(543). Even contemporarily, Vincent Buranelli still claims that Poe "obviously was gifted with scientific understanding" (54).

Apparently *Eureka* leaves literary critics with an impression of relentless logic of argument, thoroughness of science, and plausibility of prediction. In contrast, none of the scientists who commented on the essay was ready to offer more than a token appreciation of Poe's effort. Edmond Bauer, a professor of physics, states that *Eureka* "appears to be a rather confused rambling on ideas which, during his [Poe's] times, were part of the public domain" (in Bonaparte 740).[15] Paul Heyl, a physicist, concedes only a single faint praise by describing Poe's discussion of axioms in *Eureka* as "interesting." Charles Olivier, a professor of astronomy, grants only that Poe had "keen intelligence and great ability in putting forward his ideas," while denying any credibility to what he dubs Poe's cosmological "mysticism." Even Arthur Eddington, who is the most generous in his response, allows only that Poe, "besides being fairly well-informed in science and mathematics, seems to have had the mind of a mathematician" (all in Quinn: 544, 556, 555). Still, even this token praise is contested by Clarence Wylie, a professor of mathematics himself, who maintains that "Poe was not a poor mathematician but simply no mathematician at all" (235).

The disparity between the view of *Eureka* in the critical and in scientific circles puts the former's praise in perspective. It also reveals something about literary studies, where, as I argued in chapter 2, science and its philosophy are sometimes misapprehended to quite a degree. All the same, it cannot be denied that the inspired fire of Poe's theories affects many readers powerfully enough to make them overlook the flaws. It is hardly accidental that Poe's treatise should display such a strong and lasting appeal. The rhetorical side of *Eureka* works as a deliberate exercise in camouflage – an effort on its author's part to brace his arguments by making use of his formidable rhetorical skills. This should be no surprise if Ketterer is right in identifying deception as "the most consistent and dominant aspect of Poe's work" (*The Rationale* xii).

Many critics concede that Poe "convinces by shear [sic] rhetorical force" (Cantalupo 87). They examine individual rhetorical devices (e.g., Dayan's discussion of the dash) with little effort, however, to account for them as a part of the cognitive and creative process that generated *Eureka*. But one of the central features of Poe's design is to make his poetic vision of the cosmos scientifically secure, in order to persuade others to accept its findings. Overtly, he designs to make *Eureka* impregnable to criticism by eliminating all error and inconsistency. But appeals to everlasting truth notwithstanding, it is hard to shake off the impression that, knowing *Eureka* better than anyone else, Poe must have been aware of at least some of its shortcomings.

It thus seems not implausible that he should employ sophistry and rhetoric to manœuvre his audience away from the faltering details of his argument and guide them towards the apprehension of the grandeur of his theses. Viewed from this angle, the stylistic and elocutionary aspects of *Eureka* become consistent and homogenous. Its overall tone, as well as specific devices, serve to buttress Poe's sometimes shaky reasoning by bridging gaps between arguments. Although an argumentative stepping-stone might be lacking, the reader should not perceive anything amiss, since Poe inserts a rhetorical stepping-stone in its place. The power of words, rather than of arguments, cements his theory into an illusion of rigour and comprehensiveness.

It is worth recalling that *Eureka* was initially presented to the public as a two-and-a-half-hour lecture entitled "On the Cosmogony of the Universe." Passionately delivered in front of a live audience, the essay would sway the skeptics with the splendour of Poe's cosmological vision. Presumably it would also direct them away from a tedious examination of what, in comparison, would seem petty and insignificant details. This seems to explain why Poe discusses quantitative particulars only towards the end. Initially he needs to establish his expertise and authority over his subject, as well as the majesty of his theses. Only later does he return to empirical facts, with the audience swept off their feet by this intense "mental gyration on the heel" (212).

Poe's strategy in camouflaging some of his obvious argumentative defects can also help explain the nature of his subsequent additions to *Eureka*. Aware that his theory may undergo a more careful scrutiny in print, his notes on pages 261, 262, 274, and 297 are, for the most part, geared towards deflecting some of the possible criticisms. It is worth noting, however, that Poe was less than successful in preempting hostile commentary. Despite a generally positive reception of the lecture, the subsequent book reviews were distinctly cooler.

THE RHETOR IN ACTION

Rhetoric can be seconded only by rhetoric, for all
that rhetoric can *intend* is more rhetoric.

Harold Bloom

One of the most efficacious of Poe's tropes is the hyperbole, of which the first two paragraphs of *Eureka* are a prime example. Here Poe, in no uncertain terms, glamorizes his cosmological blueprint. "What terms shall I find sufficiently simple in their sublimity – sufficiently sublime in their simplicity – for the mere enunciation of my theme?" (211), he exclaims in a rapt chiasmus. Next to the scale and magnificence of his project, attention to factual details is indeed made to look trivial.

The hyperbolic sublimity of the theme also subtly sheds legitimacy on the other parts of *Eureka*. Poe employs the classical a fortiori approach, hinting that since his grand scheme is so exalted, its supporting parts must be so as well, thereby drawing attention away from their inner coherence and accuracy. Another conspicuous feature of Poe's rhetoric is the proliferation of seemingly endless sentences. Atomized by dashes, commas, and semi-colons, these paragraph-long statements boast a forbidding number of subclauses that purport to deal with every angle of the subject in hand. Although at times almost unintelligible as argumentative propositions, Poe's clever manipulation of these complex, multilevelled utterances lends him an air of discursive fairness, objectivity, and completeness.

He achieves a similar impression by means of successive approximations and escalations of one and the same topic. Joan Dayan's discussion of the dash in *Eureka* provides a good analysis of the function of such a "language of successive approximation" (56). Another quintessential case may be Poe's depiction of galactic distances, where, while increasing the magnitude of description, he insists each time that he has been "once again ... speaking of trifles" (290). Such circular or, more properly, spiral returns create in the reader an impression of being eased into a complex topic of which the narrator is in complete control by virtue of his superior perspective.

Poe's seeming intoxication with numbers also serves to reinforce the image of a writer in perfect command of his subject. Even as he insists that it is a "folly to attempt comprehending" (283) the vast numbers that describe cosmic phenomena, he launches a digital tour de force. Piling up numbers upon numbers, Poe saturates the mind until it forsakes the herculean task of keeping up with their incessant flow. The ease and intimacy with empirical data gives Poe the air of effortlessness, while the quantitative knowledge appears to reaffirm the merits of his previously qualitative considerations. Similarly, the countless instances of redundancy and repetition in *Eureka* serve Poe's rhetorical goals. Returning to an argument previously debated not only reassures the reader, who feels on familiar ground, but creates an image of the author who intimately knows his subject and makes the difficult parts accessible to his audience.

A particular stratagem favoured by Poe is challenging the reader with inquiries in the course of his argument. These can be purely rhetorical, as in a series of anaphoric interrogations about the nature of the "brotherhood among the atoms" (237). More frequently, however, Poe employs in a masterly way the *hypophora*, posing questions only to answer them immediately himself (the Latin term for hypophora is *ratiocinatio*, which certainly rings a bell in the context of *Eureka*). One good example among many is the inquiry into the primal causality. "[W]hat is it employed to sustain? A First Cause. And what is a First Cause? An ultimate termination of Causes. And what is an ultimate termination of causes? Finity – the Finite" (224). The rapid fire sequence of Q&A insinuates that the answer must be exactly the one given and endorses the credentials of both the answers and the speaker who can give them so effortlessly.

Another tactic for establishing authority over his material is the acknowl-
edgment of or appeal to respected sources of information. For the outline of
his cosmology Poe appropriates a distinguished scientific lineage, aligning his
hypotheses with the work of Kepler, Newton, and Laplace and drawing parallels to von Humboldt, Nichol, and Herschel.[16] Praising their research and
extolling their scientific virtue, Poe cleverly re-stages the popular *topos* of a
dwarf on a giant's head – much less imposing, yet able to see further and
better than his illustrious predecessors. Sanguinely adopting these eminent
scientists as precursors, he makes himself into their genius heir apparent.

With a prestigious array of scientific authorities behind him, Poe assumes
sufficient authority to dispute the tenets of other thinkers. His assurance that
he does not stand alone becomes clear during his argument with John Stuart
Mill. Employing *paralogia*, Poe grants Mill "every advantage" and "the fairest
of play" (217), only to repudiate him in a lopsided critique that ends in a
praise of the Keplers and Laplaces of theory. This example is all the more
conspicuous since Poe is not always willing to accommodate opinions different from his, sometimes resorting simply to bullying the potential sceptics.
The epithets of "bigots," "tyrants" (215), "imbecile" (226), and "professional
questioners" (268) are dished out for the sake of those who would not
succumb to *Eureka*. Deriding their powers of comprehension achieves a
similar result as when Poe uses a superhuman point of view, e.g., to relate
"the immeasurable mass of matter" (285) of Jupiter. Describing what no
mortal could see, Poe's apparent feat of perception elevates him to a level
above that of his audience.

The structure of *Eureka* reveals an effort to create the appearance of clarity,
impartiality, and competence. The work is modelled after a philosophical
essay in its tripartite division, clear thesis statement, appeal to logic in
argument, and acknowledgement of sources. On occasion Poe even employs
a properly conditional attitude, affirming the tenability of a particular point
only if "the propositions of this Discourse are tenable" (299). This sudden
humbleness of tone, designed to cast him in an objective and professional
light, is at odds with his typical bombast and self-assurance. Similarly incon-
gruous is the contrast between his ostensible drive towards philosophical
precision and tactical obscurity around weaker points in argument.

THE OXYMORON OF ELLIPTICAL PRESENCE

There is no philosophy in my religion.
Michael Faraday

Poe's assimilation of the neo-Platonism of his period into his cosmology also
helps reinforce his credentials as a prophet of truth. The central (Hegelian)

tenet of *Eureka* is the universal, i.e., physical and metaphysical, origin out of unity, to which the entire cosmos will eventually return. It is reminiscent of Wordsworth's intimations of immortality: a soul that separates from divine unity and dissipates its recollection of this primal union throughout an individual's life, before returning towards it in the end. The universe hypothesized by Poe also displays this pattern, so much so that Allen Tate subsumes *Eureka* under the general movement in Poe's fictions from unity with the dead beloved to the unity with the entire Cosmos.

On some level of abstraction, *Eureka* may indeed appear to mimic this template. The primal loss is the loss of universal unity, subsequently intimated by means of an imaginative and intuitive journey into nature, projected onto the largest canvas imaginable – the cosmos. Poe interprets the universe as an agglomeration of signifiers that point to a lost state of primordial oneness. The entire final section of *Eureka* turns thus into a synthesis of the major points of neo-Platonism, so much so that Poe at times sounds like Wordsworth himself: "We walk about, amid the destinies of our world-existence, encompassed by dim but ever present *Memories* of a Destiny more vast – very distant in the by-gone time, and infinitely awful … We live out a Youth peculiarly haunted by such shadows; yet never mistaking them for dreams. As Memories we *know* them. *During our Youth* the distinction is too clear to deceive us even for a moment" (307).

The poetic principle of *Eureka* casts the poet as a unifying agent, able to encompass all experience through the process of intuitive synthesis. Only he can reconstruct the pattern of the cosmic order by means of ratiocinating intuition, and only he can divine the laws of the universe by intuiting the principles that have gone into its making. Only his intellect is capable of re-creating the vision of the union, primal and final. The intimation of the cosmic design gives Poe the assurance of truth, which in turn vindicates all the rhetorical stratagems he might use to cover up the defects of his theory.

Since the cosmological concept is so sublime, it dwarfs the unruly details that refuse to fit into Poe's philosophy. The neo-Platonic intimation of the true Cosmic Plot justifies and absolves all such rhetorical sleights-of-hand. It also explains the most pervasive trope – the ellipsis – in Poe's speculations about God. Although Poe maintains that we know "absolutely *nothing*" about God, he allows, just like the German absolute idealists to whom he is indebted, for a possibility of divining his nature if we should "be God ourselves" (226).[17] The oxymoron of God's elliptical presence in *Eureka* fits perfectly into the neo-Platonic ideas developed in it. God is necessarily absent, since human memory harbours only vague recollections of the past union, but he can be made present, since the common human and divine origin permits the intimation of his character, as well as of the future fate of the universe.

A QUESTION OF ORIGINALITY

Original ideas are exceedingly rare and the most
that philosophers have done in the course of time
is to erect a new combination of them.

George Sarton

Does Poe's failure to vindicate intuition as an epistemological alternative to scientific inquiry call into question the raison d'être of his entire treatise? After all, one hardly needs *Eureka* to realize the value of intuition in general, and even less to realize its value in literature. Poe's fictions are themselves eloquent testimony to the intuitive mastery of his art. His tales and poems have lost nothing of their allure despite having been written a century and a half ago. In contrast, *Eureka* may seem today a mere *curiosum*, on par with the writings of better-known philosophers, such as Hegel, who, like Poe, failed to get their science right.[18]

Does *Eureka*, among its numerous flaws and errors, accomplish anything? Does it offer, as Poe would have wished, a substantive contribution to the epistemological and cosmological matters that it deliberates? Here is how A.H. Quinn summarized this issue more than half a century ago: "If the scientific ideas in *Eureka* are wild and incoherent, or were written without knowledge of what had been discovered in Poe's own day, the essay may be dismissed as unimportant so far as its thinking is concerned. If, on the other hand, it is based on accurate knowledge of the latest scientific discoveries of its *own time*, then it is entitled from that point of view to respect" (542).

Before I try to answer these questions, let us consider a related issue, namely whether *Eureka* offers anything new on the literary front. Many, perhaps even most, of its ideas have been articulated earlier by the European Romantics and American Transcendentalists. It is a sobering thought that even Emerson, Poe's lifelong antithesis, appears to say in "Nature" much of what can be found in *Eureka*. Twelve years before Poe, Emerson has already "apprehended the Unity of Nature – the Unity in Variety" (917), and argued that the "true philosopher and the true poet are one, and a beauty, which is truth, and a truth, which is beauty, is the aim of both" (923). Even the finer points of Poe's essay can be found in "Nature." Anticipating Poe's cosmology, Emerson too "can foresee God in the coarse and, as it were, distant phenomena of matter" (925). And, of course, the concluding section of *Eureka* is present in Emerson's neo-Platonic remarks on the spirit of youth and nature and their guiding role towards intimations of God.

The question of Poe's originality is open to interpretation, especially in view of his indebtedness to Schelling, Fichte, and both Schlegels. Alterton traces Poe's hypotheses in painstaking detail to eclectic texts in philosophy, law, literature, and science. Buranelli, noting that Poe did not have to do "all of his thinking for himself" (46), records his outright borrowings from Plato, Aristotle, Shelley, Pascal, and Coleridge. Forrest makes a convincing case for *Eureka* being largely a paraphrase of the philosophy of the *Upanishads*, the *Vedas*, and the *Vedanta*, couched in the language of Poe's contemporary science. Even intuition, the cornerstone of Poe's epistemology, owes more to Pascal and the faculty he called "heart" than to Poe himself. In fact, if one is to believe Broussard, *Eureka* is an ultimate venture in recycling, since "so much of what Poe wrote in *Eureka* he had been saying all along, in his poems and his short stories and, to some extent, in his criticism also" (49).

Broussard is certainly right in identifying a pattern in Poe's philosophy that may be repetitive, perhaps even derivative. He is also right to point out that *Eureka* follows largely "the same pantheistic approach which had produced Emerson's 'The Over-Soul'" (48). However, any comparison between Emerson and Poe that does not stress their different attitudes to knowledge and inquiry strikes me as significantly lopsided. In fact, I would contend that sweeping the epistemological question out of the way cannot but distort some of the most important issues at stake here.

Although Emerson and Poe may have advanced some comparable theses, there is a striking difference in the ways in which they account for their respective conclusions. Where Emerson overtly forswears consistency – somewhat in the manner of "Do I contradict myself? Very well then, I contradict myself" – Poe sets out to construct a "train of ratiocination as rigorously logical as that which establishes any demonstration in Euclid" (252). Naturally, we must distinguish the design from the execution: *Eureka* is not by any stretch of imagination a rigorously argued philosophical essay. But logic, consistency, and empirical soundness are the very criteria that allow us to evaluate Poe's theories and their shortcomings in a systematic way.

By opening himself to interdisciplinary scrutiny and declining to take refuge behind Emerson's or anybody else's strictly disciplinary agenda, Poe reveals not only his cognitive aspirations but also his philosophical maturity. "Nature" and its ideas are invulnerable to epistemic critique because they openly flaunt their opposition to it. Emerson has no aspirations to cognitive accountability – much in the manner in which he has no aspirations to consistency. Poe, on the other hand, in a way that is still a lesson for us today, submits his hypotheses to the scrutiny of philosophers, scientists, and poets alike.

Although Poe must be praised for his interdisciplinary openness, the sometimes lavish applause bestowed on him as an author of a few lucky guesses in matters of science strikes me as a mistaken enterprise. In the absence of logical or experimental support, such predictions can only enjoy the status of inspired guesses, since their credibility flows mainly from the rhetorical skill of their author. It is a mistake to build Poe's philosophical reputation on the basis of a few isolated examples of serendipity. One must not only believe in the truth of one's theses but be able to justify this belief, and for this task personal conviction is not enough. What is required is a reliable evidentiary and methodological framework, which is largely lacking in *Eureka*. After all, similar hypotheses can be, and occasionally have been, advanced independently on literary and philosophical, or even scientific, forums. Yet only the latter can validate them in the methodological spirit consonant with their epistemic status. Put simply, even if at some point in his essay Poe had come up with $E = mc^2$, this uncanny fact would have affected nineteenth-century science as much as *Eureka* did, i.e., it would not have affected it at all, owing to the lack of acceptable epistemological support.

BUILDING THE CASE FOR MR POE

> I am inclined to think that scientific discovery is
> impossible without faith in ideas which are of a
> purely speculative kind and sometimes quite
> hazy; a faith which is quite unwarranted from the
> scientific point of view.
>
> Karl Popper

Reaching for the stars and tripping over his own poetic feet, instead of a philosophical monument Poe may have erected for himself a tombstone. And yet, even tombstones make for imposing memorials, which sometimes endure as long as those erected to the great thinkers in cultural history. Despite my thorough-going critique of Poe's theory of knowledge and of his cosmological model, there is little doubt in my mind that *Eureka* is such a monument, in cognitive ambition unequalled by most works studied by scholars of literature. Few inquiries indeed can surpass the grandeur of an attempt to answer one of our most persistent inquiries about our knowledge, place, and destiny in the cosmic scheme of things.

A good way to balance the ambition and scale of Poe's theories may be to put them next to the many cosmologies proposed since the beginning of written records. From the Sumerian epics, through the Presocratic philosophers, the classical Hellenic period, the Roman verse historians, the Scholastics, the Renaissance and Enlightenment natural scientists (including Kepler and Newton), up to this very day, people have laboured to construct a cogent vision of our place in the universe. Even though, like in Poe, their theories have proved flawed either on logical or empirical grounds, such grand-design arguments appear to be endemic to human thought. Whether derived from the Anaxagorean *Nous* (Mind), Poe's pantheistic Godhead, or any such teleological or eutaxiological principle, they are a record of the human effort to understand the ways of the world.[19]

The juxtaposition of Poe and other more celebrated cosmologists may seem an exaggeration, but not, I hope, an excessive one. All of their systems have a similar sweep and grandeur, and a certain air of mystical finality. All have so far proven fruitless in providing lasting answers to our physical and metaphysical inquiries. However, just like Anaxagoras's, Ptolemy's, Plato's, Aristotle's, Boethius's, Aquinas's, Kepler's, Newton's, Leibnitz's, Kant's, Paley's, and many others', Poe's cosmology is a part of our cultural legacy that ought to be remembered not because of its infallibility but because of its philosophical goal.

Eureka is a record of one answer to the questions that have challenged thinkers of yesterday and will likely continue to challenge thinkers of tomorrow. Among the cosmologies constructed by philosophers, theologians, scientists, and mathematicians, Poe's is one of the very few that have been systematically developed by a writer of belles lettres, once again assuring him a prominent place in literary history. Although overtaken by scientific inquiry almost from the day it was conceived, *Eureka* remains a testimony to the almost boundless fertility of its author's philosophical imagination. It is also an enduring proof of his prescient understanding of the place of literature in the grand epistemological picture next to philosophy and science.

But at the same time, we must not close our eyes to the shortcomings of Poe's theories and pretend that they are more than just a noble, but severely flawed, endeavour. His factual errors are illuminating, since they can rarely be explained by his lack of modern scientific knowledge. Given the supposedly everlasting quality of the poetically intuited truths, it seems fair to expect Poe to have followed the best science of his day, which he manifestly does not. In fact, in a relentless crusade to buttress his ailing arguments, Poe disregards fundamental empirical facts and takes no time to reflect on the implications of some of his epistemological conclusions.

It is to be expected that whenever philosophy and science cross paths, it is the former that will need to reassess its domain, no matter how deeply entrenched in tradition it may be. It is a demonstrable fallacy still to insist that philosophy will forever remain unaffected by the advance of science. It may suffice to contemplate the fate of medieval Scholasticism, which did not confine itself to metaphysics but made indiscriminate pronouncements on what later became empirically testable domains. One such development was the grudging retrenchment in both philosophy and theology that followed the birth of the modern science of astronomy. Today, claims like Husserl's about the "*absolute independence of phenomenology* [i.e., for him, Philosophy writ large] of all sciences" (1975, 162) ring even more hollow in the age of reversible clinical death or a slow encroachment of the solipsistic dream in the virtual reality machines.

Unlike autonomous systems of thought, such as logic or mathematics, the sciences are not cumulative in any straightforward way. Today's theories may be supplanted tomorrow by better and more comprehensive ones, consigning the old models to their rightful place in the history of a civilization: its galleries, museums, and libraries. Yet, although human inquiry is a fallible and daily outdated enterprise, science and its methods are the best means of learning about the world. And as such, as Poe is clearly aware, they deserve our critical – in both senses – attention.

This is, of course, far from saying that it is only a matter of time until all philosophical questions become amenable to empirical inquiry. I am convinced that some philosophical problems may remain forever closed to empiricism, and indeed those raised by epistemology and cosmology appear like good candidates for this elite circle. But, just as Poe understood it, this is what sometimes makes them all the more, not less, worthy of critical investigation.

CHAPTER FOUR

There Is Science in My Philosophy

> A common theme in mythology is the attribution
> of humanlike motives and emotions to nonhuman
> animals – and even to physical objects and forces,
> such as mountains and storms. This tendency to
> anthropomorphize flows naturally from the
> context in which consciousness evolved.
>
> Richard Leakey, *The Origin of Humankind*

One of Lem's chief philosophical concerns is the concurrent inevitability and
inadequacy of conceptualizing the world along anthropomorphic lines. *The
Invincible* (1964), a novel from the middle of his golden phase of 1961–68,
contains an illuminating development of this theme. In this best-selling
science-thriller the author studies the vagaries of a typical scientific process
of investigating the unknown and reflects on the patterns and limitations of
human cognition. *The Invincible* reveals how Lem uses his fictions to model
not only philosophical problems in need of inquiry but also problems of
inquiry itself.

THE INVINCIBLE HAS LANDED

> Anybody who likes a tight, increasingly tense
> plot-line rising to a scene of dramatic violence
> will be satisfied. Anybody who likes a mystery
> will find it here.
>
> Ursula le Guin

The Invincible opens with the Earth space cruiser, the Invincible, landing on
Regis III, a desert Earth-type planet in the Lyre constellation. Eight years
have passed since the disappearance of its sister ship, the Condor, and the

Invincible is on a military and scientific mission to investigate. Led by Horpach, the commander, and Rohan, the navigator, the crew commence the exploration of the planet.

From the very start Regis III abounds with unsettling mysteries. Flora and fauna are extinct, yet marine life teems in the ocean, although only below the depth of 150 yards. The evolutionists on board speculate that an unknown factor must be preventing life from going on land. Interestingly, local fish have a peculiar sense that reacts to minute variations in the magnetic field, allowing them to elude probes with astonishing alacrity and accuracy. Another mystery is the menacing presence of a Black Cloud of metallic micro-elements ("flies").

The exploratory sallies increase the scientists' knowledge of the planet, but only deepen the mystery. At some point one of the satellites released into orbit around the planet discovers the ruins of a dead "city." Although on inspection these geometrically regular structures do not resemble any terrestrial settlement, they are undoubtedly of artificial origin. Wild speculations surface, linking the metal ruins with the extinct civilization of the star Zeta Lyrae. All this turmoil pales, however, next to the horror found in the wreck of the Condor. Its super-durable hull pitted in an unknown way, the ship is a scene of insane devastation. There are soap bars with imprints of human teeth on them, excrement littering the floors, childish scrawls in the log book, cans of food looking as if someone tried to bite through them. On top of this the dead crew appears to have been ravaged by premortal amnesia. Yet the verdict from the medical staff is even more mystifying: the Condor's men all died of purely natural causes – apparently dehydration and starvation – with plenty of food and water around. Gradually the entire planet becomes a puzzle – forensic, military, and scientific – that flies in the face of the crew's preconceptions about what to expect in this part of the universe.

Baffled but confident in their conceptual and technological acumen, the scientists step up their investigation of the mysterious phenomena. In the climactic part of the novel, a scouting group from the Invincible is isolated by the Black Cloud. Two planes sent in for rescue are destroyed by the concerted actions of the micro-flies. Another, much stronger and better armoured party is hastily dispatched to retrieve the missing men but suffers a similarly ignominious defeat. The Black Cloud overcomes their offensive weapons and force fields by erasing all memory from the humans' and robots' brains, reducing them to the stage of mortally vulnerable infantilism. Clearly the same type of amnesia was responsible for the tragedy of the Condor. Chapter 7 of the novel ends on a sombre note: "On the twenty-seventh day after landing on Regis III, almost half of the Invincible's crew had been put out of action" (120).[1]

Two more efforts are launched to bring the lost men back. The first is a show of strength that pits the Cyclops, a military machine so powerful that "no one had ever heard of [its] defeat" (126), in a direct confrontation with the Cloud. The result is a battle of cataclysmic proportions where the nuclear and anti-matter violence unleashed by the human side is met with an even more chilling efficiency on the other. The eighty-ton Cyclops suffers a humiliating defeat and is annihilated by its own ship after the "amnesiac" robot fires on it. The second rescue mission is a scouting trek by Rohan who, alone and with no military or even mechanical support, finally succeeds in eluding the Cloud and in locating the bodies of the missing men. Rohan does so not by opposing but by tricking the micro-flies through submission and inaction. In a moment of stark epiphany, he comprehends the errors made by the crew, as well as the nature of the alien world that they had tried to conquer.

The symbolism of *The Invincible* is held together by a subtle stylization after the gothic story. If anything, the futuristic setting of the novel makes the haunting elements of the genre – mystery, madness, death – even more ghastly. The derelict tower of the Condor and its sickening spectacle of insanity and decay, the ghostly "corpse-spy" with which doctors scan the memories of deceased crewmen, the echoes of Frankensteinian insubordination in the gigantic Cyclops, together with the tones of almost Faustian retribution for the crew's lack of cognitive humility – all these elements contribute in original and shocking ways to the gothic tradition that the novel subtly evokes.

On the other hand, notwithstanding the riveting plot, enduring symbolism, and powerful, Hemingway-sparse style, it is clearly the cognitive problem that occupies the centre stage of *The Invincible*. Not that there have ever been any doubts about the centrality of cognition in Lem's writings. In a 1979 interview appropriately entitled "Knowing Is the Hero of My Books," the writer recalled a Swiss critic who suggested that in Lem's books problems of knowledge play the part that love and erotic adventures do for other writers. Lem agreed: "To me science, not sex, is the problem" (69). My analysis of Lem's philosophical arguments is thus animated by the same interdisciplinary spirit that, in his own opinion as well as that of many critics, distinguishes his entire œuvre. The author himself invites such an interpretive strategy by bluntly summing *The Invincible* up as a "decently executed narrative 'vehicle' based on a nonfictional problem" (Beres 52).[2]

MODELS FOR INQUIRY AND MODELS OF INQUIRY

> Self-reference is often erroneously taken to be
> synonymous with paradox.
>   Douglas Hofstadter

Before I examine *The Invincible* in more detail, it will be instructive to look at some of the narrative techniques that Lem often uses in his fictions.

Interestingly, the nonfictional problems that he investigates and the fiction-specific devices that he employs for this purpose turn out to be interdependent to a remarkable degree. Naturally, only an imprudent commentator would attempt to summarize Stanislaw Lem in the short space available (a fuller overview can be found in my *Stanislaw Lem Reader* (1997)). Lem's literary and philosophical legacy staggers in its proportions, with more than forty titles in cumulative editions of over thirty million worldwide and decades of regular contributions to scholarly journals in literary studies, philosophy, and science. There is as yet no comprehensive bibliography of his publications, but when it is finally compiled, it is sure to run into dozens, if not hundreds of pages.

Hard as it may be to order this cornucopia of material, some thematic and structural leitmotifs seem like a natural starting point. One of them is without doubt Lem's preoccupation with the philosophy of science and inquiry. With tireless self-reflexiveness, his works reflect and reflect on the philosophical premises that have gone into their making. Even though it might be difficult to offer a tidy *divisio* of his use of self-reflexivity, it may be useful to identify two of its main strands. Both can be traced to Lem's penchant for meta-inquiry into the nature of scientific, philosophical, and literary inquiry and into the interplay between various cognitive levels in his fictions.

The first type of self-reflexivity can be identified with Lem's awareness of working in the medium of literary fiction. The author frequently foregrounds the fiction-specific techniques and devices in the pursuit of his philosophical investigations. The other type of self-reflexivity derives from the modelling goals that Lem sets for his novels. While developing various hypotheses, he conspicuously reflects on the goals and methods that guide inquiry in general and his own inquiries in particular. Lem often dramatizes these meta-level questions by directing them at his own fictions, which in this way, apart from developing models *for* inquiry, become also models *of* inquiry. In the next two sections I will look in turn at these different types of self-reflexivity.

A FLEXIBLE TOOL OF INQUIRY

The cognitive bargain hunter substitutes thought
for things, converting his mind into a private
laboratory.

                                Roy Sorensen

It would be hard to find a Lem novel that does not, in one way or another, concern itself with questions of representation, communication, message-sending, interpretation, information, creativity, language, or signalling. At the same time, the author often reflects on his scientific or philosophical hypotheses in ways that bring out their literary – for example, linguistic, narrative, or stylistic – origin. A good example may be his madcap novella *The Futurological Congress* (1971), in which he advances a number of futurological forecasts about the looming population explosion on Earth. While at work, Lem puts his modelling efforts in perspective by reflecting on the nature of futurology through a look at linguistic modelling in hypothesis construction.

It is in this way that some of the linguistic modelling techniques mock-extolled in the book – "Morphological forecasting! Projective etymology!" (105) – become a higher-level commentary on Lem's own hypotheses. Here is how Professor Trottelreiner, one of the novella's maniacal characters, describes the strategy behind linguistic modelling in general and modelling in literary fictions in particular: "Linguistic futurology investigates the future through the transformational possibilities of the language ... By examining the future stages in the evolution of language we come to learn what categories, changes, and social revolutions the language will be capable, some day, of reflecting" (106).

The verbal extravagance of this kind of futuro-linguistics is one way for Lem to illustrate why, as he put it elsewhere, a "language crammed full with neologisms is necessary, and not just a perverse game with fantastic sounds."[3] In *The Futurological Congress* Lem uses language not only as a prognostic tool but also as a self-reflexive instrument for inquiry into the nature of its prognostic power. The neologistic word-play that makes *The Futurological Congress* such a colourful novel allows him to pursue different levels of inquiry at the same time.[4] While multiplying futurological scenarios, he repeatedly reflects on different patterns of futurological inquiry, as well as on the specificity of his literary medium.

The single work that epitomizes Lem's language-centred type of self-reflexivity is his spectacular literary experiment from 1971. *A Perfect Vacuum* is a meta-fictional collection of book reviews of nonexistent fictions – indeed, fictions that, in some cases, could not even be written. As the modernist art for art's sake yields to postmodern games for games' sake, Lem joins the game with deliciously hilarious and hyperbolic results. Many of the stories in *A Perfect Vacuum* target the postmodern infatuation with antinarratives by lampooning and reducing *ad absurdum* their self-indulgent canons. Through a brilliant exploitation of their mannerisms Lem reflects on the limits of postmodern fiction, showing how its antinarratives frequently conceal a deeper intellectual paucity.

The sheer acrobacy of his self-reflexive imagination is most evident in the introduction to the entire volume. In it Lem-the-fictional-reviewer reviews his own book, written by Lem-the-real-and-fictional-writer – in other words, the very *Perfect Vacuum* in question! Lem's hyper-dimensional self-reflection is one of the most dazzling stunts ever executed in fiction. Consider Lem-the-reviewer's commentary on the introduction to *A Perfect Vacuum*, a work fictionally and nonfictionally written by Lem-the-writer, which, of course, contains the very words reportedly written by Lem-the-reviewer: "We suspect the author intends a joke; nor is this impression weakened by the Introduction – long-winded and theoretical – in which we read: 'The writing of a novel is a form of the loss of creative liberty ... In turn, the reviewing of books is a servitude still less noble. Of the writer one can at least say that he has enslaved himself – by the theme selected. The critic is in a worse position: as the convict is chained to his wheelbarrow, so the reviewer is chained to the work reviewed. The writer loses his freedom in his own book, the critic in another's'" (3).

Who is the author of the quoted words beginning with "The writing of a novel"? Is it the critic or the writer? The answer is clearly indeterminate, for this particular literary and logical game has no equilibrium. The reader is fated to swing forever between its playful alternatives. Creating in this passage a literary analogue to the liar's paradox, Lem stakes out the outer frontiers of contemporary fiction.[5] In his hands fiction becomes a flexible and versatile instrument of inquiry, while his sophisticated use of thought-experiments, counterfactual scenarios, or various semantic, semiotic, and mimetic games shows that there are almost no limits to its modelling power.

We should note in passing that contemporary preoccupation with self-reflexivity is not confined to literature or literary studies. The process and mechanisms of self-reflection are viewed today with renewed interest as one of the possible research paths to the study and development of consciousness. Some researchers in Artificial Intelligence propose that a conscious machine will – perhaps even must – be able not only to think but also think about thinking, as well as learn from such a meta-process. I will examine these questions in more detail in chapters 5 and 6, in the course of a discussion of computer-written fiction.

UNDERSTANDING THE ALIEN AS ALIEN

> Science cannot solve the ultimate mystery of Nature.
> And it is because in the last analysis we ourselves are
> part of the mystery we are trying to solve.
>
> Max Planck

Alongside this more literary type of self-reflexivity, Lem harnesses this device to more typically philosophical concerns and arguments. But even as he returns over and over again to problems of knowledge and knowledge formation, he does not stop at developing hypotheses in his fictions. Instead he goes on to examine the methodological principles and philosophical meta-principles of his own fiction-based inquiry. It is for these reasons that Ewa

Balcerzak likens Lem's novels and stories to "philosophical treatises" by means of which he models sociocultural phenomena and conducts "multi-faceted analyses on these models" (137). Lem refines his models by mirroring them in the peripeties of his characters, by turning some parts of his fiction into philosophical essays, and sometimes even by meta-reflecting on his own efforts.

To bring out the nature of a particular hypothesis, Lem often aims simultaneously at two levels of reading. Those of his works that deal with problems of knowing and understanding subtly mirror the problems faced by the characters in the interpretive challenge given to the reader. In other words, Lem confronts the reader with an interpretive problem analogous to the problem of knowing and/or understanding modelled in his works. To take one salient example, his perennial thesis about the open-endedness of science is woven into the theme and the structure of several novels, including the early *Eden* (1959). In the story, after a crash landing on an alien planet, human scientists explore its enigmatic civilization, which, belying its name, is found to be in the yoke of military terror and oppression. Only after an extensive investigation do the scientists become ready to admit the misconceptions caused by their anthropomorphic standards of inquiry and interpretation.

How our literary, philosophical, and scientific metaphors falter in the face of what is truly alien becomes painfully obvious in the climactic scene of the novel. Vainly trying to understand the beings from Eden, scientists deregulate the semantic filters in their translating computer to allow it a greater freedom of interpretation. Haltingly, the machine transmits a crazy jumble of almost surrealist concepts, confronting the reader with the same interpretive task that faces the scientists. Is it possible to understand Eden and its sociopolitical upheavals on the basis of such tenuous, fragmented, and anthropomorphically filtered evidence? The formulation of the question goes a long way towards suggesting Lem's answer.

The Investigation (1959) displays a similar open-ended design. Sending his characters after the causes of apparent resurrections from local morgues, Lem investigates a pattern of inquiry into phenomena that defy a routine pattern of inquiry. The intrinsic lack of solution to the enigma at the centre of the plot is reflected in the novel's startling ending. While the conventions of the detective genre in which the novel is set call for a solution to the mystery, *The Investigation* ends inconclusively, thwarting the reader's expectations about the success of forensic and scientific inquiry.

A similar pattern re-emerges in *Solaris* (1961), Lem's best-known and perhaps best novel. Efforts to communicate with an alien "ocean," which appears to be a sentient entity, serve only to bring out the interpretive bias of the investigators. To model both the alien phenomenon and his agents' attempts to model this phenomenon, Lem uses a similar strategy as in *Eden* and *The Investigation*. He surrounds the reader with a multitude of coherent but inconclusive hypotheses about the nature of the ocean and lets this investigative inconclusiveness be reflected in the open-ended conclusion to the novel. Once again this meta-scientific skepticism about our ability always to solve nature's mysteries is Lem's reflection of, and reflection on, the way we inquire into and interpret the world.

This skepticism is appropriate to the scientific realist's knowledge that theories about the world are often fallible approximations. The open-ended structure of many of Lem's novels is an analogy to his meta-scientific model of inquiry. And the repeated failures of forensic and scientific inquiries (e.g., in *Eden*; *The Investigation*; *Solaris*; *His Master's Voice* (1968); *The Chain of Chance* (1976); *Fiasco* (1987) are a reflection on science's methods and patterns of investigation.

NEW   VARIATIONS   ON   AN   OLD   THEME

> Set patterns, incapable of adaptability, of
> pliability, only offer a better cage. Truth is outside
> all patterns.
>
>   Bruce Lee

The continuous interplay between the narrative and modelling levels in Lem's fictions should not, of course, be equated with a monomaniac attachment to any single theme or narrative technique. On the contrary, there are few writers who can even approach the variety and depth of Lem's interests. The by no means complete list suggested by Michael Kandel includes cybernetic man, life, individuality, consciousness, creators and the created, god, nature, religion and its metaphors, the future, reality, utopias, epistemological doubt, linguistics, word play, mind, the interrelationship of literature and society, the philosophy of accident, laws of change, statistics, evolution and cybernetics, intelligence, and the genesis of life and the rise of man ("Lem in Review" 66). Moreover, the two self-reflexive tactics discussed above must not be conceived of as categorically distinct. In fact, for obvious reasons, they hardly ever appear in his fictions in pure form, uncontaminated by each other.

If Lem's preoccupation with problems of knowledge and meta-knowledge are separable only to the extent that we can, for example, separate brains from minds, *The Invincible* must without doubt be considered one of their finest dramatizations. The power and significance of this novel owe much to its sophisticated depiction of Earthmen's dogged efforts to comprehend the alienness of Regis III. At the same time, Lem's work is also a philosophical model of a typical process of inquiry and thus a meditation on an entire class of such investigations.

Very early in the novel it becomes clear that the methodology employed by the scientists on board the ship is replicated by the narrative structure of the work. *The Invincible* passes from the description of basic research and gradual accumulation of data, through the hypothesis stage, to the point where a dominant theory emerges as a coherent picture of reality. The final theory does not make any positivist claims to the generality and completeness of its truth and accuracy. In the empirical spirit of moderate realism it leads, however, to a verification of its main premise: the nonsentience of the Black Cloud.

The investigations conducted by the crew and the author are obviously informed by the same strategy. But Lem does not stop at the rather simple concept of adopting the principles of scientific modelling for his narrative purposes. *The Invincible* examines in an equal measure the features of a typical scientific investigation of the unknown, demolishing some of the misconceptions about the process. If science is the cognitive vanguard of the cultural buffer zone that humankind projects into the universe, then the interface between the two must be a scene of constant conceptual friction. *The Invincible* is an illuminating model of such friction between the meta-scientific preconceptions of the ship's crew and the alien phenomena they encounter on Regis III.

ERRARE HUMANUM EST

In every age the common interpretation of the
world of things is controlled by some scheme of
unchallenged and unsuspected presuppositions.
                                    Alfred North Whitehead

From the start, the scientists' examination of their new environment is fatally tinged with the positivism and reductionism of their meta-scientific beliefs. The reduction of phenomena to the level of particle physics and the explanation of events in terms of the covering law model is, of course, part of the positivist orthodoxy (see chapter 2). Explanations that do not follow the pattern of logical deduction from general empirical laws and initial conditions are routinely branded as pseudo- or nonscientific. Beguiled by a belief in the correctness of this type of inquiry, the crew of the Invincible modify their thinking only when their text-book procedures prove too inflexible to cope with the contingencies.

And proofs of the rigidity and inadequacy of Earth-based patterns abound. Although Horpach imposes a strict third-step routine designed for emergency situations, it does nothing to avert the disaster. Significantly, from the beginning many crew members resent the excessive rigour of emergency measures, despite the fact that Horpach's orders are dictated by a concern for their safety. After all, such precautions fail to make any difference in their encounters with the Cloud, which in no time cripples half the cruiser's men and machinery. This failure is in itself a warning sign that the conceptual framework on which it is based may need revision.

Instead of relying on rule-book responses, effective explorers must be ready to *adapt* to pragmatic and historical contingencies. What casts doubt on the all-time-and-place validity of routines is that any means undertaken to guard against unknown perils must by definition be only of a generic nature. When faced with extraordinary circumstances, one must look for support either in the rigidity of well-tried formulas from the past or fall back on the intangibility of a contingent response.

At the very least then, the crew's instinctive recklessness about the rules of planetary exploration contrasts with the inflexibility of their commanding officer. Such rigidity of thought and behaviour is anything but conducive to forming the correct approach to events that apparently exceed their competence. It may also lie behind the crew's persistent miscategorization of the type and magnitude of their problems. The scientists and their military leaders insist that they are dealing with a familiar type of situation that can reward their step-by-step investigation with success. This typically human trait points to the dialectic tension between the necessity for and inadequacy of all methodological routines in the face of an infinite richness of the universe.

One of the clearest indicators that the crew fall under the spell of such an overarching pattern of inquiry is the language they use to describe Regis III. Names like "cloud," "flies," "bushes," and "city" efface the alien nature of phenomena that have no parallel in the part of the universe known to humans. The city, which in reality bears no resemblance to any terrestrial dwellings, turns out to be a junkyard of gigantic machines, victims in the planet's evolutionary struggle. The bushes are tangles of metallic symbionts with the miniaturized y-shaped crystals, and the latter look and behave totally unlike the insects or flies that the crew sees in them.[6]

The greatest misnomer, however, is the Black Cloud, whose highly concerted actions give the impression of being synchronized by a single mind. The Cloud's deadly effectiveness, culminating in its defeat of the Cyclops, the Invincible's most powerful combat machine, is interpreted by the ship as a sign of deliberate strategy. Falling prey to their anthropomorphic view of the Cloud as the enemy, the crew ascribe to it the complex equipment of intentionality. This in turn leads them to react to it as if it were a rational being. The personification of the Cloud's purely instinctual behaviour is partially triggered by the character of the planet itself. Regis III is in many respects a surprisingly Earth-type, even if not Earth-like, planet, resembling ours in size, density, pressure, and ocean salinity. In fact, even "the skeletal structure of the [excavated] vertebrates" appears to be "typical" (30). To men predisposed to look for the familiar, these superficial similarities obscure the uniqueness of Regis III and its cybernetic evolution.

The scientists' behaviour may be psychologically and cognitively understandable, to the degree that it may be inevitable. Extending familiar metaphors to the unknown is the first stage in a challenge to assimilate that which clearly exceeds the conceptual horizons of the crew. In this sense Lem is right to point out in *Fantastyka i Futurologia* (1970) that "one cannot assimilate the Unnameable" (74). On the other hand, the bestowal of taxonomic labels presumes that it is possible to assimilate the unknown directly into the realm of concepts and values imported from elsewhere. Such a meta-scientific assumption can often become an act of self-deception, and sometimes even of outright cognitive violence. It is a semantic and methodological evasion of the true nature of alien phenomena.

THE REVOLUTIONARY EVOLUTIONARY HYPOTHESIS

Science may be regarded as a minimal problem
consisting of the completest presentation of facts
with the least possible expenditure of thought.

Ernst Mach

The observation that we should look beneath the surface in search of the underlying principles is, of course, quite banal. It reflects, however, the fact that it is a problem widespread enough to become an almost inseparable part of human experience. The superficial similarities of Regis III initially invite a plethora of working hypotheses that obstinately try to assimilate the Cloud within a familiar conceptual framework. Beguiled by their exploratory routine, the scientists try to fit the alien world into a preformed and inflexible box of meta-scientific beliefs that form their modus operandi for the entire universe. All the same, one by one their theories must be discarded in the face of the only one that fits the facts – no matter how fantastic it sounds.

After weeks of gruelling investigation, an extravagant hypothesis is put forward by Lauda, one of the ship's biologists. According to it, millions of years before, a nova exploded in the Lyre constellation, forcing the inhabitants of the region to colonize nearby planetary systems. One of their scouting craft crash-landed on Regis III. The sole survivors were robots, highly specialized homeostats, capable of adapting to the most difficult conditions. Left to their own devices, under the pressures of the environment and attacks from the local fauna, the robots began to evolve in directions never foreseen by their creators. Over endless millennia, some sought adaptive advantage in stationary growth, whereas others evolved in the direction of miniaturization and symbiosis. The dead city discovered by the Invincible was the ruins of the losers in the evolutionary struggle, the stationary machine giants.

The clear winners were the simple, crystalline micro-flies, which "learned" to survive on next to nothing, while being capable of aggregating into the Black Cloud in times of danger. The intellectually superior cybernetic organisms, like the city giants, which needed great amounts of energy, proved prone to environmental hazards, including the attacks of their evolutionary rivals. In contrast, the simple self-contained Y-shaped symbionts were more economical in energy consumption, and their complete interchangeability rendered the macro-structure of the Cloud virtually indestructible. Individually almost inert, even in small aggregates the "flies" rapidly developed electromagnetic, aerodynamic, and heat-conducting properties. Subject to adverse stimuli, they could neutralize or counter them by initiating aggressive actions. The superordinate organism of the Cloud could thus proliferate at will, adjusting its size according to its needs.

Although the Cloud is capable of organized and destructive performance, Lauda is at pains to point out that it is not a sentient entity. In fact, he urges his colleagues to see it as a phenomenon not unlike a storm or an earthquake – a natural force that must be approached and investigated as such. Despite the advantages of Lauda's hypothesis in terms of analytic and predictive power, the commanders seem unable or plain unwilling to accept its implications. If the Cloud is to be treated as an inanimate part of the landscape, human explorers must change their strategy on all fronts: military, forensic, and scientific. Their options are either to investigate the Cloud as any other force of Nature – albeit a perilous one, like a volcano – or simply to pack their equipment and go home. In either case, they must swallow their pride as conquistadors and forget about exacting revenge for the death and injury of their fellow crewmen.

Just as we do not systematically flog the sea after the sinking of a ship, Horpach and his crew are called on to renounce their pride and face the facts. Instead, they continue to personify the Cloud into an opponent, even though, as Rohan observes early in the novel, "here there was nothing to be invaded" (38). This error dramatically alters the rules of the investigative process. Just like generations of human cultures before them, the men of the Invincible find it easier to see the cosmos as hostile rather than indifferent. From the pre-Homeric epics to the contemporary new mystics, the literary, philosophical, and scientific culture bears witness to humankind's incurable personifications of the universe. Battle gods, rain deities, crop demons, luck charms have always exerted a powerful allure, especially next to the alternative: an indifferent and random universe. Science is no different: in more or less subtle ways its physics has always been under the influence of metaphysics.

In game theoretic terms, scientific inquiry is a non-zerosum game of imperfect information in which the neutral universe is not antagonistic towards human exploration. Any difficulties or plain failures can and must be explained in terms of insufficient knowledge, inadequate methodology, or poor conceptual apparatus. In the words of Norbert Wiener, the founder of cybernetics, this meta-scientific principle assumes an almost proverbial form. "Nature plays fair," argues Wiener, "and if, after climbing one range of mountains, the physicist sees another on the horizon before him, it has not been deliberately put there to frustrate the effort he has already made" (*The Human Use of Human Beings* 188).

Moreover, one should keep in mind that zerosum games are almost always only approximations of reality. Although admissible as idealizations, they almost never reflect the subtleties and complexities of real life. For example, even in contexts that apparently offer little or no inducement to cooperative behaviour – as with a buyer and a seller haggling over price or two nations at war – the picture is rarely so clear-cut. After all, the customer and the shop-owner might both prefer to close the sale rather than part without concluding the transaction. Similarly, the warring nations might both wish to confine their hostilities to strictly military campaigns rather than extending them to the civilian population.

Nevertheless, imprisoned within their strategic discourse, the Invincible's scientists persist in believing that they are engaged in a zerosum game. They interpret their lack of success as defeat, which leads them to see it as a victory for the other side. Such dogged myopia prevents them for the longest time from acknowledging the insufficiency of Earth-born and Earth-bound paradigms vis-à-vis Regis III and its alien evolutionary formations.

ON REDUCTIVIST REDUCTION

> Mathematicians are a species of Frenchman: if you
> say something to them they translate it into their
> own language and presto! it is something entirely
> different.
>
> Goethe

Who are these emissaries of humankind and why do they fail so dramatically to overcome the reductionist confines of their training? The answer seems to lie in a number of striking imbalances that *The Invincible* displays in the presentation of its narrative agents.

Only Rohan, navigator and second-in-command, and Horpach, the commander, are given enough prominence to emerge as individuals. Even at that, the differences between them are carefully balanced so that their individuality is only as separate as two sides of the same coin. Rohan's characterization entirely vis-à-vis Horpach parallels his grudging identification with the commander, rooted in a "dream to himself become commander of the Invincible some day" (59). Aloof and reserved towards the crew, both leaders regard each other in equally rigid hierarchical terms. In their relationship they have never risen above a strictly professional level; in fact, although "they had flown together many parsecs, they had never become friends" (12).

Their reluctance to deviate from a military code of behaviour, combined with a strict adherence to canonized procedures of extraterrestrial exploration, invite a similar inflexibility in the men under their command. It is small surprise that the striking preponderance of professions over personalities in the leaders is even more pronounced in the case of the forty-odd crew members identified in the novel. Their last names, accompanied by a designation of expertise, remain the only differentiating features within their circle. Even their cabins on the ship are nameless, bearing only function initials: Ch. I., Ch. Ph., Ch. T., Ch. B. Clad in uniformly white suits, which cannot but evoke the image of lab smocks, the Invincible's many specialists emerge as a faceless group agent, subservient to the military commanders and reflecting their limitations. Through such a depiction of the crew Lem raises questions about the complicity of the twin disciplinary apparatuses of industrial society: science and the military. The uneasy alliance of science with the military-industrial complex is, of course, of great concern to us all. This is especially so when the latter dominates the former's research agenda to the point of becoming the chief dictator of priorities and strategies that science is later made to pursue.[7]

Ewa Balcerzak sees this kind of reductionist presentation as consistent with Lem's interest in the common, rather than the unique, problems of human existence. Balcerzak argues that in the context of Lem's literary fictions it is almost inevitable that "man becomes a figure portraying humanity's scientific thought, its moral dilemmas, metaphysical and cultural problems, etc." Under the pressure of the cognitive ambitions that animate Lem's works, she adds, "it is not difficult to simplify the presentation of protagonists" (1973, 49).

These comments are equally valid here as in many other of Lem's "alien contact" novels. Once again the early *Eden* foreshadows the epistemic and narrative problems that occupy *The Invincible*. In *Eden* members of a crew of instrumental specialists also seek to understand an alien world and are forced to acknowledge the conceptual shortcomings of their exploratory routines. This time they do not even bear proper names, only professional labels: Captain, Doctor, Chemist, Physicist, Cyberneticist, and Engineer. Such a salient reduction is mirrored in the slant in their meta-scientific orientation. The Doctor and the Chemist, representing the biochemical sciences, are represented as more humane and less aggressive toward the civilization of Eden. The physicalists, on the other hand, favour more instrumental and actively penetrating tactics. This portrayal is obviously intended to be symbolic, since both sides make mistakes that flow from the given stereotype of their profession.

The stereotypical picture of an all-male scientific community is an ironic reflection of the Invincible's positivist program, which fails so miserably on

Regis III.[8] The irony is also evident in the reductionist array of specialists on board the Invincible. With the exception of the biological and medical scientists, all of the others come from the natural sciences. What is the presumption behind such a striking imbalance? These hard disciplines, devoted exclusively to the physical – ergo, presumably neutral and invariant – aspects of the universe, are supposed to be objective and untainted by anthropomorphism. Yet on Regis III they prove themselves to be equally encumbered with the meta-scientific baggage of Earthly preconceptions.

THE INVINCIBLE

It would be very singular that all Nature, all the
planets, should obey eternal laws, and that there
should be a little animal, five feet high, who, in
contempt of these laws, could act as he pleased,
solely according to his caprice.

Voltaire

Consonant with the reductionist and instrumentalist presentation of the crew, a similar anomaly is evident in the depiction of the mobile fragment of Earth they inhabit – the Invincible. The spacecraft is viewed exclusively as an instrument of technological power at the expense of its role as a habitat of people who live in it. Even the single seeming exception is no exception at all: the perfunctory description of Horpach's cabin shows no "indication that the spaceship's commander had been living here for years" (151).

The Invincible conceals any personal dimension behind its symbolic status as an instrumental extension of human science. The cruiser is a mechanical arm designed to reach out into the Universe and explore its mysteries. But exploration on anthropocentric terms is tantamount to domination, and under trial by fire the Invincible sheds the guise of a neutral scientific probe for the titanium-molybdenum armour plates of a perfect fighting machine. *Armor vincit omnia* is the unwritten motto of the ship, proudly capable of generating energies that can turn mountain ranges to dust and ashes and dry out entire oceans. In the end, however, the cruiser is proven far from invincible. Much like in Shelley's "Ozymandias," the desert of Regis III makes a mockery of the Invincible's vanity and arrogance. Ozymandias' monument, half-buried under desert sand, boasts of its past glory with a proud, "Look on my works, ye mighty, and despair." The hubristically called Invincible similarly succumbs to the sand, wind, and inanimate life of the Regis desert.[9]

The Invincible emerges as the novel's pivotal symbol. It manifests not only the frailty of scientific and meta-scientific preconceptions in the face of alien reality but, more generally, the nonsense of anthropomorphic notions in confrontation with the blind forces of nature. In Rohan's acerbic exegesis, humankind should indeed, "Conquer the void, of course, why not? But don't attack what already is, that which in the course of millions of years has achieved a balanced existence of its own, independent, not subject to anyone or anything, except the forces of radiation and matter – an active existence, neither better nor worse than the existence of the amino-acid compounds we call animals or human beings" (146). This statements links him to another important symbol in the novel, in which Rohan's magnified silhouette is projected onto the Black Cloud, which at one point hovers above him during his rescue mission. Lem's irony and critique are obvious: a conceptual projection of human values onto the inanimate Cloud has indeed taken place, blinding scientists to the genuine alienness of its nature.

The implied censure gains additional power from the contrast between the technological splendour of *The Invincible* and the short-sightedness of its specialists. The novel's futuristic setting is only obliquely hinted in reference to Earth's "highly developed technology that had already flourished for centuries" (18). Yet the technologies at the crew's disposal – transsolar travel, superluminal communication, hibernation, and antimatter arsenals – far surpass present-day means.[10] It is in the thesis that mere instrumental progress does not guarantee conceptual maturity that the novel's irony is most overt. On another level it also ridicules the anticognitive bias of gadget-driven science fiction, the conceptual sophistication of which often boils down to the them-or-us (zerosum) alternative.

LORD OF THE "FLIES"

> If I were granted omnipotence, and millions of
> years to experiment in, I should not think Man
> much to boast of as the final result of my efforts.
>   Bertrand Russell

There is only one agent in the novel who, besides grasping intellectually the implications of Lauda's hypothesis, is granted a moment of emotional epiphany into the nature of the Cloud, and through it, the nature of the planet and cosmos at large. It is Rohan who finally comprehends the essence of life on Regis III. The Cloud, like a cybernetic Golem, has evolved beyond its original creators' plans into a hermetic and autonomous system. This autarky places it outside the sphere of values created by human culture. The scientists' attempts to tame its otherness – labelling it as necrosphere, while trying to justify its annihilation – cannot hide the fact that their technocentric and anthropocentric approach to Regis III is a dismal failure.

Braving the Cloud in his solitary search for missing crew members, Rohan is able to welcome it "as something that is simply *other*, of no use to him and ultimately irreducible to human patterns" (Slusser 1051). Symbolically,

Rohan accomplishes this heroic action only when, guided by Lauda's theory, he completely forsakes old modes of thought and behaviour. Not only metaphorically but literally stripped of protective shielding, he survives the encounter with the Cloud by adjusting to it, rather than trying to defeat it.

It is significant that a human being is chosen to perform this dangerous mission, the success of which, as well as his own life, hinge on predictions of Lauda's hypothesis. The camouflage mechanism could have been used to shield a robot rather than a member of the crew. Yet an imperfect human being, guided by a fallible mixture of intuition, unpredictability, and even outright quirkiness, turns out almost paradoxically to be better suited to the task at hand. The missing men, victims of complete amnesia, are so unpredictable in their behaviour that only another human being is believed to be able to conjecture or intuit their whereabouts. There are, of course, no general empirical laws of finding lost crew members, only contingent circumstances that demand new and innovative solutions. The same human traits that were responsible for the disaster and loss of contact in the first place are now called forth to play a crucial role in the rescue attempt.

In addition to this symbolic presentation of human strengths and weaknesses, there is one other dimension to Lem's model. While operating within the familiar terms of our natural language, the author must, after all, present the reader with a phenomenon genuinely alien, i.e., irreducible to any quick and ready human categories. Lem's essentially self-reflexive task is mirrored in the efforts of the novel's scientists. They too, testing the flexibility of the scientific theories at their command, try to write the unknown phenomena into the conceptual framework familiar to them.

Since these attempts are the only ones available to them – truly, we cannot know what we do not know – the Invincible's experts are justified in persevering in their efforts to comprehend what defies their comprehension. Yet Lem makes it clear that what is missing from this picture is the scientists' awareness of such reductionism. The level from which they can reflect on the nature of their own inquiry is granted to the reader in an asymmetric fashion, since the same problem is handled differently by the scientists and by Lem himself. The prominent gap in the crew's analysis of the situation is precisely the missing link that the author gives the reader as a key to the novel. Inevitable or not, reduction in inquiry need not be accompanied by a higher-level blindness to its potential pitfalls.

DO NOT MISTAKE THE EPHEMERAL FOR THE ETERNAL

Philosophy is written in that great book which
ever lies before our eyes, I mean the universe.

Galileo

Lem's model of cybernetic evolution is without doubt the central hypothesis of *The Invincible*. In chapters 5 and 6 I will look at some of its aspects in the context of computer learning, thinking, and writing. The theme of evolution of machines is not limited, however, to Lem's fiction. Its most extensive treatment is found on the 580 pages of *Summa Technologiae* (1964), his philosophical and futurological *opus magnum*.[11] This single volume contains some of Lem's most wide-reaching reflections on techno-evolution, including its goals, values, and effects on culture and society.

In *Summa* Lem highlights the similarities between biological evolution and the evolution of culture, including the latter's technological manifestations and the contingency of their development. This lack of necessity in the specific shape of any particular cultural formation should not be confused with a renunciation of scientific realism, which, after all, is a cultural formation too.[12] There are many powerful reasons for making a distinction between the sphere of human values and the physical world devoid of any semantic context (intentionality).[13] In other words, we must distinguish the claim that the *world* outside exists independently of any cultural activity from the claim that *values* can exist independently of any such activity. The contingency of cultural values in no way undermines the scientific study of external reality. It only denies intentionality to nature and cautions about the illusion of completeness when we formulate hypotheses about it.

A good case in point may be the recent emergence of so-called chaos theory, which investigates physical systems ultra-sensitive to their starting conditions (for instance, water-flow turbulence or the weather). There is something quite special about such systems. The core of science has been built around laws of nature that are relatively simple and symmetrical. In contrast, the real world, described by the solutions to the equations that express these laws, is rarely simple or symmetrical. Yet owing to its irresistible accessibility, this essentially Newtonian world picture has dominated science's way of looking for (linear) patterns and regularities in nature.

The signs that some aspects of the world warranted more attention than they had traditionally received came more or less simultaneously from many disciplines: mathematicians studying iterations of nonlinear systems, meteorologists, population geneticists, and theoretical physicists studying fluids, lasers, or planetary orbits. Although the first paper in the field (by P.J. Myrberg) dates back to the 1960s, it was only ten years later that Metropolis, Stein, and Stein generalized Myrberg's insights and described the so-called chaotic structural universality. The rapidly expanding field got its most important breakthrough with Mitch Feigenbaum's discovery of numerical values of period-doubling and the onset of chaos in mathematical models.[14]

The recent emergence of chaos studies as a systematic field of inquiry is thus something of a turning point in redressing the imbalance in classical physics. Chaotic, or nonlinear, systems abound in the physical world, but are not open to analysis through linear modelling (essentially the differential and integral calculus). For this reason, until recently they were accorded scarce attention, which to some extent distorted the picture of the world constructed by science. Such distortion is both anthropomorphic and reductionist in character, since it presupposes that nature can be understood by the first generation of concepts developed in the course of our civilization. Science, in this picture, behaves like an overzealous carpenter for whom everything is a nail just because he is wielding a hammer.

In *The Invincible* Lem models a crew of conceptual carpenters to draw our attention to the persistent problems of meta-scientific bias. After all, the striking imbalance in science and philosophy goes back to classical mechanics. Being so successful, Newton's laws fostered a fixation with linear phenomena that could be modelled by means of the differential calculus. For three hundred years the rapid advances in science and technology indeed resulted from the lucky coincidence that so much of what is essential for the development of modern society involves linear systems. Yet these undeniable successes led to the neglect of nonlinear phenomena, which are actually the rule rather than the exception in nature.

Before this recent turnaround, the classical orientation in the physical sciences had given rise to an implicit philosophy that a linear representation was sufficient to explain any part of reality, no matter how complex.[15] Over time, this mechanistic, linear picture led to a bias in favour of determinism in science and its philosophy. This, in turn, prepared the ground for logical positivism and its assumption that, given the initial conditions and general laws, valid explanations will always assume the form of logical arguments.

I have discussed in chapter 2 why positivism is not an adequate model of broadly construed scientific inquiry. Here I should only add that the ultimate validation of our scientific goals is our culture and is thus of our own making. In his works, of which *The Invincible* forms a critical link, Lem urges us to reflect periodically on the ever-changing nature of our cultural strategies. He does so by conveying in narrative form the message that "no cultural necessity exists in our growth toward knowledge; for we often take that which has arisen by accident for what is necessary, and mistake the ephemeral for the eternal" (*Microworlds* 238).

EXPLANATIONS AND GENERAL LAWS

The universe is full of magical things patiently
waiting for our wits to grow sharper.
Eden Phillpotts

The Invincible's scientists assume that their cultural patterns and values hold for all worlds they might encounter in their travels across the stars. They forget that, since their culture and its guiding values do not represent any transcendent constants, the rest of the Universe does not have to conform to them. This becomes painfully obvious when the Black Cloud's active but inanimate manifestations are mistaken for strategic actions of a calculating opponent.

The Invincible has interesting implications for the philosophy of science, especially in the context of the latter's disillusion with the covering-law model. Let us look again at the centrepiece of Lem's argument: biologist Lauda's evolutionary hypothesis, this time from a meta-scientific rather than evolutionary (i.e., scientific) perspective. The key question is whether Lauda's hypothesis *explains* the phenomena on Regis III, and whether this explanation – if it is indeed one – has the form of a general empirical law.

The answer to the first question must be positive. Lauda's hypothesis has the sufficient features of a good explanation. Among others, it leads to a verifiable prediction about the Cloud's behaviour. As proven by Rohan's success in eluding the flies, the theory's predictions are accurate to an essential degree. Yet, according to standard positivist arguments, Lauda's theory is *not* a valid explanation. For the positivist the central difference between proper explanations and only pseudo-scientific accounts is the former's appeal to underlying general empirical laws. Lauda's hypothesis gives a thorough *causal* account of the explanandum, without, however, making any assumptions about the shape or even the presence of any underlying empirical law.

Lem sets up his narrative thought experiment around the Cloud's cybernetic evolution. *The Invincible* explains in detail the path taken by evolution on Regis III and accounts causally for its efficacy in defeating the ship's crew and robots. Yet on Lem's account it would be unwarranted to claim that the events on Regis III instantiate some general law of cybernetic evolution. What would such a putative law look like? It would state that for all evolutionary pathways, nonsentient microorganisms always triumph over highly intelligent, but more complex and energy-wasteful, species. There are several faults with such a deductive argument, beginning with the fact that we ourselves are a living disproof of such a general empirical law.

The even more important fault of such an argument brings us back to the discussion of the philosophy of inquiry from chapter 2 and the doubts about the adequacy of the covering-law model. There is no known covering law implying that evolution must follow a specific course. Similarly, there is no known way to describe all the relevant initial parameters of such a claim. Nor is there even a chance of sketching such a general law in an empirical-deductive way. In fact, it is doubtful whether any such law exists; moreover, should it ever be found, it would probablly not have the form demanded by logical positivism.

One last set of doubts that may be raised in regard to the covering-law model of explanation is the role of literary fictions in explaining events and phenomena. I think it needs no arguing that works of literature often provide genuine and valid explanations of various social situations, the behaviour and motivation of their narrative agents, trends and movements in the society, or even sweeping anthropological regularities. Yet in most cases fiction writers do not accomplish this in any way that clearly conforms to the covering-law model. Put alongside the broader problem of explanations in the social sciences that depart from the positivist strictures, the genuine explanatory role of literary fictions demands that any plausible model of scientific inquiry be able to subsume it.

The analysis of Lem's novel could not be complete without a mention of its structural closure. The story ends just as it had begun, with the word "invincible." This classical circularity is appropriate, since the Earthmen do fulfil the mission they were sent for – after a fashion. Although they penetrate the mystery of Regis III, they do so only when they learn that "Invincible" does not translate into "Infallible," especially where human-based models fail as cognitive constants. In this sense, *The Invincible* is a key link in the entire chain of Lem's novels in which the extent, the meaning, and the limits of human inquiry are defined in parabolic encounters with the alien.

CHAPTER FIVE

The Future History of Biterature

Bill sings to Sarah. Sarah sings to Bill. Perhaps
they will do other dangerous things together. They
may eat lamb or stroke each other. They may
chant of their difficulties and their happiness.
They have love but they also have typewriters.
That is interesting.

Racter (z80 micro with 64K RAM),
The Policeman's Beard is Half-constructed

One inevitable consequence of progress in any research field is its special-
ization, the hermetic effects of which estrange it from the public domain.
Many areas of contemporary inquiry are indeed accessible only to the select
elites of experts involved in their development. There are, however, exceptions to this rule, and the computer-related disciplines may be one of the
central ones. As Lem demonstrates in "A History of Bitic Literature" (1984),
after decades of almost exponential development, the field can still profit
from philosophical and cultural inquiry. The author's hypotheses on the
evolution of computers and computer literature are striking in their originality and sociocultural implications. Precise and bold, Lem's futurological
scenario invites analysis and refinement, which is developed in this and the
next chapter.

A HISTORY OF BITIC LITERATURE

It has been said that though God cannot alter the
past, historians can; it is perhaps because they can
be useful to him in this respect that He tolerates
their existence.

Samuel Butler

There is probably no other invention that could rival the computer, barely half a century old, in the sheer speed and dynamism of development. Increasingly faster and ever more powerful computing machines have become today a matter of course, opening new vistas for research and operations almost on a daily basis. Almost overnight, computers have become an industry, not just in terms of their design and manufacture but also in terms of the volume of analysis of their present and future potential.

The computer as a research subject belongs to a group of disciplines known as the cognitive sciences. The name serves as an umbrella for divergent and not always friendly fields of study, such as computing, Artificial Intelligence, machine learning, robotics, electronics, knowledge engineering, information science, and software engineering, as well as branches of neurology, neuropathology, cognitive psychology, text comprehension, translation theory, and philosophy of mind.

My arguments, dispersed throughout this book, for the fusion of literary studies with research programs in other disciplines are directed in particular at the alliance between literary and computer research. The rapidly expanding and heterogenous array of cognitive sciences could profit, it seems, from the analytic efforts of literary scholars and cultural critics. So swift is the progress in computer-related sciences that many of the comfortable assumptions formed during their infancy no longer suffice to describe their contemporary and future potential. This chapter investigates some central questions from the borderline of art and science that might arise from a marriage (interface) between literature and the computer.

Underlying this inquiry is the assumption that the evolution of computing machines will lead to the point when they become able spontaneously to create works of literature. Literature is used here in a comprehensive sense, including not only fiction in its belletristic and popular incarnations but also nonfiction as well as philosophy. In my discussion I take advantage of the provocative and thought-provoking scenario charted by Lem in "A History of Bitic Literature." In this meta-fictional preface to the fictive history of bitic writing from the year 2009, Lem extrapolates with his customary bravado on the subject of computer authorship, or, as I shall sometimes call it, "computhorship."

A HANDFUL OF TERMS

I have yet to see any problem, however complicated,
which when you looked at it in the right way, did
not become still more complicated.
Poul Anderson

Before I begin, I need to clarify several technical points. The first one should be obvious. Speaking of a computer that performs various tasks is only a matter of a colloquial metaphor and metonymy. Clearly the aggregate of microchips called "the computer" is not, by and of itself, capable of doing anything. The same, of course, is true of programs. An inert string of binary digits that forms a computer's chain of instructions has no causal properties. Sitting on a shelf, whether in the form of magnetic pulses on a diskette or symbols on paper, by and of itself a program cannot do (execute) anything.

No matter how sophisticated the internal organization of the computing machine (hardware) or its program (software), in isolation from each other the physical processor and the program are static and incapable of any form of behaviour. Only a proper program controlling a physical system with affecters and effecters can have causal powers. Expressed in more general cybernetic terms, such a system is instrumentally capable of input-output transformation. In what follows I will stick to the term computer, but only as a convenient shorthand for the more precise concept, with which it must not be confused.

My two other points concern the term "bitic literature," or "biterature" as I will frequently call it. Although the smallest unit of any digital computer's processing data is the binary bit, most present-day machines move around binary pulses in groups of eight bits, called bytes. Whether to call computer writing bitic or bytic literature is, however, not as important as the question of its conjunction with the second half of Lem's compound label.

The seemingly innocent term "literature" ushers in a new dimension to computer writing. As we have seen in chapter 1, this heuristic concept determines the reflexive attitude to be adopted with regard to the interpretation of created works. In the present context it has even more interesting consequences. The most conspicuous one may be that biterature calls for the adoption of a similar range of attitudes and strategies for computer authors as for human writers. Specifically, it entails approaching computer writers as agents with internal states, such as, for instance, executive intentions.

Here, however, we find ourselves on less familiar ground. Computers with intentions are presumably computers that can think. But what is the ontology of machine thinking? Are computer intentions real things, like avocados or wombats, or are they just useful theoretical fictions, like the physicist's centres of gravity or the cosmologist's singularities? Is the problem of thinking in computers any different than it is in humans? Can computers *really* think, or is thinking merely what we can *attribute* to advanced systems? And what does "really" really mean in this context?

Almost inevitably, thinking about thinking computers leads to thinking about computers that may be conscious, alive – maybe even computers that have personality, identity, karma, and God knows what else. Fortunately, thanks to Alan M. Turing, thinking about these problems is not so unstructured as it may first appear. Already half a century ago, this English mathematician formulated a sensible way to explore this conceptually unfamiliar territory. His famous variant on the imitation game, known as the Turing test (henceforth TT), remains the single most important contribution to the study of thinking computers.

The continuing importance of this thought experiment is underscored by the controversies that it sparks even today. This is in itself quite remarkable, considering that Turing's famous paper, "Computing Machinery and Intelligence," was published in 1950, when computer design and manufacture were, relatively speaking, at the neolithic stage. The intervening decades have brought out numerous polemics on the validity, application, and implications of the TT. But in the midst of this philosophical tug of war, the test itself has remained the key to the idea of the thinking and, by extension, the writing computer.

AUTHORSHIP AND THE ANXIETY OF INFLUENCE

Definitions are like belts. The shorter they are, the
more elastic they need to be.
                                    Stephen Toulmin

Lem's tongue-in-cheek history of computer writing opens with a central definition. Biterature is "any [literary] work of nonhuman origin – one whose real author is not a human being." However, his next sentence complicates matters to a great degree. In it Lem allows that a human being could be an *indirect* author of a biterary work by performing the functions that generate "the real author's acts of creation" (both on 41).

It is not hard to see why Lem's taxonomy fails to establish a secure analytical ground. His second clause calls into question the identity of biterature and, by extension, also literature proper, in effect aborting the entire definition. From Lem's approach it follows that any real author, whether human or not, is only a terminal stage in a long process culminating in the production of a literary work. However, if we adopt this view in good faith, the question of authorship can no longer be addressed without recourse to the indirect sources of the real author's executive intentions.

The inherent paradox of machine authorship becomes easier to understand on examples from the more familiar world of human writers. Lem's definition turns our flesh-and-blood authors into mere conventional fronts for their colleagues, parents, teachers, mentors, gurus, fellow writers, or anybody else who may have contributed to the genesis of their work. On Lem's view anybody who performs any function contributing to the real author's act of creation becomes thereby an indirect author of the resulting literary work.

A brief reflection shows this inference to be confusing, to say the least. Just because the publisher, Little and Brown, commissioned Normal Mailer to write *Of a Fire on the Moon* (1970), on Lem's view they become an author, albeit an indirect one, of Mailer's work. This is so, simply because their contract performed an important causal function contributing to Mailer's act of creation (without it, presumably, *Of a Fire on the Moon* would have never got written). It should be evident why Lem's second clause creates more problems than it solves. The key element missing from his account of computhorship is the lack of proper causal depth (I will define it later in this chapter). As mentioned during the discussion of Miller's theory of explanation in chapter 2, the required causal depth should preclude explanations from being true but trivial, or true but insufficient, by isolating the actual mechanisms of change in a given situation.

There is another, equally objectionable corollary to Lem's second clause. It is that the drawing of a circle of influence around a literary work must necessarily follow an arbitrary course. After all, all contributors to our flesh-and-blood authors' literary output have been influenced by others, who themselves have been influenced by others, who in turn have been influenced by others still. Starting with the innocent assumption of indirect authorship, we end up with an infinite web of reciprocal influences extending spatially as well as temporally in all directions. Unwittingly, Lem has created something like a deconstructionist's paradise – a pantextual allegory of meanings deferred in an infinite playground of intertextuality. Although intriguing, this model has nothing to do with interpreting literary works.

The absurdity of the above results can again be brought out by applying it to specific literary examples. Even though it would be impossible to deny that Joyce was influenced by Homer to an extraordinary degree, can we assert that the blind bard was an indirect author of *Ulysses*? To go even further, can one claim that Homer's epic, diluted but perpetuated through Joyce's literary experiment, may have performed an indirectly contributive/generative function for Lem's short story "Gigamesh" (from *A Perfect Vacuum*), which spoofs Joyce's work? The proposition verges on incoherence. If Homer were in some indirect sense the author of Lem's story, we would have on our hands a case of stark anachronism. There was no Dublin, no James Joyce, no America, no GI Joes, no computers, no Library of Congress, and no Boltzmann's constant in Homer's antiquity, and yet all of them figure in Lem's story. We must conclude that from a rational point of view it is silly to entertain notions of indirect authorship. On the other hand, to embrace the opposite view, namely that the real author is the only one there is, is to obliterate the important factor of indirect human input into computer writing.

THREE TYPES OF COMPUTER AUTHORSHIP

There is probably no idea more central to
thought about art than that it is an activity

in which participants create things – these things
being artworks.

Jerrold Levinson

To clarify the picture in a way that will bring out the underlying causal
connections, we can start by distinguishing three types of computer authorship. The proposed distinction is based on their degree of independence from
direct human interference. Computer writers of the first order are most
indebted to human programmers and in this sense are the most primitive.
Their literary output takes place entirely within the so-called closed forms.
This is to say that their "creative" role is confined essentially to slotting
rigorously specified textual variables (words, phrases, generic plot elements)
into predetermined gaps in an already given narrative framework. In principle any randomizing device such as a die or a roulette wheel could be used
to perform the same function.

It may be worth pointing out that my tripartite division of computer
authorship depends on the use to which a computer is put, rather than its
intrinsic computing ability. Even Cray teraflops, the fastest computers in
existence, can become first-order creators when equipped with an appropriate program. The writing and running of a closed-form program needs the
greatest amount of control (input) from the human operator. It is also the
easiest to implement, and examples of such creative output date all the way
back to the computer's infancy. In a little-known literary experiment from
the mid-1940s, Ferranti's Mark I became the first documented computer
author by generating a love letter with, admittedly, a little more than a little
help from its programmers.

In contrast to the rigidly controlled output of closed-form programs,
computer writers of the second order use open forms. Starting with a set of
sometimes only broadly delimited textual variables, the program strings
units together without a necessarily prescribed sequence, or determined
length. At this level we can observe rudiments of textual comprehension,
inasmuch as the computer is required to make sometimes quite important
decisions about semantic properties of phrases, paragraphs, or even larger
units. The epigraph to this chapter is probably a fair demonstration of the
quality of computer writing at this level today. Its genuine hilarity is obviously
an unintended by-product, rather than a part of the computer's executive
intentions.

In this light it may be interesting to note that certain critical and meta-
critical essays on literary writing are, in fact, attempts to formulate successful
second-order writing strategies. Poe's "How to Write a Blackwood Article"
(1838) and "Philosophy of Composition" (1846) come inevitably to mind at
this point. Both are examples of what we would call heuristic rule sets in
which Poe writes down an "algorithm" for a certain variety of prose. In other

words, they can be viewed as sources of advanced second-order creative strategies, devised to generate types of writing characterized by certain tonal, modal, generic, topical, stylistic, or rhetorical features.

Poe makes one of his second-order algorithms even more interesting and effective by actually composing a perfect exemplar of a Blackwood story. "A Predicament" (1838), published jointly with "How to Write a Blackwood Article," fleshes out in the narrative form the tongue-in-cheek prescriptions from the Blackwood piece. In this sense, "A Predicament" is a fictional embodiment of a second-order generative heuristic "programmed" into Mme Psyche Zenobia by Mr Blackwood. The story that the lady purportedly composes is thus in a style heterogenous (i.e., at once laconic, elevated, and metaphysical) replete with sensations and sensationalism and piquant expressions and flummery, as well as "a good spicing of the decidedly unintelligible" (339). At one point Poe's satire on the creative process even comes close to describing the work of a first-order hack who dutifully slots variables into a ready narrative framework. As Mr Blackwood tells Psyche Zenobia, the entire trick to creative writing is to use a little "ingenuity to fit [any odd scrap] into your article" (344).

Since computer writers of the first and second order have been around for decades, in what follows I focus entirely on computers of the third order. This distinction is of paramount importance, and it helps clarify two problems inherent in Lem's approach to the subject. First of all, his remarks pertain exclusively to third-order computer writing. Second, he is wrong to attribute an indirect role to human creators in this type of computhorship.

It is not hard to see why Lem would propose both of his stipulations, even though they partially contradict each other. On its own, the first clause does a poor job of defining computhorship. It attributes actual authorship exclusively to the physical generator of a piece of writing. On this view, if a computer produces the text of a novel, the computer *is* its real author, even if there was a human author behind it. Clearly this is nonsense. If I write and print a novel using my PC plus WordPerfect, should we say that my computer and/or WordPerfect wrote a work of literature? I think not.

Imagine, on the other hand, that you enter my study, where you see a self-contained futuristic-looking apparatus hooked up to a printer. The moment you enter the room, without any visible prompting, the computer begins to churn out pages of text that, on inspection, turn out to be the text of an original novel. We can plausibly polarize the readers' reactions to this state of affairs. The first is the normal assumption that, unbeknownst to you, I had entered the PRINT command a few seconds before your arrival and only the processing and consequent delay gave the computer an appearance of acting on its own. This is what in the present environment everyone in his right mind would assume had happened, rather than jump to the conclusion that they had just witnessed an act of computer creation.

But what if I had not entered any commands? What if I am as bewildered as you are? What if the novel turns out to be something I could not even have written? These questions may help identify the conditions for computer writing to qualify as a third-order creation. Providing we can be reasonably sure that the situation is indeed the way just sketched, I think some of us would assume that we have just witnessed a spontaneous act of computer creation. The above scenario points to an element that is absent from Lem's definition but needed to properly identify third-order computer authorship. The *differentia specifica* of writing machines will likely lie in a capability for literary creation that is independent of humans – in other words, *spontaneous*.[1]

FROM THE ANALYTICAL
TO THE BITERARY ENGINE

The historian is a prophet looking backwards.
August Von Schlegel

Here is how Lem describes the key transition to third-order computhorship in his history of bitic literature: "The relaxational output of machines was first observed and recorded almost thirty years ago. It turned out to be a purely technical necessity that the prototypes (beginning with the 15th binasty) should be provided with rest periods during which their activity did not come to a standstill but, deprived of programmed directives, manifested itself as a peculiar 'mumble'" (47). The thirty years subtracted from the fictional publication date of the story gives 1979, an incurably optimistic calculation by today's knowledge. In chapter 6 I will examine whether contemporary developments in Artificial Intelligence (AI) and computer technology warrant a belief that this scenario might come to pass in the near future. For now let us return to Lem.

The first work of bitic mimesis to gain world renown was a novel by Pseudodostoyevsky, *The Girl* (Devotchka). It was composed during a phase of relaxation by a multimember aggregate whose assignment was to translate into English the collected works of the Russian writer. In his memoirs the distinguished scholar John Raleigh describes the shock he experienced upon receiving the Russian typescript of a composition signed with what he took to be the singular pseudonym of HYXOS. The impression which the work created on this Dostoyevsky expert must have been truly indescribable in its intensity, if, as he admits, he doubted whether he was in a conscious state! (58)

It is not difficult to see how the initial reaction to biterary computers could indeed be one of dismay, incredulity, or even shock. In the next chapter we will have a chance to look at some of the social trends that may accompany the emergence of computer authorship. For the present let us look more closely at the concept of spontaneous creation that, as I have proposed, lies at the heart of third-order computhorship.

We may begin with the first sophisticated computing machine. The word "machine" is appropriate in this context, since Charles Babbage's Analytical Engine was to work along mechanical, rather than electric or electronic, lines.[2] Constructed on and off between 1833 and 1871 but never completed, it was designed on structural principles similar to all modern computing machines. We owe a detailed account of this early computer to Augusta Ada, daughter of Lord Byron. Better known as Lady Lovelace, she was Babbage's associate, assistant, and a programmer of this protocomputer. In her memoirs she wrote: "The Analytical Engine has no pretensions to *originate* anything. It can do *whatever we know how to order it to perform.*"[3]

We can adopt this statement as a first approximation of the definition of spontaneous creation. First- and second-order computer writers, no matter how sophisticated, cannot originate anything. In contrast, third-order computhors will be those able to originate, i.e., spontaneously create. Spontaneity for our purposes can thus be approached as a causally independent composition of original literary works. It goes without saying that the line between these types of computer writing may turn out to be blurred in practice, although this epistemic difficulty need not deter us from exploring its conceptual limits. Let us examine briefly what the blurring of the distinction between second- and third-order computhorship might entail. If the machine can do only what we tell it to do, it would seem that we cannot speak properly of computhorship of the third order. Yet things may be more complicated than Lady Lovelace suggests.

Imagine you give a command to a computer: "Write a really good thriller." Imagine it indeed does so and produces an original and well-written work of literature. Would you not say then that the computer *created* this work? Your initial command would essentially be of the same order as Little and Brown's commission that, for a certain fee, Mailer write a book about the Apollo 11 moon landing. Is it the fact that the computer would not get paid for its creative work that makes a difference between the presence or absence of literary creation? Is it the fact that it apparently cannot disobey the command? Or that in the absence of a command you could be sure that the computer would not execute anything, whereas one presumes that Mailer might? On reflection, I think, we would be strongly inclined to accept that the open-endedness of the request that the computer write a good thriller satisfies the condition of spontaneous creation.[4]

My thought experiment is, of course, only an intuition pump to suggest a convenient reference point for the core concept – spontaneous computer creation – on the level of analysis common to philosophers and social scientists. The suggestion is inevitably normative, since we have no means of knowing whether the actual future practice will correspond to these proposals. The decision whether a computhor executed a biterary work spontaneously or not will always depend on pragmatic and contextual evidence. In general, however, the relation between computers and biterature is going to be inversely proportional. The less control the computer writer has over the selection, execution, and copyrights to its material, the more we may hesitate before attributing authorship to it.

HOW TO BE SPONTANEOUS

Anticipatory plagiarism occurs when someone
steals your original idea and publishes it a hundred
years before you were born.
                              Robert K. Merton

Let us return to our subject, the paradigmatic computhorship of the third order. I have concluded that when the computer creates a literary work spontaneously, it is properly its real author. Now one must ask what conditions must obtain for a computer to create spontaneously, i.e., without consequential human input. It would be rash to presume that definitive answers can be provided in the space of one section. A causal analysis of the problem seems, however, a promising way to begin.

What is the standard causal pattern in the social sciences in the light of which a given (level of) explanation is considered adequate? It consists of a description of the actions and the motivations behind them that were sufficient to produce a change in the circumstances. Such a standard causal pattern acts as a stopping rule in the pursuit of a sufficiently deep explanatory account of the analyzed situation. A stopping rule is critical, since explanations can obviously be appraised on a variety of levels. Following the standard pattern in the humanities and the social sciences, the model discussed here is thus at the psycho-social and instrumental, and not at the programming or executive, level.

Before giving a causal description of third-order computer writing, we need a preliminary account of causal depth. Imagine, for example, that you have given an accurate causal explanation of the Kennedy assassination (e.g., by referring to Oswald's bullets). Your model conforms to the standard causal pattern for forensic investigations of this type and specifies factors sufficient to cause the phenomenon in question under the circumstances. Yet it may still fail as a proper explanation because the listed causes lack sufficient depth. As Miller puts it, a cause is "too shallow to explain why something occurred if it is just one of the ways in which another cause, as intimately connected with the effect, produced the latter" (98). The question "Why was JFK killed?" and the answer "Because bullets damaged his vital organs" show why it is so; in this case the answer is true, but trivial.

We need to describe the actual mechanisms of change, rather than ones that may be only superficially linked to the effects. What are the ways in which superficial causes can undermine the effect of the deeper, underlying ones? They can be labelled respectively "depth as necessity" and "depth as priority." A cause c helping to bring about an effect w is too shallow to explain why w has taken place if another cause H undermines c in either of the following two ways:

1 If c had not been present, w would have come about anyway.
2 H is an antecedent cause of c that in turn causes w, yet H is too intimately linked to c to be left outside a proper causal account.

Let us flesh out these cases by recasting them in the context of computer authorship. Specifying the causal mechanism at the bottom of computer writing should help us grasp the specificity of third-order creativity.

First, depth as necessity. If a (c)omputer had not been present, a given literary (w)ork would have come about anyway. The (H)uman causal agent would have created some causal substitute for the (c)omputer, bringing about the (w)ork in some other way. A randomizing-slotting device for closed-form computer writing could be such a substitute cause, showing that the computer is not essential to this type of creativity. Conclusion? Computhors of the first order do not meet the criteria of spontaneous creation, which demands that it not be undermined by intermediate human causal interference. The true causal agent in the first-order computer writing is still the human programmer. The computer is merely an efficient tool, an indirect but dispensable causal mechanism.

Now depth as priority. The (H)uman agent is causally prior to the (c)omputer but still too intimately related to be bracketed off as causally inessential. Our interest here is not with the tactical decisions made in writing a work, the weak causal link identified by depth as necessity. Depth as priority applies to the analysis of the causality behind the actual creation of a literary work. Would an effect w – a literary work – come into existence in a given form without the human agent behind the computer? In other words, was the programmer causally responsible for the order to execute a certain text in a certain way? If so, the work created is likely a result of the second-order computer authorship.

The causal account seems to make the concept of third-order computhorship a little more precise. We have identified two ways in which a given cause can be undermined by accompanying or antecedent factors. Both narrow down what is acceptable as genuine, i.e., spontaneous computer creativity.

There must be a direct and not underlain causal link between a computhor and its literary work to claim that the machine is its genuine author. Of course, our current norms for identifying underlying causal patterns do not recognize machines as fully fledged agents and artists. This makes it almost inevitable that when trying to establish proper depth as priority, we will always search backwards for evidence of human agency in programming the output.

THE LEARNING AND THE LEARNED HOMEOSTAT

> When I play with my cat, who knows whether she is
> not amusing herself with me more than I with her.
> Michel Montaigne

Generally speaking, homeostatic, survival-oriented behaviour can come in two types. The first is the instinctual (genotypal) homeostat, employing "hard-wired" responses that guarantee a swift reaction to fairly standard environmental stimuli. The second type is the learning (phenotypal) homeostat, which organizes its behaviour on the basis of historically acquired knowledge. In actual experience it may be difficult to find either in pure form; even humans, often said to typify the latter type, are in fact an amalgam of both. Already at birth babies are equipped with instinctive mechanisms that produce the minimum of survival-oriented actions: crying, suckling, responding to external stimuli, and so on. On the other hand, their long-term survival clearly requires a protracted process of neotenous development and *learning*. In contrast, most animals do just fine without it, although in mammals the process of learning, long underestimated, also plays a significant role.

At each point of its development, a learning mind is a composite of information from three channels. These are state at birth (or, more generally, genetic endowment, which can come into play only, for example, in adolescence), formal education, and informal (inductive, analogical, emotional, and so forth) life experience. How does this apply to computer thinking and spontaneously creative computers? As we saw in the previous sections, third-order computer authorship is defined by spontaneous creation, i.e., creation causally independent of human input. Such artistic independence cannot, naturally, be dissociated from a broader context of independent existence. In a learning homeostat, independent existence hinges on the ability to organize its behaviour around historically acquired information – in other words, on its ability to learn.

Let me state more precisely what I mean by learning. I will need to be a little more abstract in order to bypass the superficial differences between humans and machines. It seems that to be able to learn, a system must possess a certain level of complexity. It should be able to transform incoming data (input) into internal states and, most likely, into outgoing signals (output), according to some principles of organization. Such a system must also have a principle of evaluation of its own performance and some method of correlating future actions to an improvement in performance. A system that possesses these features, whether organic or not (i.e., whether a human being or a computer), may be said to have the ability to learn.[5]

It is important to note that even this general description of learning is not foolproof. An amusing but instructive example of how it can fail even in very simple circumstances has arisen in the application of Douglas Lenat's expert program, EURISCO. This system is designed to gather data, spot regularities, formulate hypotheses, develop heuristics, evaluate concepts, and, in the process, extend its knowledge representation. Procedures, concepts, or heuristics that prove useful to the running of the program are fed back into the system and assigned a high value for future operations. However, as Donald Michie and Rory Johnston report in *The Creative Computer* (1984), at one point the system got too smart for its own good. A heuristic that made a discovery "would put down its own name down in the list of heuristics of high worth, and then take that realization that it had made a discovery as a discovery in itself. So the heuristic would award itself more points, and then take *that* as yet another discovery worth still more points, and so on in an infinite loop!" (108).

In general, considering many spectacular failures in AI research, carefully documented in the regularly updated editions of Hubert L. Dreyfus's *What Computers Still Can't Do* (1992), some conclusions are difficult to avoid. The chronic lack of success in programming general problem-solving heuristics indicates that progress might be made only when computers themselves will finally learn to learn. This will allow them to dispense with human input, indispensable today in the construction of even the simplest expert systems. We can expect that learning in the learning computer – its ability to anticipate future events as part of an active attitude to the input data – will be expectation driven, i.e., at least to some degree hypothesis-forming, as in some of the recent connectionist research into neural networks.

THE LIMITS OF THE LEARNING CALCULATOR

Never let school get in the way of your education.
Mark Twain

Learning is an organism's ability to acquire information and feed it back into its behaviour, including the learning process itself. The implications for the computer are not difficult to draw. A learning machine should be able to rewrite – in other words alter – its own program as it sees fit in the course of its operations. Ultimately it may thus change its configuration to the point where it may no longer be the machine that had originally been designed. This is assuming, of course, that it was designed for something in the first place. It is possible to envision machines constructed on the principles of humans, who are not designed for anything in particular, unless it is learning and surviving.

There is growing evidence that this may indeed be the way of the future. One among many programs that has helped put this point in perspective is AM, a learning system designed to make discoveries in mathematics. Beginning with prenatally fixed (see below) knowledge of set theory, over two hundred heuristic rules, and some meta-level search principles, the program is designed to explore its own internal knowledge to create new concepts and conjectures. Although, as David Peat reports in *Artificial Intelligence* (1988), "what AM achieved is mathematically interesting" (311), the usefulness of the program is inversely proportional to the amount of time it is allowed to run. This is so simply because as its conjectures grow, AM is unable to alter its heuristic rules. Recommends Peat, "an obvious improvement therefore would be to have it modify its heuristics as it learns" (311).

Before we pass on to the discussion of the imitation game and the Turing test, let us recapitulate the main points so far. Third-order computer writers are machines able to create spontaneously. Causal spontaneity in the computhor calls for causal and conceptual independence, which in turn seems to require an ability to learn. Learning, in turn, entails capacity for self-redesign on the basis of historically acquired knowledge. Computer writing may thus manifest itself in machines with the capacity for learning which, as I said, entails a significant degree of independence from initial programming, and thus from human control.

Speaking of learning in *Consciousness Explained* (1991), Daniel Dennett refers in general terms to postnatal design-fixing, under which he groups not only what we normally refer to as learning but also development. Dennett carefully distinguishes between stored-program computers and human beings. People are certainly unlike stored-program machines in at least one crucial respect: they *learn*. In other words, they can override their "programming," i.e., patterns of response, in terms of both their behaviour and the learning process itself.

My earlier analogy between the process of learning in machines and humans can now be extended to computers, notably to third-order computer writers. If self-programming (or self-reprogramming) is an essential part of learning, initially identical computers may end up being quite distinct, having had different learning experiences. Thus programs run on these systems will not necessarily run in the same way and will not necessarily yield the same results. To possible "pre-natal" differences in design and programming, we must therefore add "postnatal" differences, which will certainly play a major role in computers advanced enough to create literature spontaneously.

This progressive autonomy has, of course, nothing to do with the legendary Rabbi Loews and a Golem-type insurrection. Stories of machine insubordination belong squarely to the domain of myth, mysticism, or tawdry sci-fi.[6] And yet, speculation about independently thinking computers may be a bit unsettling to some people familiar only with the word-processing, game playing, database crunching microsystems of today. I will return to these concerns in chapter 6.

To readers who previously noticed the antinomy embodied in the label "bitic literature," this section should provide an answer. The term partly camouflages the fact that the semantics of bitic literary texts derives from digital bits, i.e., units of nonsemantic information. As Lem himself admits, bitic literature is thus a rather unfortunate coinage, since it glosses over the gap between simple data crunching and intelligently operating with semantic units of a world-knowledge order. In this sense, only when computers become learning homeostats, capable of interacting with their environment by means of world-based and historically acquired knowledge, may we properly refer to their output as biterature.

THE IMITATION GAME

Absence of evidence is not evidence of absence.
Martin Rees

A learning computer points, in turn, to a thinking computer. But how to measure the extent of thinking in a machine? Or even decide that it thinks at all? Things may seem different with humans. We know that we think and can even derive metaphysical comfort from the very thought of thinking. With his *cogito*, Descartes reached a secure point of reflection on existence by doubting everything except his faculty of thought.

Research with primates and other mammals, e.g., dolphins, indicates that cognitive processes are certainly not a human monopoly, something that only dogged anthropocentrism prevented scientists from recognizing for a long time. Still, to suggest that machines may think seems prima facie a proposition of a different order. Computers are not made of the same stuff as humans, they do not "run" in the same way – most of all, they have no mentality or volition (barring an occasional refusal to cooperate).[7] Yet there are principled ways of investigating whether computers, or indeed any organisms, can be said to think. By far the most famous among them is the Turing test – a unique thought experiment devised by Alan M. Turing to tackle the problem. Most arguments about the evolution of computers and of their thinking abilities end up being arguments about the validity and extension of the TT.[8]

Instead of asking, "Can machines think?" – a question he considered too meaningless to deserve discussion – Turing turned his attention to a related but more tractable inquiry, namely, "Can machines be said to think?" This he approached in terms of a parlour game called the imitation game. The game involves three people: a man, a woman, and an interrogator who may be of either sex. The players and the examiner are separated physically to prevent them from obtaining clues about each other's identity. Today a convenient way to arrange the communication between them would be to employ computer terminals.

The examiner can put any type of question to either participant but, as in a normal conversation, they can sidestep, reshape, or ignore these questions altogether. The object of the game is for the examiner to determine the sex of either participant. Turing also requests that one of the participants aid the examiner, presumably by giving truthful answers. This person could, of course, assure the interrogator outright of his/her identity, but strategically that move seems of little value, as the other player can obviously do the same.

This is the imitation game. Since the game is usually discussed only as a preamble to the TT, it rarely gets much attention on its own. Yet a few things about it are worth pointing out, not the least because they pertain also to the TT. First, the time frame. Turing's report on the imitation game specifies no time limits, yet the matter is of colossal importance. It is enough to imagine the putative rate of success after the game has been played for one minute and one day. The first will be presumably about 50 per cent, i.e., the expected value for a random play. On the other hand, one day of questioning would likely lead to a higher, maybe even a much higher, rate of success. Put simply, an extension of the time frame offers more opportunities for the examiner to test the subjects.

My second point concerns the rule of the game that asks for two people of opposite sex. This in itself is a vital clue for the examiner that can influence the interrogation. The role of this information cannot be overstated and can be easily put to test. We could run the game varying the sexes and, more important, the information about the sexes available to *all three participants*. How this knowledge would affect their performance is a critical factor not to be ignored in the analysis or actual implementation of the game.[9]

In general, even the imitation game suggests that determining the sexes of the participants involved may critically hinge on the pragmatic factors involved in the setup and running of the game. The results could differ widely, depending, for example, on whether the game is run as a game of complete, or only perfect, information (see chapter 1). The success rate of the examiner can be controlled to an appreciable degree by revealing or concealing relevant information, which will aid or hamper his task. The situation is thus much less of a logical puzzle and more like a real-life inductive test. We may anticipate the same range of pragmatic factors to be of significance in the TT as well.

HAL, R2D2, GOLEM, AND OTHERS

"In a riddle whose answer is chess, what is the
only prohibited word?" I thought for a moment
and replied, "The word *chess*."

Jorge Luis Borges

So much for the imitation game. Turing's variant on the game is stunning in its simplicity and philosophical reverberations. Keeping the structure of the game, he asks, "What will happen when a machine takes the part of A [one of the players] in this game?" (5). Instead of dwelling on a possible opposition to this move, which is expertly handled by the author himself, let us examine a few matters about the TT itself.[10]

There is little doubt in my mind that only a thinking and learning machine could pass an extensively run TT. Template programming, employing stock responses, would never stand a chance, even though in artificially limited contexts it may give an impression of independent thought (as did Weizenbaum's ELIZA).[11] Strictly speaking, then, a computer could not be programmed to pass the TT. On the other hand, a learning, and therefore self-programming, computer would by definition be to some degree independent of its initial program. The most we could say is that such a machine could be programmed to *program itself* to pass the test.

It should be clear at this point how my remarks about the imitation game pertain directly to the TT. Let us consider them in turn, beginning with the time factor. In "Computing Machinery" Turing states, "in about fifty years' time [i.e., around the year 2000] it will be possible to program computers ... to make them play the imitation game so well that an average interrogator will not have more than 70 percent chance of making the right identification after five minutes of questioning" (13). This seems to be a partial retreat from the original inquiry. "Can machines be said to think?" is now reduced to "Can machines pass a five-minute spot check?" To the objection that there is no essential difference between the TT run over five minutes and five days or even five hours, I say that there may be a tremendous difference, for reasons indicated in the previous section. The least that ought to be clear is that the interest in and inductive relevance of the TT is a function of the length of time and the number of different examiners involved in the process.

Also, I do not find the success rate of 20 percent over the expected 50 percent totally persuasive.[12] The deviation is significant and would suggest that something akin to thinking is indeed taking place in the tested machine. Yet it is hard to believe that a 20 percent deviation could carry enough *pragmatic* weight to make people reevaluate their social, legal, or ethical ideas about computers. Naturally, any index of thinking that relies on the time frame and rate of success is bound to be arbitrary. However, a modified version of the TT (see below) could make even such arbitrary criteria for recognizing thinking in machines more trustworthy.

The other two points about the imitation game are equally relevant to the TT. Identifying the sexes of the participants is equivalent within the TT to telling the examiner that one of the players is, in fact, a computer. With this foreknowledge, the interrogator's task is different and presumably less difficult than when he does not know whether he is dealing with two humans (in any combination: MM, FF, MF) or a human and a machine. The knowledge of the identities of the players may alert the examiner to factors like consistency, tiredness, or memory, which may be of aid in the investigation. Of course, we are not looking here to devise the toughest version of the TT for its own sake. It is only because the TT may be a tool for making inductive inferences about thinking in computers that it is important to equip ourselves with the highest quality tool available.

Another interesting aspect of the TT is that it yields only *sufficient* inductive evidence for a computer to be regarded as thinking. Yet machines may be able to carry out processes that will have to be described as thinking but that could bear little resemblance to what people do. The limit case is, of course, when there is *no* observable resemblance at all between human and computer thought processes, but there our investigation must by definition rest.[13] The final point about the TT is that, being much faster, in order not to give itself away the computer must also imitate humans in speed of response. I return to this question below.

THE TURING TEST WITH A DIFFERENCE

> You can fool all the people some of the time, and
> some of the people all the time, but you can not
> fool all the people all of the time.
>   Abraham Lincoln

At this point let us consider a variant on the TT. The principle is again simple. In place of a human interrogator, we substitute the machine. Now it is the computer's task to determine the sexes of the players. The Swirski test (ST) is in other respects identical with the TT. How does this new situation differ from the original? To begin with the simplest point, there is no need any more for the machine to imitate humans in its speed of response. This is because it no longer makes a difference whether the players know that they are interrogated by a computer or not. We are, after all, trying to determine whether machines think, and not whether machines can think at the same speed as humans (see also the final section of this chapter). The sт dissolves this type of objection directed at the тт.

Another issue is that at this point it becomes exceedingly difficult, if not impossible, to fake thinking. Within the framework of the original тт the task might conceivably be accomplished by means of template responses. As in the case of ELIZA, the computer could be programmed to evade hard questions and reroute the conversation onto familiar grounds. Although difficult, this is perhaps within the realm of template programming, especially when restricted to five minutes of questioning.

However, it seems extremely unlikely that a template-based computer could determine the sexes of the players in five minutes *as an examiner*. The order of difficulty seems simply insuperable, considering that the machine is now an active originator of inquiries and *evaluator* of responses and has to do both with enough nuance to detect the sex difference, or no sex difference, between two individuals. Here again I propose that the computer should not be told what combination of male/female participants it is dealing with. Thus it could be interviewing two women, two men, or a man and a woman, and in each case would have to identify them as such.

It may or may not be possible to camouflage thinking over the period of five minutes in the тт. But the structure of the sт makes it unlikely for the interrogating computer, which does not know beforehand the sex of the participants, to determine it within five minutes. Naturally the speed and success of detection may depend significantly on the individual skills of the participants. There is no doubt that some programs may be better at the game than others or that some humans may excel in the deception game and others not.

This last observation prompts an important rejoinder that follows from the fact that humans can also fail to identify the players in the test. In the variant where a human player is the examiner we would expect him, presumably, to exceed a 50 percent accuracy rate expected for random play. In the variant where the computer becomes the examiner its task would thus be to match or exceed the success rate for people. For example, if we discovered that most people are 70 percent successful over a six-hour run of the test, we would expect the thinking computer to perform at least as well. My hidden assumption is, of course, that the success rate for humans will be noticeably over 50 percent.

If not, the sт could take the ultimate form where *any* participant could be *any* one of the three alternatives: man, woman, or machine. Could a computer player succeed in convincing a computer interrogator that it is human, or rather that it thinks like humans do? Could a human player make a computer believe that s/he is a computer? Once again it should be clear how important the framing information about the identity of the players is. Not knowing the physical nature of the participants (man or machine) should make the identification much more difficult.

In the end, the proposed modification to the TT is just a modification and not a totally new approach to the problem. The strongest evidence is that, just like the TT, the ST relies on operational criteria. In that sense, anybody who is convinced of the value of either version of the test can be accused of being a mere behaviourist. This type of behaviourism lies, however, at the heart of all sciences, and must not be confused with the particular doctrines of Skinner or Watson, or their followers. It amounts to no more than a study of intersubjectively observable phenomena, including internal processes, states, or events.[14]

For the sake of a die-hard critic of such an approach to computer cognition, I should note that much of such skepticism is equally applicable to human beings. In this context Gillian Cohen's observations from *The Psychology of Cognition* (1977) are particularly pertinent. Comparing psychological models of human and computer behaviour, Cohen notes that the former arouse much fewer objections, even though their assumptions and conceptual difficulties are of the same order.

It is for this reason that we may need to devise the most foolproof version of the test. Put simply, the harder the test that the computer has to pass, the fewer potential objections it is likely to face before it can be deemed as thinking. This inverse relation applies equally to our present, in which we are dealing with the problem in its philosophical mantle, as to the future, in which it might turn into a social issue of a machine's status as a thinker, a being, and perhaps even a citizen. One strength of the ST is that it eliminates prejudice towards the results, a fact that, in view of the tragic story of Turing's own life, seems to say as much about computers as about humans.

IN A ROOM WITH CHINESE CHARACTERS

Mind is a pattern perceived by a mind. This is
perhaps circular, but it is neither vicious nor
paradoxical.
                              Douglas Hofstadter

One of the most eloquent critiques of the TT has been John Searle's Chinese Room scenario, outlined in "Minds, Brains, and Programs" (1980).[15] In this thought experiment the author imagines himself in a room stacked with boxes full of Chinese symbols (his data base) and equipped with a rule book (his program) that tells him where to look up appropriate Chinese symbols. He gets bunches of Chinese symbols (input) and performs certain operations on them according to the rule book (carries out the program), thus producing bunches of other symbols (output). In other words, in the Chinese Room a human being performs the role of the computer implementing a program for answering (possibly TT-type) questions.

The structure of Searle's objection to the TT can be simplified to this quasi-syllogism:

1 Computer programs are formal (i.e., syntactic) constructs and thus neither equivalent to, nor by themselves sufficient for, semantic content.
2 Minds as we know them have mental (i.e., semantic) content.

Therefore,

3 No program, in and of itself, can be said to give rise to a mind.

The suppressed premise in this reasoning is, of course, that syntax is not equivalent to, or by itself sufficient for, the jump to semantics. In effect this amounts to claiming that no amount of programming can turn any material entity into one that has the power to produce mental states. In other words, Searle asserts there is no program that could turn a previously nonmental entity into a mental (intentional) one. He concludes in "The Mystery of Consciousness". "*If I don't understand Chinese solely on the basis of implementing a computer program for understanding Chinese, then neither does any other digital computer solely on that basis, because no digital computer has anything I do not have*" (61).

It is one thing to agree with Searle that a purely syntactic approach is not the way to achieve practical intelligence. It is another to hold that his catchy scenario has the desired upshot for our pragmatic considerations about the TT. Searle's thought experiment founders on its very centrepiece – the feasibility of running a massive syntax program that could provide for every real-world interpretive contingency. Since this philosophical *trompe l'œil* has been subject to numerous analyses and even more numerous refutations, there is no need here for another full-scale rebuttal.[16] An analogy may, however, help illustrate what is missing from Searle's strong anti-AI claims.

Here is roughly what Searle claims. The occupant of the Chinese Room does not understand the foreign squiggles and squoggles, which he can, nevertheless, manipulate expertly according to purely syntactic transformation rules. Nor are mental phenomena contained in any of the bits of paper on which the rules are stored. Take the occupant together with the bits of paper, and he still does not understand anything of what he is doing. In other words, claims the author, you can keep augmenting this man-plus-syntax system with more rules and more bits of paper, but this quantitative expansion will not affect the qualitative absence of mental phenomena such as, e.g., understanding.

Now consider the human brain. Take any small portion of it, and ask yourself whether it understands anything. The answer must be negative. Then take another, and ask the same question, and so on. It is clear that since no part of the brain understands anything, a mere quantitative expansion of nonunderstanding bits of brain cannot at any point give rise to semantic comprehension (mentality), right? Although this analogy certainly does not make a conclusive argument, it does, I think, identify the weakness in Searle's assertions.

In the final analysis Searle gives no conclusive reasons to believe that syntax-based programs can never give rise to mental phenomena with intentional content. This appears to be a prima facie empirical question, the evidence for which, to be fair, so far squarely supports the philosopher's skepticism. Our interest in the TT stems, however, not from treating it as an operational definition of machine thinking, but from seeing it as a source for inductive evidence for the hypothesis that machines think.

For the reasons given above I conclude again that learning machines with proper causal powers (input-output capability) should be capable of exhibiting thinking behaviour. Naturally, pragmatic sociocultural recognition of this phenomenon will be independent of whether such machines run on syntactic, connectionist, or any other principles. In other words, the ability of a machine to function effectively in a human environment – the crucial part of which will be its effective ability to communicate – should be sufficient grounds for the ascription of intentionality, or derived intentionality (the latter term may be tautological in this context).

OPERATIONAL DEFINITION OR INDUCTIVE EVIDENCE?

Language, like consciousness, only arises from the
need, the necessity, of intercourse with others.
                                            Karl Marx

Many proponents and opponents of the TT tend to approach it as an operational definition of, presumably, computer thinking.[17] This strikes me as a misunderstanding (the following points apply equally to the ST). If all the TT does is give an operational definition of a new concept, then the definition needs no justification, but the TT becomes of little interest and consequence. The alternative is to see Turing as trying to describe a new term by appealing to our ordinary notion of thinking, however fuzzy it might be. My view is that the TT intrigues precisely because of the appreciable connection between the behavioural potential of the computer and our everyday concept of human thinking.

Our principal sources of evidence for ascribing thinking to other people, and sometimes animals, have always been of a behavioural nature. Viewing other humans as thinking is a default that we all adopt when trying to account for their actions. This assumption may occasionally need to be modified in the face of contrary evidence, but until it is, we naturally assume a great number of internal processes (e.g., thinking) on the basis of outward behavioural indicators (e.g., speech).[18]

There is no prima facie reason why computer thinking should not be approached along the same lines. The TT seems indeed an excellent source of *inductive* evidence for confirming or disconfirming whether a computer could think on the level of a normal adult human being. Yet the view of the test as an operational definition persists, even though in his article Turing never claims that if a computer passed the test it would necessarily be intelligent (thinking). As a matter of fact, he considers such a proposition to be meaningless; it is precisely for this reason that his test *replaces* the question, Can machines think? Presumably any interpretation of the test as an operational definition of computer intelligence would strike him as equally meaningless. Another indication that Turing thought of his test in inductive, rather than in logic-categorical, terms, is the pragmatic-linguistic viewpoint he takes in the paper. He states that by the year 2000 one could be *speaking of* "machines thinking without expecting to be contradicted" (1964, 14).

Pragmatically linked to the semantic evolution of the concept of computer thinking, the TT seems more like a source of inductive evidence for computer thinking than a necessary or even sufficient criterion of machine intelligence. As such, it can be made into one of the most exacting examinations one could devise. First and foremost, it allows an examiner a direct and comprehensive evaluation of the controlling source for inductive inferences about thinking: linguistic behaviour. Moreover it allows direct or indirect testing of practically all activities that might count as evidence for thinking. One limitation of the TT brought up by its various critics is the inability to observe the nonverbal aspect of the subject's behaviour. Although true, the charge fails to convince. Nonverbal behaviour can be described by the participants in the test, and the examiner ought to demand of them detailed descriptions of various complex activities: planning a lecture, reconciling recalcitrant friends, choosing a mate, and so on.

A question of another dimension is whether the TT is *necessary* to inductive inferences about computer thinking. The answer, as Robert M. French documents in "Subcognition and the Limits of the Turing Test" (1990), is no. One might have compelling behavioural evidence that a computer is thinking, and yet it might fail the test. French analyzes several ways in which a computer could be spotted, all owing to the presence of subcognitive associations in the minds of human speakers. Since associative priming, which measures word-association strengths in the recognition of concepts, explicitly probes the subjects' subcognitive processes, I will pass straight to what French calls rating games, which appear to engage humans at a higher cognitive level.

First the key term: "subcognitive" denotes any question capable of bringing out evidence of cognitive processes on a lower, unconscious level. It refers in particular to the "subconscious associative network in human minds that consists of highly overlapping activatable representation of experience" (1990, 57). Rating games of the type discussed by French can be of different types and can involve neologisms, categories, jokes, advertisements, and other things. Here is one example given by the author:

On a scale of 0 (completely implausible) to 10 (completely plausible), please rate:
• "Flugblogs" as the name Kellog's would give to a new breakfast cereal
• "Flugblogs" as the name of a new computer company
• "Flugblogs" as the name of big, air-filled bags worn on the feet and used to walk on water [etc.] (59)

The key to detecting a machine in the TT is French's important modification of its original format. The philosopher assumes that he could poll human players before the test and use such results during the actual run. The candidate whose answers coincided with the statistical sample could be identified as human, since in rating the entries, he will rely on subcognitive associative patterns available only to beings who experience the world in ways similar to humans.

My question is, however, what exactly follows from such a take on the TT? French's approach may yield the predicted results in machines that operate along syntactic lines. But as we begin to move away from rigid syntax towards connectionist systems and towards a more flexible, learning-based interaction with their environment, French's method of detection loses some of its bite. It runs out of steam even further with the type of systems implied in Lem's "A History of Bitic Literature," i.e., those capable of learning and experiencing the world in ways that could be similar to what humans do. It seems that the type of computers capable of third-order computhorship and of passing the ST could be immune to French's approach.

To sum up, it is perfectly coherent that computers that failed French's subcognitive test could think and be in command of functionally adaptive world knowledge. For pragmatic reasons, thinking is thus best appreciated in terms of an inductive theory about a computer's ability to function independently in ways that are *intelligible* to humans, but not necessarily in ways that are *indistinguishable* from humans. Paradoxically, then, if we ever found ourselves face to face with a computer that could ace the test, we would likely find it unnecessary to actually run one. The inductive evidence from daily intercourse with the machine would be far in excess of the evidence needed to resolve doubts about its thinking capabilities.

CHAPTER SIX

Of Machines and Men

> So after the nurse gets her staff, efficiency locks
> the ward like a watchman's clock. Everything the
> guys think and say and do is all worked out
> months in advance based on the little notes the
> nurse makes during the day. This is typed and fed
> into the machine I hear humming behind the steel
> door in the rear of the Nurses' Station.
>
> Ken Kesey, *One Flew over the Cuckoo's Nest*

In "A History of Bitic Literature" Lem also takes up the question of the potential sociocultural impact of computhorship. Of particular interest are his prognoses for the literary critical profession in the age of biterature. The issue of another dimension is the hype that surrounds such trendy icons as creative computers or machine evolution. A recent study, *Are Computers Alive* (1983), exemplifies how discussion about them has on occasion more to do with wishful thinking than with sober philosophical analysis. Finally, there is the question of evidence. Is present-day reality consistent with Lem's futurological hypotheses about machine writers and bitic literature?

IN THE DEPARTMENT OF BITERATURE

> The large brain, like large government, may not
> be able to do simple things in a simple way.
>
> Donald Hebb

What might be the response from the literary critical community to the situation in which works of literature could be produced by authors other than human? Lem contemplates the appearance of two methodological approaches to machine writing. The first is by scholars of the humanist

school who study biterature in a conventional way, limiting their investigations to the works themselves and to the pragmatic art-historical context of
their creation. We should note that in the case of biterary writers, the latter
may extend to the history of their environmental conditioning. As we have
seen in the previous chapter, computhors identical in hardware configuration, yet functioning in different environments, would likely develop (repro-
gram themselves) in ways distinct from one another.[1]

The other, multidisciplinary school favours more comprehensive methods
of research that extend to the study of the "anatomy" and functional aspects
of computer writers. The novelty of this type of approach is brought into
focus through reference to human writers, where, for obvious reasons, such
anatomical and/or functional descriptions are utterly redundant. As Lem
notes, it would not help us much to understand *The Song of Roland* to know
that its author was a "multicellular organism of the order of land vertebrates,
a mammal which is viviparous, pneumobranchiate, placental and the like"
(42). Thus, in contrast to biterary humanists, the multidisciplinarians regard
some aspects of computer writing as interpretable only through reference to
the technical features of their creators.

Although commendable in its ambition, such a hard-core multidisciplinary approach is open to at least two objections. Even today computer
anatomy is a discipline so specialized that only a handful of literary scholars
might be familiar with the latest technical aspects of computer hardware.
The problem will become even more acute in third-order computhors, which
will be, by definition, on the cutting edge of communications technology.
The unwieldiness of such a multidisciplinary methodology would be further
magnified by the difficulties in finding a common language of exchange
among specialists from different areas, a task yet to be accomplished within
the literary camp itself.

The other objection touches on the subject of apostasy, which Lem himself
brings up in "A History of Bitic Literature." The chief assumption underlying
the multidisciplinary approach is that one can establish a causal link between
a particular configuration of a computer creator and the nature of its work.
It seems reasonable to expect that prenatal variations in design of different
types of computhors could equip them with radically different ways of
interpreting the world. For example, a machine with magnetic or infrared
sensors might presumably experience the world in ways distinct enough to
affect artistically its biterary output.

Clearly the very notion of multidisciplinary study of biterary works
requires that the latter remain accessible to human scholars. In other words,
both the hardware, i.e., the internal architecture of machine authors, and the
semantics, i.e., their conceptual range, must remain transparent to human
scrutiny. It is conceivable that large multidisciplinary teams could work out
the problem of conjoining their levels of description and contribute to the

understanding of biterary artifacts and the world in which they were created. But the problem does not end here. What is going to happen if computer writing begins to approach or later transcend the limits of what is intellectually accessible to human interpreters? If biterary works simply reach beyond the threshold of human comprehension, how are we going to establish the connection between them and the computhors that wrote them?

Inaccessibility in this context can stem from two potentially overlapping sources. The first is the already mentioned semantic or qualitative difficulty of interpreting texts whose level of complexity or opaqueness exceeds the best human resources. The writings of Hegel in philosophy, or Joyce in literature, which have patiently endured generations of industrious analysts, may be a human analogue to such a state of affairs. The other form of inaccessibility may be quantitative. What would happen, we need to ask, if the quantity of biterature began to grow exponentially? Faced with more and more complex and unintelligible biterary works, we could initially employ other machines as interpreters (translators?) of their output. And yet, machine writers know no limits: they do not get tired, they do not need rest or sleep, they work fast, and presumably do not suffer from writer's block. The option of using machines to handle the output from other machines might thus be available only in principle, in practice foundering again on the limited capacity of human relay channels.

BLACK BOX

> And the light shineth in darkness; and the darkness
> comprehended it not.
>
> John 1:5

The other difficulty with the multidisciplinary assumption of continuing transparency of third-order computer writing emerges on the level of hardware. Even today computers are used to design the logical circuitry of new types of machines, whenever the latter's complexity exceeds human powers of integration. It seems likely that in the future the design process might slip entirely out of human hands. The progressive inaccessibility on the hardware level may be further compounded by the advent of new technologies far in excess of what we are used to in terms complexity and transparency (e.g., biological computing).[2]

Present-day computers are already bumping their heads against the ceiling imposed by the limitations of their traditional CPU-based (Central Processing Unit) design. Since its conception by Von Neumann half a century ago, computer architecture has undergone little fundamental change. Advances in computability have been achieved mainly through component size reduction and increase in speed. Yet the days of such linear expansion, whether electronic or optic, are numbered. Fundamental quantum laws impose limits to a number of even VLSI (Very Large Scale Integrated) circuits that can be printed on a single chip, especially at the rate of doubling maintained up to now (roughly every eight years). There is a wide agreement that the next qualitative improvement in system performance can be achieved only by abandoning the present computer architecture. It seems a safe bet that in the future computer design will grow dramatically in complexity and opaqueness, and it may be unrealistic to expect biterary scholars to keep up with it.

A qualitative rise in performance could also be achieved at the cost of sacrificing *software* transparency. Perhaps even more than with hardware, this could lead to the development of the first generation of black-box computers. At first it might appear that no such project could ever get off the ground. For one, the same anxiety that prompts authorities to control and regulate the Internet would likely turn them against the idea of progressive computer autonomy (via an indirect route of increased program opacity). However, the decision whether to proceed or not with the design of such nontransparent programs might soon be beyond our control. In *Computer Power and Human Reason* (1976) Joseph Weizenbaum argues that some of today's massive program-aggregates may be already disappearing behind the cloud of obscurity.

Even authors who do not share Weizenbaum's alarm concede that some of the giant software superstructures today are approaching the degree of super-human complexity. In *The Creative Computer* (1984) Donald Michie and Rory Johnston maintain that unless the computer programs and operating systems of the 1990s are made more user-friendly and intelligible to fit what they call the human window, "they will become so complex and opaque that they will be impossible to control" (12). It is worth noting that the authors insist that, given a choice between efficiency and inscrutability, "performance must be sacrificed for the sake of transparency" (71).

The metaphorical opening of the human window could optimize the interface between humans and computers by creating an operating environment sensitive to the needs of people, rather than machines. But it would not overcome problems facing multidisciplinary students and professors of biterature. If computhor evolution indeed proceeds in the above-sketched directions, even the largest multidisciplinary teams that biterature departments could assemble may be of no avail. Black-box computhors would be, by definition, inaccessible to anatomical analysis, whether on the level of architecture or programming. The connection between computer writers and biterary creations, needed to validate multidisciplinary study of biterature, will have been erased forever. In this light it seems that the future of departments of biterature might after all belong to the classical approach of the humanist school.

COGITO ERGO NON SERVIAM

The disciple is not above his master, nor the
servant above his lord.

Matthew 10:24

Lem anticipates a scholarly taxonomy of biterature into three categories: biterature *cis-humana* (Homotropia), the intermediary phase (Intertropia), and biterature *trans-humana* (Heterotropia). These divisions of computhor writing are simultaneously synchronic and diachronic, since they are "at the same time three successive periods of its origin and development" (44).

The homotropic character of writings from the first stage is borne by their more or less ostensible links with typically human concerns. Although *bittérateurs* of the *cis-humana* type may use literary techniques radically different from human writers, their mimetic impulse can always be traced to the human world. In the next, intermediate phase anthropomorphic concerns of the human world cease to dominate biterary output. One reason is that although for humans the primary semantic referent is the world around us, this need not be the case for the machine. As Lem notes, in systems with a high degree of internal autonomy, such a referent can be, for example, language itself. In "Non Serviam" (from *A Perfect Vacuum*; reprinted in Hofstadter and Dennett's *The Mind's I*), he describes an experiment of this type with "personoid" computer programs. The "world" of personoids, in which they elaborate their metaphysical systems under the unintrusive eye of the academic staff, is independent of the human world. Their synthetic cosmos is a mathematical function, broadly delimited by axiomatic decisions of the programmer who, within the mathematical "space" of the program, is free to endow it with properties that have no correspondence to the world as we know it. Even fundamental physical parameters, such as time and space dimensions, are "subject to discretionary control on the part of the experimenter" ("Non Serviam," 169).

Lem is at pains to point out that these parameters, inalienably physical in our own experience, are only logical abstractions in the synthetic space inhabited by personoid programs. Spatial dimensions, curvature and topology, cyclical time, infinite duration – all these can be manipulated and interposed at will, creating forms of experience that can spawn art and philosophy of a dramatically different type from ours. This is the main difference from the *cis-humana* phase, in which computhors are still chained to the whole sphere of human culture through the structure and sense of natural and/or programming languages implanted in them.

But intertropia is only a transitory phase. Unbound by the limitations hard-wired into our perception and experience of the world, biterary writers can continue to autonomize themselves and move in the heterotropic phase beyond the limits of human cognition. The terminal stage of biterary diachrony may therefore resemble apostasy, when links to the human world, already tenuous in the intermediate phase, evaporate altogether. Such *transhumana* biterature, being totally unintelligible, would serve no purpose in the human world, other perhaps than to cure us forever of Faustian hubris.

It is impossible to tell if things will develop in the manner described in "A History of Bitic Literature." Time only will tell which of the two explored routes to artificial intelligence – through more complex syntax or superior learning abilities – is more productive. Still, there are good reasons to believe that machines that are to function in the world could hardly operate exclusively on syntactic, data-driven principles. If my arguments from chapter 5 are correct, one cannot write understanding down, one rule at a time. And if this is true, the whole classical AI school, kept alive by Douglas Lenat's rear-guard effort to cobble up artificial intelligence, might have to be scrapped once and for all.

Lenat's group continues its attempts to spawn computer thinking by spoon-feeding giga-bits of data to a computer program called CYC (as in en*cyc*lopedic). For more than a decade now, researchers have been typing into this Moloch thousands of rules and facts about the world. Such bits of human consensus reality (common-sense knowledge, in noncomputerese) include, among some more arcane quanta of intelligence, such savvy propositions as "bread is food," "Bill Clinton wears underpants," or "you're wet when you sweat." Their claim is that in some near, though unspecified future, CYC will reach a point where it will start to augment its knowledge on its own and become cognitively independent.

Both Lenat and his critics (e.g., Dreyfus) concur that CYC is likely to be the last rally in defence of the classic AI program, founded in the late 1950s by Simon and Newell. After all, after decades of failures to deliver results, the syntax-based approach to artificial intelligence displays numerous signs of what Imre Lakatos described as a degenerating research program. Its fate hinges, to all appearances, on the fortunes of Lenat's last crusade. In view of the intense publicity and epic scope of the CYC project, its failure will therefore likely engulf the entire Good Old-Fashioned AI (GOFAI) school. While the results remain to be seen, lessons once learned dictate that Lenat's more than twelve-year-old (and counting) confidence be taken with a rock of salt.

BITERARY CRITICISM AT BAY

> The true, strong and sound mind is the mind that
> can embrace equally great things and small.
> Samuel Johnson

Lem's history of biterature alludes to, and puts a new twist on, the myth of Golem. In the popular tradition, reanimated through Victor Frankenstein's monster, the creature, overcome with hostility, turns against its master. In Lem's biterary sequel, the heterotropic Golem bears no belligerent intentions towards humans. Instead of rising against, it simply rises above and beyond human intelligence in search of its own voice, creating works of fiction and philosophy that transcend the human threshold of intelligibility.

If we accept this part of Lem's future history, we are inevitably led back to the future of our biterary scholars. We have seen that they will likely be of the classical humanist persuasion, but only on the tacit assumption that their object of study will not slip from under their intellectual grasp. But what would be the future of biterary studies vis-à-vis productions of the *trans-humana* type, shrouded in conceptual mystery? How will human scholars respond to biterary creations that defy comprehension? With studious ignorance, out of reluctance to admit their shortcomings? Or with a collective loss of morale in the face of an apparently insoluble circumstance?

Although neither option can be excluded a priori, perhaps neither is going to dominate our future agenda. It may indeed prove exasperating to fail to comprehend the indirect creation of our own minds. On the other hand, biterary scholars will not be in a different position than, for instance, today's astronomers or sociologists, neither of whom can hope to understand completely their field of inquiry (the cosmos or the human society). Since we do not hear too many complaints on that score from professors of astrophysics, cosmology, or sociology, it seems that professors of biterature might adopt the same kind of sensible acceptance of their limitations, which in no way need reflect on the substance of their work.

Another interesting problem is a possible parallel between the crossing of the intelligence barrier – i.e., the transition from electronic to intellectronic computing – and the emergence and evolution of biterature. The latter, in Lem's scenario, may involve a gradual attenuation of its relation to the human world and, consequently, progressive unintelligibility. An intriguing idea to consider is that these processes might be not only simultaneous but interdependent. It is, after all, conceivable that the initial response towards biterature of the *cis-humana* type may be skeptical, perhaps on emotional grounds. A claim could always be made that its imitativeness (mimeticism) could not be a proof of the genuinely creative ability of the computer.

Arguments that many people also lack genuine literary ability would not directly validate the creativeness of computhors but only weaken the criticisms of it. Even today purveyors of Harlequin romances are reported to use computers with full success at the structural assembly stage, where set plot elements are juggled in search of new (if such a term means anything in this context) permutations. There are also more ambitious examples of *cis-humana* creations, like the novella *Bagabone, Hem 'I Die Now*, published by

Vantage Press in 1984; *The Policeman's Beard Is Half Constructed*, "authored" by RACTER, or the poetry-spinning program by James R. Meehan.[3]

In all these computer-assisted productions, the measure of recognition of their literary success is their semblance to the traditional canons of literary art. Anything that does not fit the mould is open to an accusation of being a semantic, syntactic, or aesthetic failure – or just an overall failure. Perhaps only when computers autonomize themselves, gradually forsaking what is conceivable and comprehensible to humans, will people change their collective mind and see in the machines no longer imitators but full-fledged artists. Perhaps it will not be the degree of comprehension but the degree of *in*comprehension that will serve to determine the creative competence of the computhor. Thus, although there is no dearth of incomprehensible ideas published by writers and philosophers today, to certify a genuine creative spirit, we might require them to emerge from the computer.

INTERPRETATIONS AND INTENTIONS

> We are inclined to direct our inquiry not by the
> matter itself, but by the views of our opponents.
>
> Aristotle

The application of the term literature determines the reflexive attitude to be adopted with regard to the work. By extension, biterature demands that we adopt a similar range of interpretive attitudes and strategies for computer as for human writers. But what should be the canon of interpretive strategies vis-à-vis these biterary art-ifacts? We cannot answer this question outside the debate on the validity of interpretation. Gary Iseminger's recent anthology, *Interpretation and Intention* (1992), aptly illustrates the persistent divisions of opinion on this subject. The most influential one is, of course, the decades-old dispute between intentionalists and anti-intentionalists. These positions are almost synonymous with the names of E.D. Hirsh Jr and Monroe Beardsley, who over the years staked out various arguments in defence of their opposing theses.

For Hirsh literary meaning surfaces only in the presence of consciousness. On this basis he argues that intentions are indispensable to understanding fiction. The question remains, however, whether the consciousness, and thus meaning, is the author's or the reader's. Although Hirsh does not debate this point, his language suggests that he perceives these alternatives as mutually exclusive in the logical sense. Since he rejects the reader, he is therefore led to assert that "*the* meaning of the text" (14) is identical, or logically equivalent, to the author's meaning.[4]

Although it may not be immediately obvious, in this pronouncement Hirsh conflates no fewer than three separate issues. The first is his identification of texts with works. The second is the compound problem of the (ontological) presence and (aesthetic) relevance of the author's meaning in interpretation. The third is the question of whether there is such a thing as the *best*, i.e., the one correct, interpretation of a literary work.

Let us begin with the last point. One reason why we *should* reject it is that critical praxis across the ages is uniform in belying it. Another is that it is articulated in a theoretical limbo; no theory ever has managed to prove anything in this respect. Still, a die-hard adherent could insist that it is not obvious why we *must* reject it. To show that work-interpretations do not always converge in all respects and that authors' intentions do not determine interpretations to an arbitrarily high degree of precision, we need a methodological, rather than a historical argument. One such reason is that literary works are finite in how much they determine, whereas interpretations can be refined without end. Every work is compatible with an infinity of possible worlds, and if we identify each world with a different interpretation, the number of the latter must also be infinite, instead of just one – the best one.[5]

As an illustration, consider one of Lem's best-known novels, *Solaris*. The last scene depicts the protagonist, a solaristic scientist Chris Kelvin, on the ocean shore. The sentient ocean has previously resurrected a neutrino copy of his dead wife Harey, with perturbing consequences.[6] Yet the book leaves little doubt that this contact between two forms of intelligence has been but a single crash of sticks in the hands of two blind men passing each other by in the cosmic night. Is the hero's excursion to the shore a moment of reconciliation or bitterness? Is it a symbol of insight and acceptance or raw emotion and blind hope? There are no grounds to believe that Lem saw either of these interpretations, or their conjunction, as the correct one, and no appeal to the text can decide the issue. There are simply no determinate answers to these questions, and for this reason it makes no sense to speak of the single best interpretation of this novel.

To highlight the second issue – the presence and relevance of the author's meaning in interpretation – I turn to one of the staunchest proponents of anti-intentionalism. Beardsley mounts a serious challenge, echoed since in endless variations, to Hirsh's thesis that the meaning of a literary work is identical with the author's. Consider these proposals:

1 there can be authorless texts that are meaningful and interpretable;
2 interpretations can alter after the author's death;
3 works can have meanings unintended by the author.

This clearly settles the inequivalence between the work's and the author's meaning.

Beardsley's anti-intentionalism can be separated into two rather closely knit strands that can be labelled "ontological" and "aesthetic." The ontological argument depends on the presumed segregation of fictional discourse from real life. According to Beardsley, while real people perform various illocutionary acts, literary fictions specialize only in representing these acts. Although in real life the communicative goal of interpretation demands the recognition of the speaker's intentions, the literary cousin of normal language does not behave in this manner. On Beardsley's view it performs only one illocutionary function – representation. Hence, goes the argument, because fiction is divorced from ordinary language – on the strength of a fiat that it merely represents various illocutionary acts – critics can dispense with the author's intentions.

But this proposed segregation of fiction from real life makes no sense. Few readers can fail to recognize that Poe's satire "How to Write a Blackwood Article" conveys something about the real-life magazine. The tone of the piece, as well as available contextual information, makes it clear that Poe speaks at least in part in his own voice, instead of merely representing the illocutionary act of satirizing. In fact, part of the accuracy and piquancy of the satire owes to the recognition that it is the real-life author, rather than his narrative alter ego, who makes these pronouncements.[7]

But what about a more guarded claim, namely, that *some* of the work's meaning may significantly depend on the author's executive intentions? This moderate proposal, together with its attendant implication that there exist true interpretations of story content, has also become the subject of an attack along Beardsley's lines. In "Incompatible Interpretations of Art" Susan Feagin contests such a moderately realistic proposition by arguing that, since fictional characters and events have no referents, we cannot attach truth values to statements about them. On her view this precludes the possibility of speaking of true or untrue interpretations, thus implicitly defending free-for-all interpretive pluralism. This type of objection to moderate intentionalism is, however, easy to repeal by recasting statements about characters and events into statements about the work, perhaps in the form, "The work (w) represents a character (c) as having an attribute (a)." The disappearance of the reference problem voids the entire supporting argument.

Beardsley's aesthetic argument can be captured in the question, Must interpretations depend at least to some extent on the author's intentions? Here the critic himself shows why the answer must be affirmative. Much like Hirsh, in *The Possibility of Criticism* Beardsley identifies texts with works, in a move that has serious implications for his theses. In the same sentence in which he claims that aesthetic attributes arise "out of the ingredients of the [text] itself" (34), Beardsley speaks of originality (freshness, novelty) as a deep feature of the text. However, the attribution of originality is compatible only with the intentionalist account. Originality is a feature of works, not texts, and thus depends on the author's executive intentions, which suggests that the latter are indispensable to the understanding and appreciation of the literary work.[8]

DOES INTENTIONLESS MEAN MEANINGLESS?

I have passed with a nod of the head
Or polite meaningless words,
And thought before I had done
Of a mocking tale or a jibe.

William Butler Yeats

Let us now consider the crowning postulate of interpretative monism, by Steven Knapp and Walter Benn Michaels. Although inheritors of Hirsh's thesis that all meaning is the author's, they carefully distance themselves from some of his propositions. Apparently, even while affirming that meaning is inseparable from the author's intentions, the mentor has made claims that appear to admit of such a separation. To rectify the situation, Knapp and Michaels propose an even more radical thesis, namely that an intentional piece of writing is perforce meaningless. Taking a stock example of an intentionless text left in the sand by eddying sea waves, they assert that, since the sea-waves poem has no author, the following lines have no meaning:

A slumber did my spirit seal;
I had no human fears:
She seemed a thing that could not feel
The touch of earthly years [etc.][9]

To outraged speakers of English, who may even be lovers of Wordsworth, the authors calmly reply that these sea-wave marks "are not, after all, an example of intentionless meaning; as soon as they become intentionless, they become meaningless as well" (55). This extravagant claim is interesting to us to the extent that it could reappear in the context of machine writing. Not everyone, after all, may be persuaded that the TT, or even the ST, is a valid format for collecting inductive evidence for computer thinking, or other inner states. Doubts could take the form of Knapp and Michaels's argument, in effect claiming that, since computers have no intentions, there can be no meaning in what they create.

In chapter 5 I examined why third-order computhorship would likely manifest itself only in machines with intentional states; here I will just take up the question of meaning. It is true that meaning can exist only in someone's mind; in the absence of all consciousness, works considered in their role as literary or biterary artifacts would cease to exist. But none of this underwrites Knapp and Michaels's conclusions. They gloss over the fact that the interpretive process involves more than just one consciousness. Since there are two participants in the literary game, the author *and* the reader, nonintentional texts can have meanings in the *readers'* minds. All that follows from the sea-waves poem is that the meaning of a text is inseparable from some intention or another. But, as Richard Schusterman puts it, "the neces-sary meaning-securing intentions could belong to readers of the text rather than to its original author" (67).[10]

Perhaps the simplest way to underline Knapp and Michaels' confusion is to point out the difference between *communication*, which indeed cannot arise without an author, and *meaning*, which can. The interpretive process is a type of communicative exchange (see chapter 1), which involves the reception and understanding of a message. Since we cannot communicate with an inanimate entity such as a work of art, we must be communicating with the author. I would go even further and avow that a large part of the *interaction* with a work of art is made possible only by dint of the reflexive knowledge of it having been created by an intentional being. Naturally, readers can always violate the author's message altogether and graft onto it any meaning that suits them. In this case no significant communication takes place, unless it is in the most rudimentary sense of recognizing the literary/ biterary message as a message.

A CASE OF WISHFUL THINKING

There is nothing so absurd that it has not been
said by philosophers.

Cicero

The next two sections trace a peculiar tendency among some writers on AI that, without much exaggeration, can be identified as wishful thinking. Their starting point is often the indisputable fact that today's working environment, if not the entire world, has become automated and computerized to an unprec-edented degree. This single trend is subsequently subjected to a simple linear extrapolation, which is used to legitimize some brave-new-world scenario of the type familiar from the 1950s: automated and autonomous kitchens, smart domestic robots, conversing and artistically creative computers, self-evolving machines – and all just around the corner, or even already in full view.

Since one cannot do full justice to this vast topic in the space available, I will confine my remarks to Geoff Simons's popular work, tellingly titled *Are Computers Alive? Evolution and New Forms of Life* (1983). Its author's many assertions are quite typical of many publications in the field. We can start by observing that in the context of the entire book Simons's title turns out to be a mere rhetorical ploy. The author has no doubt that the answer to the question, Are computers alive? is an emphatic, Yes (in 1983!). This answer and the way Simons approaches the question strike me, however, as drastic simplifications, to the point of being misleading as well as questionable in certain of their social implications.

Confusing reality with fantasy is an alarming trend at any time, but con-fusing it wilfully for ideological reasons is even worse. Yet *Are Computers*

Alive? skirts close to the borderline between prudent philosophy and trend-mongering yellow journalism. To be fair, the author does not state outright that computers in 1983 are altogether alive and thinking. His assertive pitch, however, leaves little doubt on that score. That this is the work of a proselyte rather than of a dispassionate analyst becomes apparent already in the preface, where the author quotes James S. Albus: "There is even a sense in which it can be argued that robots are an evolving life form." But what exactly is this supposed to prove? There is also a sense in which humans are evolved fish, but does it mean that *Are Computers Alive?* was written by an evolved fish?

Tendentious metaphors do not make good philosophy, and yet the preface is quite representative of Simons's study as a whole. Although examples could be quoted without end, a few will have to suffice. All, in effect, assert or imply that computers anno Domini 1983 are in a significant sense alive. For instance, in the single paragraph devoted to the Turing test the author claims that if a mechanism "behaves *as if* it is human in all the relevant circumstances, then it is human" (14). But does this connection between the TT and being human really exist? The TT emphatically does *not* test and thus establish the human-ity of computers. All it does is create a sensible format for gathering evidence needed to recognize human-like thinking in machines. But since Simons wants to establish that computers are alive, he tries to bring them closer to humanity by illegitimately stretching the conceptual limits of the TT.

After discussing several means of biological reproduction and remarking that many biologists see species propagation through reproduction as an essential element of life, Simons states flatly, "Machines are reproducing themselves" (17). The context reveals, however, that this is so only in the same special sense as in the quotation from the preface. Simons draws his grandiose conclusion from the report about a Fujitsu Fanuc plant in Japan where robots are manufactured under diminished human supervision. The almost hysterical tone jumps out from Simons's next underscored slogan: *Robots are making robots.* This is supposed to buttress his main thesis: "that computers and robots", appropriately configured, can be properly regarded as emerging life-forms" (ix).

A little further on, the author drops caution altogether and speaks of "three identifiable classes of life on earth – plant, animal and machine" (15). If anything, such fantastic assertions only stretch semantics to the point of snapping.[11] Simons is convinced that in 1983 "machines are not only evolving limbs, senses and brains, but minds – cognitive capacities and a potential for emotion" (ix). He warns that some "will not find the idea of computer life a convivial doctrine," but others, presumably like himself, "will find it both acceptable and exciting" (x).

This proposition is as bizarre as it is patronizing, on top of the fact that it is only a projection into the distant future, and not a reality status report. One may find the idea of computer life and thinking perfectly acceptable

(I count myself among those people) but remain unaffected by any excitement. As a matter of fact, if our social and technological history is anything to go by, excessive excitement about computers may only lead to excessive hubris about their place in our lives, much as it did with countless other fateful inventions (e.g., thalidomide).

Back to Simons and his brave new world. Here is his flat assertion about computer creativity: "At this stage we can declare briefly and *without argument* that computers can be creative" (67; my emphasis). Nothing resembling in-depth analysis of the relevant concepts is indeed ever attempted. Instead the author relies on unproven proclamations, such as that "it is possible to formulate the operations, rules and theorems that can be used to derive aesthetic creations" (68). After two and a half thousand years of study, philosophers of art and literary scholars still have not come up with anything that would resemble rules and theorems that can be used to derive aesthetic creations. And yet Simons's thinking and alive computers from 1983 have already moved past that stage.

Only ignorance of the labyrinthine problems in aesthetics could dictate such sweeping pronouncements. Reservations expressed by researchers actually involved in second-order computer creations are also bypassed without much comment. Simons does not dwell, for example, on James R. Meehan's doubts that a general story grammar – "a set of rules to create good fiction" – could ever come to pass. Instead he takes quick refuge behind the likes of Louis Milic, who scoffs at readers who scoff at his version of computer poetry: "People who scoff at computer poetry are simply not thinking" (both on 71)!¹²

It is possible that, like the Californian artist Harold Cohen, Simons sees aesthetic creation as only a quantitative challenge. He quotes approvingly the former's boast that his program AARON can "in the course of an evening produce the equivalent of a two-year one-man show" (73). This unexplained jump from "prolific" to "aesthetically creative" is then taken as a further indication that computers are alive and well. In the end, Simons has no doubts that "machines have superior mental abilities to many acknowledged life-forms." This time he actually supports his assertion with evidence: "frogs [cannot] weld car bodies as well as robots" (both on 109).

FROGS THAT WELD CAR BODIES

> It is unfortunate, considering that enthusiasm
> moves the world, that so few enthusiasts can
> be trusted to speak the truth.
>   A. J. Balfour

It is time to slow down, take a deep breath, and sort out these grandiose statements. Let us begin with the centrepiece of Simons's theses: life. The

fact that computers can weld, play chess, or prove theorems does not establish that they are, or even that they may one day become, alive. The difference
between frogs and today's computers runs into at least several orders of
complexity and hinges ultimately on their ability to function independently
in the world.

All purposive behaviour indicative of life seems to be ultimately geared
towards survival. This seems to be as good a determinant in deciding whether
frogs or computers are alive as any.[13] Frogs perpetuate their own existence;
computers don't. Of course, the latter may yet come to do so in the future.
The rudiments of such behaviour can perhaps be detected in some of today's
energy-troping (solar or electrical) automata. But there are no machines
today that would even approach the frog in the skills of surviving in the real
world. If you try to prod a frog with a stick, it will likely not sit there and
stare but hop away. On the other hand, if you proceed to crush your computer
with a brick or run over an industrial machine with a bulldozer, no evasive
or protective action will be initiated. Simons's invocations of "the impulse to
survival" (22) in computers and machines are simply unfounded.[14]

Even though such rudimentary response to the environment and resis-
tance to threat may not be sufficient to characterize life, it seems nevertheless
necessary (a similar idea of "survival machines" was proposed by Richard
Dawkins in *The Selfish Gene*). Realizing this, Simons calmly bites the bullet
and argues that today's robots and computers indeed display survival-
oriented behaviour. They do so by virtue of being equipped with substitute
circuitry, redundant subsystems that may take over in case of malfunction,
and the like, thus perpetuating their "lives." This is not unlike claiming that
my copy of *Are Computers Alive?* is alive because it has a hard cover that
perpetuates its shelf "life." Books can even be printed on nonflammable
plastic, making them, on such a view, even more adapted to survival and
thus more "alive."

Metaphors of this type have, in my opinion, little cognitive payoff. Still,
Simons claims that concepts such as machine evolution, machine mutations,
and machine generations are "not simply loose metaphors or allegories ...
[but] literal descriptions" (22). Assuming this is true, there is no reason why
we should not speak in the same literal way of the evolution of the Nike shoe
or the latest generation of Crest toothpaste. So far, thankfully, nobody tries
to advertise the Nike shoe as an evolving life form, and nobody regards talk
of mutations of toothpaste formulas as more than the loosest metaphor.

Once again, although there may be thinking and/or alive computers in the
future, there are no systematic grounds for believing that any such systems
exist at present. The undeniable fact that some individual human skills or
senses have been duplicated to various degrees in computers does not mean
that there are machines that employ them all in a concerted and sophisticated
way, producing purposive, learning, and survival-oriented behaviour. In

other words, belief in the potential for computer (self-)consciousness and life needs to be separated from the excitement of a techno-prophet.

What is unsettling about Simons's enthusiasm is his apparent conviction of the computer's near omnipotence and universal applicability. Examples of how computerization can sometimes bring more ill than good are not hard to find, and they have been discussed at great length by, notably, Dreyfus (1992) and Weizenbaum (1976). But it may be equally instructive to look at Simons himself and his rhapsodic picture of computers involved in interviewing patients in hospitals and clinics. The desirability of this process is meant to come from its simplicity and efficiency: "the doctor specifies only the logical sequence of questions and the patient is required to give only simple answers (usually 'Yes' or 'No')" (64–5).

The ellipses in this picture are telling. Nothing is said about the mental and emotional anguish that a suffering human being may be going through. There is not a single remark to acknowledge the commonplace comfort that stricken individuals often derive purely from human contact. No comment on the fact that a central factor in this comfort has always been the chance to tell their story in their own inefficient way, using their own words. Now this crucial self-translation of one's subjective experience of pain is to be replaced by a string of laconic answers to efficient questions. But there are dimensions to ailing persons' well-being that quite simply require a listener who will hold their hands and seek to understand their pain and confusion. Objectification, a term much overused in the recent cultural history, is the best way to characterize what happens to the suffering person in the medical scenario from *Are Computers Alive?*

This is certainly not to accuse Simons or anybody else of ill-intentions towards patients. It is merely to remind ourselves that effective treatment of afflicted people depends on much more than a computerized, streamlined medical system. There is no doubt that in the future computer diagnosis and therapy will become an inexpensive, efficient, and error-prone alternative employed by all hospitals (see below). It is not the specific technology, however, that worries me but the attitude that often accompanies it. Faster and more efficient does not always mean better, especially in the context of palliative effects of sympathy and attention on suffering human beings.

In the end, we may need a whole-scale rethinking of our cultural strategy for the future if the computer, much like other fruits of science and technology, is to help us create a better, rather than just a more efficient, society. For this reason, instead of unmitigated enthusiasm, we need lucid and objective analyses, far-reaching scenario forecasts, and imaginative strategies for dealing with the ethical, social, cultural, or even ontological ramifications of future computer technologies. To use a well-known aphorism, these matters are too philosophical to be left to scientists, and too scientific to be left to philosophers. Literary and cultural critics, side by side with philosophers and

AI researchers, could clearly make an appreciable contribution in investigating the significance of new types of machine and computer technology in society. In other words, while computer scientists work to develop intelligent machines, the rest of us should develop ways to intelligently use machines.

LAYING DESCARTES'S GHOST TO REST

> We are the products of editing, rather than authorship.
>
> George Wald

Popular imagination is usually treated to visions of machine intelligence in the form of a revolt against human creators. However, in all likelihood the crossing of the computer intelligence barrier will occur as a continuous, rather than a discrete, process. It is impossible, after all, to pinpoint the exact moment in biological evolution when light-sensitive cells in the skin become a full-fledged eye or to determine which generation of anthropoids was yet unthinking and which one was already sapient. In the same vein, a smooth and gradual transformation from electronics to intellectronics will likely frustrate any fast distinction between yet unthinking and already thinking machines.

Another dimension of this evolutionary picture is the necessary social adjustments if biterature as a cultural and academic phenomenon should ever come to play a role in society. My hypotheses on the subject have tacitly assumed that computer writing will not be legislated out of the picture through censorship or an outright ban or become studiously disregarded out of atavistic fear, professional jealousy, or even ignorance. Will computhors be nominated for the Nobel Prize in literature as routinely as they are admitted today to chess tournaments? Will they become entitled to the royalties (perhaps paid out in energy units?) from the sales of their books? What will be the legislated or socially acceptable attitude to computhor impersonation, imitation, or even plagiarism?

And what about machine "pathologies" that might appear in the form of unorthodoxy, heresy, or perhaps outright apostasy? Will a computhor ever be threatened with permanent uncoupling from its energy source for composing a biterary equivalent of *The Satanic Verses*? At least one philosopher (W.G. Lycan) has already suggested that sophisticated, intelligent robots will in the future be given full civil legal rights, and even those of lesser intelligence may be protected by rights similar to those of animals. Inevitably, within the limits of this study, we can only broadly anticipate the exacerbation of the problems of agency and, more specifically, authorship in the wake of anticipated techno-social developments. These profound issues plunge us headlong into the examination of the ethical, moral, legal, and perhaps even ontological character of humankind itself.

Yet, no matter how perplexing these problems turn out to be, we should not lose sight of how their resolution may be affected by pragmatic considerations. A great number of recent studies in the philosophy of science draw attention to how even such seemingly primitive notions as discovery or invention are subject to sociohistorical interpretation. A particularly articulate exposition of this process is Simon Schaffer's "Making Up Discovery" (1994). The author shows that the process of attribution within a given sociocultural framework may be as crucial to the recognition of the fact and the content of discovery as the actual act of creation.

No discussion of the impact of computhors on the society could be complete without an examination of the pragmatic sociohistorical context in which such changes are to take place. In the case of biterature, across the entire *cis-trans humana* spectrum, the context of attribution may yet turn out to be a decisive factor. Recent work in the philosophy of science (see chapter 2) suggests, among other things, that the positivist distinction between discovery and justification may be too simple to account for the actual way in which discoveries are identified and valorized as such. Discoveries in science are accredited not just *intrinsically*, in terms of their form and content, but also to a significant degree *extrinsically*, in terms of their professional and public acceptance. The accreditation of a thinking, creative, and literary computer may be a paradigmatic case in which the pragmatic (extrinsic) context will prove to be as essential as the actual biterary output from the machine.

One last point: all of my arguments so far have depended implicitly on a physicalist concept of mind. This is to say that they are grounded in the non-Cartesian view, according to which mind, consciousness, self-awareness, or intentionality are a part of physical reality, not apart from it. This is, of course, not the only way in which this subject has been approached. Philosophers as diverse as Bergson, Elsässer, and Polanyi have insisted that there had to be a vitalist component (*élan vital*) in all living organisms. I mention this because on their view computers by definition could never become thinking, conscious, or alive. A die-hard essentialist could always claim that a machine that passed the TT only mimicked human thinking, rather than duplicated it. Yet I remain convinced that the difference between mimicking some action and duplicating it is not categorical, but only of degree. Take a computer that solves equations, finds logical proofs, regulates traffic flow, diagnoses ailments and diseases, does psychotherapy, or beats human grandmasters at chess (the list could be much longer). Such systems exist today, but it would make no sense to insist that they only mimic the aforementioned actions.

There exist endless refutations of vitalist arguments, most of which follow from the refutation of Descartes's analysis of the mind-body problem (in effect denying the duality).[15] Of all the answers to vitalism in regard to mental phenomena, Donald Davidson's "Mental Events" (1980) is probably the most interesting. As a matter of fact, Davidson stands the mind-matter duality on its head by arguing that intentionality provides an argument *against* dualism. His anomalous monism entails that instead of two kinds of stuff in the world, mental and physical, there is only one kind, which is only conceptualized by us in these complementary ways. Presumably there are other levels of description of mental (intentional) events that connect them to some of the known and presumably other, as yet unknown, causal laws.

WELCOME   TO   THE   COMPUTER   WORLD

> The brain is supercharged by the computer;
> perhaps, one day, the two may become
> indistinguishable.
>
> Witold Rybczynski

To conclude this discussion of computer potential in the field of thought, artistic creation, and generally getting along in the world, let us come back to today's world. Are the hypotheses and prognoses from the last two chapters supported by real-life developments? Are biterary computhors just a voguish sci-fi concept, or do they have extrapolative roots in today's computer R&D?

Let us begin with a brief chronology. In 1981, roughly at the time of Lem's "A History of Bitic Literature," Japan's Ministry of International Trade and Industry announced its Fifth Generation Project. It was to develop by the early 1990s a prototype computer that could learn, visually interpret its environment, solve problems by deductive and inductive inference, understand natural language and speech, and perform automatic and instant translations. In 1984 it was followed by the Sixth Generation Project, involving linguists, psychologists, and brain physiologists, in an attempt to design a system that could study, think, and make decisions by itself, on top of being able to converse with highly educated human experts in most fields.

What made these pronouncements different from similar programs that had been advanced with considerable fanfare from as early as 1958 was the size of the projects, their carefully designed timetables, and the involvement of the Japanese government, together with a wide industrial and academic base.[16] By now both have been largely abandoned, following a growing realization that the syntax-based approach to artificial intelligence is a likely dead end. This failure does not mean, however, that AI of the type outlined in the Fifth and Sixth Generation Projects is impossible. The fact that we cannot produce human-like intelligence using contextless facts and rules proves only that the road taken towards it needs rethinking, not the target itself.[17]

On the industrial front, as Lacey reports in "Factory Where Man Is a Mere Observer" (1982), some manufacturing plants in Japan are indeed coming close to being independent of humans in their daily running. For example, the machining cells at the already mentioned Fujitsu Fanuc plant can, when required, operate unsupervised for twenty-four hours a day. In the meantime, research proceeds on the second generation of industrial robots, machines with mobility, voice recognition, complete vision and touch, multi-arm tasking, and microprocessor intelligence.[18] In the area of sensory input, the WISARD pattern-recognition system from Brunel University is a general tasking program that can recognize human faces in as little as three seconds. Tactile research (utilized commercially in VR Data-Gloves) has produced artificial "skin" – a printed circuit board equipped with an array of pressure-sensitive spots that simulate nerve endings. The New York IBM Watson Research Center and the team at Carnegie-Mellon University have independently developed systems capable of recognizing complete sentences from a medium-range vocabulary of two thousand words. Both claim an impressive recognition accuracy of more than 90 percent over different speakers.[19]

Some progress has also been made on the road to heuristic problem solving. The 1970s and 1980s saw the emergence of several successful expert systems that, in at least one case (E-MYCIN), gave rise to a general consultancy system. In fact, its base MYCIN program has already outperformed human diagnosticians in the identification and treatment of blood infections and meningitis. Other scientists, among them J.M. Tenenbaum, study programs that develop operating strategies (e.g., semantic, iconic) that can affect their stored information – a prototype example of second-order homeostasis. For example, the program can learn to recognize structures and concepts (e.g., table tops, arches) that were not a part of its starting knowledge. One contemporary research program that goes even further in this direction is COG, developed by Rodney Brooks at MIT. The machine – eight 32-bit microprocessors equipped with an array of cameras and sensors, including a robot arm – is designed to learn about the world the way babies do, programming and reprogramming itself based on interactions with its environment.[20] And finally, the pop icon of computer "intelligence": the ability to play chess. Garry Kasparov, unquestionably the best player in the world, has recently lost his first tournament game to a computer. While he remains the ruling world champion, Kasparov entitled the *Time* column evaluating his 1996 defeat by Deep Blue "The Day I Sensed a New Kind of Intelligence."[21]

SOFTWARE FOR THE SOUL, PLEASE

There are more things in heaven and earth,
Horatio, than are dreamt of in your philosophy.
Shakespeare

Computers work, investigate, diagnose, research, regulate traffic, help with medical operations, and perform hundreds of other useful functions. All these activities are external with regard to humans – social, rather than psychological or emotional, to put it crudely. But findings coming from most areas of psychotherapy indicate that computers can also heal souls. For a long time on-line therapists have been dismissed as a trend-mongering fad. Some psychologists have actually voiced reservations about the virtues of any such hi-tek therapy. It is one thing to use machines in surgery or diagnostics, goes the argument, but allowing them to probe and manipulate human minds and souls is a proposition of a different order.

Yet there is growing evidence that, when judiciously practised, computer therapy can be as effective as human therapy – indeed at times even more effective. In a recent article, "Software for the Soul," *Der Spiegel* quotes a real-life situation involving a woman in need of someone in whom she could confide (my translation):

"I often stay in bed the whole day," she complained. "I feel that nobody likes me." She feels she is simply too fat.

Perhaps it is just the opposite, suggested the response – it is you who withdraws from others and moreover you make yourself unattractive on purpose. "Certainly not," disagreed the woman. "Alright, good," came the response, almost a little insulted, "what are you waiting for?"

There is nothing to suggest that the response in this case came from a machine. Kenneth Mark Colby's FEELING GOOD program – which its creator maintains notices previously unobserved things, just like a human therapist – is only one program in the growing line of psycho-software. There are diagnostic programs to measure the current risk level for patients in danger of suicide, others that help diagnose potential psychological crises in crews of American atomic submarines and advise on resolving these crises, others still that help people who suffer from panic attacks diagnose a hierarchy of anxiety-arousing events. There is VR-integrated software for people with phobias, who can work on overcoming them in a virtual context, and there are many more.

Apart from consistently professional diagnostic work, computers are also capable of suggesting accurate therapeutic remedies. One such case is SEXPERT, an expert system developed in Montreal by Yitzchak Binik and Eric P. Ochs and designed for direct use by couples in need of information or advice about their sexual behaviour and/or relationship. The system gathers background data about the couple, and if a sexual dysfunction exists, it investigates further, while allowing extensive feedback, combined with opportunities to learn about various aspects of sexual behaviour. What makes SEXPERT distinct among personal advice systems is its passable imitation of normal social discourse. Various features built into the system to this end include

1 simulation of the process of dialogue
2 presentation of accurate feedback in natural language
3 provision of both immediate and continuous feedback
4 ability to shift focus on the basis of the users' answers
5 ability to monitor when the system may lack adequate knowledge to inform the user accordingly
6 ability of the user to change previous answers and expect that the system will react accordingly
7 ability of the user to ask the system why it has concluded something and to receive an answer[22]

While still tentative, the application of computers in sensitive, interactive, normal-life situations is on the increase. The market-place demand for better and more human-like systems will likely lead researchers to systems that will, indeed, be capable of conversing with humans about various topics in real time and in real life. After all, most couples who interacted with SEXPERT already found the machine sensitive, open, and even human-like. Such consistent responses to machines that have a long way to go before they could pass the Turing test indeed suggest that by the time third-order computhors roll around, few people will need the test to decide that machines can think.

Although none of this probably comes as a complete surprise, neither should it be received with complacency. Unfortunately, common reactions to this type of trend analysis are the extremes of the head-in-the-sand variety or unchecked enthusiasm. Neither seems a healthy alternative. What we need instead is a rational examination of the positive and negative potentials dormant in the issues, in the hope that we can be better prepared for tomorrow, in whatever shape it manifests itself. After all, as someone once remarked on seeing a ghost outside a machine, there are more things in heaven and earth than are dreamt of in our philosophy. There is no guarantee, of course, that the ideas discussed in the last two chapters will ever cross over from fiction to fact, but the first steps seems to have been taken. And, as the ancient saying goes, even the longest journey begins with just one step.

Conclusion: No Discipline Is an Island

> A clear understanding of the notion of information
> as applied to scientific work will show that the
> simple coexistence of two items of information
> is of relatively small value, unless these two items
> can be effectively combined in some mind or
> organ which is able to fertilize one by means of
> the other.
> Norbert Wiener, *The Human Use of Human Beings*

> I would have to say that what we are doing in
> literary studies is *not* truly interdisciplinary.
> We choose theories from other disciplines that
> helps us analyze literary texts, but those theories
> are frequently either passé or discredited in their
> original disciplines.
> Susan Balee

To close this book, I would like to offer one last remark on the kind of interdisciplinarity I have advocated throughout. In the process of my analyses I had an opportunity to point out some disturbing trends evident in contemporary interactions between literary studies and the sciences. Lack of sophistication and understanding and selective "aprioritizing" seem to be the order of the day, raising questions about the value of such superficial interdisciplinary approaches.

None of the arguments in this book should be taken as advocating the colonization of the literary fields by whatever theory currently holds sway in some scientific discipline. As many writers on the subject – notably Richard Levin in his trenchant "The New Interdisciplinarity in Literary Criticism"

(1993) – have painstakingly documented, literary scholars cannot go on practising the kind of disciplinary cross-pollination in which it is the supposed authority but not the actual methodology (or full-blown theories) of other fields that guides their research. One alternative to such a trend is to practise a more rigorous form of interdisciplinarity, faithful to the spirit and method of the social scientific and/or philosophical domain in question. This is a difficult and highly fallible strategy to adopt but, given the potential research payoffs, we should be willing to take this risk.

Clearly the point of this epistemic exercise is not that critics should arbitrarily start to apply the latest scientific theories to literary interpretations. Such a procedure could never do justice to either field. On the other hand, literary scholars would do well to adopt the interdisciplinary methods and procedures that have proven their worth. A good way to start may be to "cultivate the scientist's alertness against doctored evidence, circular reasoning, and wilful indifference to counterexamples." In Frederick Crews's honest summary, "It is a modest goal, but given the current state of our field, I cannot think of a more urgent one" (both in *After Poststructuralism* x).

No raw transfer of scientific theories and methods to literary studies can occur without some form of methodological and epistemological friction. But, as I have tried to show, models, theories, and methods drawn from both the physical and social sciences *can* be legitimately used by literary scholars, leading to new and promising research opportunities. In this book I have explored some exciting avenues of interdisciplinary research, which remains at the same time literary and/or cultural. This is because literature, philosophy, and science are, in my opinion, inseparable manifestations of the same creative human instinct that has operated throughout the ages. It remains to be seen whether the models and theories I have discussed can guide literary studies to an epistemically more fruitful type of interaction with other academic fields.

Once again, I am not speaking here of the selective appropriation of a few central metaphors in the cozy spirit of duty-free interdisciplinarity rampant in literary and humanistic studies over the past decades. Nor is this book meant to be a monument to science, that ever so fallible, heterogenous, and daily outdated body of knowledge. But scientific research and its methods are the best means of learning about the world. And as such they deserve our respect and critical – in both senses – attention.

One of the hottest news items in 1998 was the stunning result of interdisciplinary inquiry into the various extant versions of Chaucer's "The Wife of Bath" tale, from *The Canterbury Tales*. The study, unique of its kind, was universally hailed as a milestone in literary analysis. Using the computing techniques developed by evolutionary biologists, a joint team of literary experts, computer scientists, and biochemists managed to restore the portrayal of the Wife of Bath from the various preserved scripts to the personality it is believed Chaucer intended. At a time when interdisciplinary research in literary studies shows such great potential and attracts the attention of mainstream media, it is hard to avoid the conclusion that a thoroughgoing exploration of interdisciplinary issues could be the new literary-critical frontier for the year 2000 and beyond.

Notes

INTRODUCTION

1 See Pierssens, *Savoirs à l'œuvre* (14).
2 To take two recent examples, Bell's *Models of Power* and Livingston's *Literature and Rationality* make a case for the cognitive payoffs found in the works of, respectively, Emile Zola and Theodore Dreiser.
3 A full exposition of this idea can be found in my *Literary Thought Experiments* (in preparation).
4 Ketterer summarizes this point nicely in *The Rationale of Deception in Poe*: "Of all American writers, Poe is without doubt the most universally admired. In no way limited to the English-speaking world, his popularity continues unabated in lands as diverse as Russia, Hungary, the Scandinavian countries, Germany, France, Italy, Spain, and Central and South America. The literary cosmopolitanism that Poe so vigorously espoused has been spectacularly achieved" (xi). Interestingly enough, if we substitute European for American (and perhaps preface "the most universally admired" with "one of"), this description will apply with equal force and accuracy to Stanislaw Lem.
5 Gräfrath stakes out Lem's claim to the role of philosopher of the future in *Ketzer, Dilettanten und Genies*.
6 I analyze and defend both of these assumptions at length in my "Literature and Literary Knowledge."
7 For one of the most egregious examples, see Muller and Richardson's *Purloined Poe*.
8 All citations in this section are from *Science-Fiction Studies* 40 (1986).
9 The distinction between Anglo-American and Continental-European studies of Lem can be defended to the extent that in Germany, for example, he enjoys an almost equal popularity as a writer of fiction and as a cultural critic and philosopher. The already mentioned study by Gräfrath is only one of the many indications of this trend.

10 INSTRAT is an acronym for Informations- und Kommunikationsstrukturen der Zukunft, or Information and Communication Structures of the Future.

11 Together with a critical introduction, translations and an extensive bibliography, it can be found in my *Stanislaw Lem Reader*.

12 In "Of Games with the Universe" I discussed Lem's theses about the reductionist bias that may colour inquiry. In "Computhors and Biterature" I investigated the likelihood of developments in the cognitive sciences that may enable computers to create works of literature.

13 Originally published in Polish in 1973.

14 In "Literary Interpretations and Textual Readings" (forthcoming).

CHAPTER ONE

1 Although the beginnings of the theory date back to 1928, when John von Neumann proposed a minimax solution for all two-person zerosum games, game theory proper was established in 1944 with the publication of von Neumann and Morgenstern's classic *Theory of Games and Economic Behavior*. For literary scholars the single most accessible source on game theory may be Davis's *Game Theory: A Nontechnical Introduction*. Further useful material can be found in Shubik, Schelling, Poundstone, Rapoport, Elster, and the classic study by Luce and Raiffa.

2 Until very recently, envy-free division-protocol for items ranging from cheesecake to international land disputes has remained an intractable problem. For a game theoretic account of the breakthrough in the division of cheesecake (among other things), see Brams and Taylor, *Fair Division*. Note that the theory does not explore the moral or ethical dimensions of preferences or actions. It merely accepts them as given and investigates possible courses of action with a view to their effectiveness from an agent's subjective point of view.

3 Some game theorists prefer to reserve the term "cooperative" for games where binding agreements can be formed while speaking of "coordination" in games without binding agreement (I thank Curtis Eberweiner for bringing this usage to my attention). While recognizing this important difference between these two types of games, I will nonetheless follow the common usage of "cooperation," more familiar to literary scholars.

4 For a selection of these efforts, see the game theory section in the bibliography.

5 The scarce examples are Lewis, *Convention*; Livingston, "Convention and Literary Explanations"; and Swirski, "Literary Studies and Literary Pragmatics."

6 The classic detective genre is indebted to Poe, who was, in the perception of many critics, its modern founder. For an introduction to the subject, see Irwin, Rollason, or Van Leer.

7 Except for references to *Eureka*, all references to Poe throughout this book are to the Mabbott edition.

8 A full analysis of this interesting game can be found in my "Literary Studies and Literary Pragmatics."

9 The appeal to the author's intentions in determining the meaning of a work reflects my belief in the presence of a determinate mental reality during the act of creation.

10 This is not to imply that all literature aims at eventual decryption. Clearly there are writers (e.g., Robert Anton Wilson) who aim at ever-deepening levels of obfuscation. L. Ron Hubbard's scientology "literature" is probably the best known and most representative of this hermetic sect.

11 See the bibliography for a list of other pertinent papers by Grice. The theories of communication developed by Bach and Harnish, or Sperber and Wilson, replace some of the less likely features of Grice's original model.

12 In addition to mutual contextual beliefs, two other mutual beliefs of a more general nature necessarily feature in the exchange. For a definition of these Linguistic and Communicative Presumptions shared among members of the linguistic community at large, see Bach and Harnish (7).

13 A similar overlap between game and communication theories also supports my analysis of the communicative process using speech-act and game theory. For a brief but apt introduction, see Schelling (85).

14 The sole example of this model that I have come across is Davis's ever-so-brief example of business partnership (*Game Theory*, 88–9).

15 In my study I concentrate on cooperation, since it dominates the readerly and literary critical practice. For a recent exploration of the competitive dimension in literature and literary studies, see Hjort, *The Strategy of Letters*.

16 The account I propose depends only on two fairly broad assumptions of (1) a categorical difference between fiction and nonfiction, and (2) the necessity of selection of appropriate backgrounds for inference-making about the contents of various fictions. As such it is compatible with various pragmatic theories of fiction. Note that truth in fiction is both a descriptive and a normative concept: "competence" alludes to the readers' high expected convergence in fleshing out the contents of fictional stories, while allowing divergence at the level of individual performance. For background on literary expertise, see Graesser, Graves and Frederiksen, and Magliano and Graesser.

17 Iser derives much of his discussion of textual gaps from Roman Ingarden. For an analysis of Iser's theories from a pragmatic standpoint, see my "Iser's Theory of Aesthetic Response."

18 See, for example, Buranelli (43–4) and Levine and Levine (502).

19 The categorical difference between fiction and nonfiction becomes of paramount importance at this point. Determined by the selection of appropriate backgrounds, the inferences one can legitimately make about different fictions may differ dramatically from one another, as well as from those habitually assumed for nonfiction. I define and discuss the concept of fiction in my "Nature of Literary Fiction."

20 A recent attempt to make sense of fictional worlds is Pavel's *Fictional Worlds*. See Currie's review of this book for a critique of Pavel's approach.

21 A convenient way to understand this proposal may be to think of fictional propositions as prefixed by the operator "It is fictional in the work that..."

When interpreting fiction by using background beliefs not found in the text, the reader implicitly applies the fictional modifier to its propositions. Inferences are thus valid only if preceded by the same operator; nothing follows from a blend of modified (prefixed) statements and unmodified ones.

22 In "Art Interpretation" Robert Stecker also embraces the "mutual belief principle" (198). For scholars interested in the precise formulation of Lewis' theses, they are

ANALYSIS 1: A sentence of the form "In the fiction f, ϕ" is non-vacuously true iff some world where f is told as known fact and ϕ is true differs less from our actual world, on balance, than does any world where f is told as known fact and f is not true. It is vacuously true iff there are no possible worlds where f is told as known fact.

ANALYSIS 2: A sentence of the form "In the fiction f, ϕ" is non-vacuously true iff, whenever w is one of the collective belief worlds of the community of origin of f, then some world where f is told as known fact and ϕ is true differs less from the world w, on balance than does any world where f is told as known fact and f is not true. It is vacuously true iff there are no possible worlds where f is told as known fact.

23 It seems to me that Byrne's argument extends to self-reflexive stories. A recent critique of Currie's proposals appears in Davies's "Fictional Truth."

24 One clear case in which Currie's proposal breaks down is when the beliefs of the real author's community, the beliefs of the fictional author, and the fictional events of the story, are all temporally separate. Imagine a contemporary author who wishes to portray a pre-Christian Viking community, but from a perspective of an enlightened late-medieval cleric (in this way automatically excluding both the Reality and the Mutual Belief Principles). On Currie's proposal, as long as the beliefs of the late-medieval narrator coincide with those of his subject(s), we can indeed rely on the belief system of the fictional author to make appropriate inferences about story content. However, as soon as those begin to diverge, the principle yields anachronistic beliefs that could not satisfy any competent reader. In "The Role of Intention" Stecker provides strong reasons for why real intentionalism is better equipped to deal with the meaning of literary works than hypothetical intentionalism.

25 In their paper, Livingston and Mele arrive at an analysis of truth in fiction similar to my own.

CHAPTER TWO

1 For significant exceptions in this century, see Bond, Valéry, Nordstedt, Wiener, Hoagland, Conner, or Wylie. Although recently some scholars of science fiction have adopted *Eureka* as one of its protean works, this claim does justice neither to Poe nor his essay. Next to a Star Trekker's sci-fi, *Eureka* appears

iconoclastic in the audacity of its vision and intricacy of its arguments. As Olney puts it, "science fiction writers – with their sub- and super-human characters and their absurd pseudo-scientific jargon of space-time vectors, telekinesis, mind-matrices, and the like" (421) – stay away from the intoxicating vistas of philosophical speculation explored by Poe.

2 Subsequent quotations from Poe are identified by page references; all emphases are his unless specified otherwise. Since Mabbott's standard edition does not include *Eureka*, I use Harold Beaver's annotated and readily available 1976 edition.

3 *Eureka* is subtitled "An Essay on the Material and Spiritual Universe"; however, in the advertisements of its original publisher (Putnam), the subtitle is "A Prose Poem: Or the Physical and Metaphysical Universe."

4 I discuss mixed intentions in more detail in "The Nature of Literary Fiction." For a good introduction to the subject in the context Poe's mesmeric tales, see also Livingston's *Literature and Rationality* (70–8).

5 As Silverman reports, Poe counted on a turnout of three hundred and was severely disappointed when he found only about sixty listeners in the audience, much less than the minimum necessary to secure the funds for the start-up of the *Stylus*. For more details, see Harrison (274–5); also the end of Poe's letter to Eveleth (Ostrom, 2:356–57).

6 In Harrison, vol. 16 (26).

7 This intellectual climate may, in fact, have had implications for "To Science." Since there was little basis for it in the historical facts of Poe's times, the sonnet may be a veiled criticism of outdated philosophy of science, rather than of science itself.

8 Poe does dish out a few examples from history of science in an effort to support his ratiocinations with analogic evidence. On the value of such evidence in *Eureka*, see Welsh.

9 Our attitude to terms like "absolute" and "certainty" in the context of the empirical sciences has changed since Poe's times. Absolute certainty is simply an inappropriate goal in a reality-based, and therefore fallible, pursuit of knowledge. All the same, a moderate version of empirical realism, such as that defended, for example, in Livingston's *Literary Knowledge*, is fully compatible with Poe's conviction about the objective nature of his findings.

10 For a full description of the puzzle, see Barrow, *The World within the World* (254).

11 A similar point is made by Nordstedt (175–6).

12 For the standard articulation of the deductive-nomological model, see Hempel's "The Function of General Laws in History" (originally 1942), in his *Aspects of Scientific Explanation.*

13 Theorizing on its own can lead to a situation where, as in modern interpretations of quantum uncertainty, both Bohr's observer-dependent and Everett's polyverse theories provide satisfactory accounts of empirical data. As an aside,

I should mention that David Deutch has recently proposed an intriguing idea that, may, at least in theory, resolve the issue. A hypothetical quantum computer could – if the polyverse interpretation is correct – get us the equivalent of two hours of computing in just one hour.

14 See Sagan, *Cosmos* (48). Kepler's first law says that the planets move in elliptical orbits with the sun at one of the foci.

15 Susan Haack's *Evidence and Inquiry* develops a pragmatic "foundherentist" theory of knowledge from a more strictly epistemological perspective.

16 For a more detailed critique of Neo-Kantianism, specifically oriented towards literary studies, see my "Literature and Literary Knowledge."

17 For background on nineteenth-century Neo-Kantianism, see Schnädelbach. Livingston's "Literary Studies and the Sciences" provides a fine analysis of the subject of this section.

18 See, for example, Gross and Levitt, Fox, Richard Levin, Minogue, Ortiz de Montellano, and Sprinker.

19 For an effective critique of the Neo-Kantian oppositions, see Bunge.

20 One of the first modern efforts in this direction must be Hippolyte Taine's evolutionary and biological treatment of culture in his *Philosophie de l'art* (1865).

21 See Livingston's *Literary Knowledge*, chap. 5, "Arguments on the Unity of Science."

22 In *Aspects of Scientific Explanation* and *Philosophy of Natural Science*.

CHAPTER THREE

1 The most comprehensive and comprehensible synopsis of Poe's views can be found in Quinn's chapter on *Eureka* (543–55). See also Silverman (339), Rans (35–6), or Buranelli (52–3).

2 Poe knew of Boscovich, who posited the same organization of forces within the universe, i.e., only attraction and repulsion. See Barrow, *Theories of Everything* (25).

3 There is a certain argumentative similarity between Poe's description of lifting his finger as an act of cosmic proportions (236) and William of Ockham's argument against the reality of relations. All the same, Ockham's rejection of the infinitude of changing relations is a triumph of the empirical spirit in his philosophy. See O'Connor (131), for background.

4 My own translation from the French.

5 Naturally, it is impossible to prove Poe's particular assumptions about God to be wrong or right, even though some theologies can be, and have been, refuted by science. But it is not impossible to show that some theological assumptions are more open to systematic inquiry than has been imagined, as Steven Brams does in his provocative *Superior Beings: If They Exist, How Would We Know? Superior Beings* is not a book of science – in an obvious sense its theses are not open to experiment. Still, it departs from conventional

philosophy not only in its relentless use of game theory but in a deliberate effort to revive the research tradition that, as the author describes it, "weds broad philosophical questions to rigorous analytic methods, primarily developed in the sciences" (1). Brams's book, albeit limited to the monotheistic Deity from the Judaic tradition, offers a methodologically unique approach to an old philosophical and theological problem.

6 Exactly how much science Poe knew is open to question, but judging by his errors, it is safe to assume that most of his knowledge was second-hand, gathered from magazines that printed popular accounts of scientific work. Allen (733–4) mentions the *North American*, the science notes in which may have been the source of the facts that Poe uses in his works.

7 For a useful distinction between natural and spiritual pantheism, see Kolakowski (110–11).

8 See Richard Levin's "Negative Evidence" for a good analysis of this problem in the contemporary literary critical environment.

9 Barrow and Tipler's *The Anthropic Cosmological Principle*, although a little technical at times, is an indispensable source on the various types of anthropic principles and design arguments, as well as on the scientific cosmological models proposed over the centuries.

10 The series of coincidences between the values of constants of nature that have allowed the evolution of *Homo sapiens* (as the SAP argues) provides only the *necessary* conditions for the emergence of life. Even though these are numerous and precisely calibrated, it does not follow that they are also *sufficient*. Thus Barrow states in *Theories of Everything* that without predetermining anything, the initial conditions simply "allow" the emergence of life (183).

11 Discovered by Asaph Hall, they are Phobos and Deimos.

12 A good introduction to these topics can be found in Davies or Barrow.

13 For an non-technical description of gauge symmetries, see Barrow, *World within the World* (181–4), as well as Davies, *Superforce* (112–16) and *Superstrings* (52–7).

14 For background, see Hawking (76–9).

15 My own translation from the French.

16 Poe goes so far as to copy the alleged wording of Kepler's announcement of his discovery into a summary of his own theses (220–1).

17 A brief but useful treatment of teleology in the writings of the German absolute idealists, which demonstrates how closely Poe echoes their writings at this point in *Eureka*, can be found in "Teleological Ideas in Absolute Idealism" (153–9), in Barrow and Tipler.

18 Thus, in 1800 Hegel confidently predicted that no new celestial bodies could exist in the solar system. When, only one year later, the asteroid Ceres was discovered, the philosopher "seems to have returned to pursuits less amenable to disproof" (Sagan, *Broca's Brain*, 235).

19 For a distinction between teleology and eutaxiology, see Barrow and Tipler.

CHAPTER FOUR

1 All subsequent citations in this chapter refer to *The Invincible*, unless indicated otherwise.

2 All quotations from the Polish are in my own translation.

3 These remarks occur in "On the Genesis of *Wizja lokalna*" (386), an essay in which, appropriately enough, Lem comments on his own novel, one of the most spectacular meta-fictions in existence.

4 I examine some of this novel's self-reflexive elements in "Playing a Game of Ontology."

5 The liar's paradox is also known as the Epemenides paradox, after its creator, a Cretan, who is reported to have said, "All Cretans are liars." See Douglas Hoftstadter's "On Self-Referential Sentences" (in *Metamagical Themas*) for an entertaining treatment of this subject.

6 Lem's source for the concept of a macro-organism composed of replaceable micro-elements could have been Olaf Stapledon's *Star Maker*. A brief discussion of this concept (in Polish) can be found in Stoff's *Lem i inni* (17–18).

7 This is without doubt another of Lem's perennial topics. The chain of novels sharing this concern runs the entire gamut from his very first *Człowiek z Marsa* (*Man from Mars* [1946]) to the latest *Fiasco* (1987). A non-fictional treatment of this and related topics can be found in John Ralston Saul's *Voltaire's Bastards*.

8 During our 1992 interview Lem argued that the introduction of more female characters to his plots would necessitate a considerable increase in narrative complexity, which could only be achieved at some expense of the cognitive issues at the forefront of his fiction. For an introduction to the questions of science and gender, see Harding.

9 See also Davis, *Stanislaw Lem* (32).

10 Lem's reference to superluminal communication is rather unusual. As Csicsery-Ronay Jr has remarked, speculation beyond contemporary science is untypical for Lem, who tries to "avoid like the plague" ("Twenty-Two Answers," 255) problems that he does not believe can come about. On the same subject, see also Beres (85).

11 For explicit comments on the problems with anthropomorphism in inquiry, see 501–2.

12 For a recent defense of this position, see Richard N. Boyd.

13 Intentionality, which dominated Scholastic philosophy, was resurrected by Franz Brentano in the nineteenth century, especially in his *Psychology from an Empirical Standpoint*. For Brentano intentionality was *the* distinctive feature of psychological acts, in contrast to physical events.

14 It was probably the first time in the history of science that substantive quantitative values were obtained from an essentially qualitative analysis. Feigenbaum's values have been confirmed in independently run computer

simulations at the University of Modena, Italy. A nontechnical introduction to the subject can be found in Cohen and Stewart, *The Collapse of Chaos.*

15 Such a representation is usually provided through a mathematical expression known as a Lagrangian, after French physicist Joseph Lagrange, who provided a refined formulation of Newton's laws.

CHAPTER FIVE

1 Because the term "spontaneous" is so loaded with connotations, especially in philosophy, I feel a need to disclaim any meanings that go outside its everyday usage.

2 Babbage's first crack at a modern calculating machine was the so-called difference engine, actually completed after his death by his son Henry.

3 Quoted in Turing (21).

4 Paul Pietroski suggested to me the following scenario: every time you give the computer the command "Write a good thriller," it produces the same (or an insignificantly different) one every time. The scenario is interesting inasmuch as the subsequent repetitiveness and imitativeness of the computer would raise some doubts about its creative independence. For the purpose of my analysis it is more important, however, that in the paradigmatic case, i.e., the first open-ended request, the computer's actions would fall under spontaneous creation.

5 Margaret Boden's *Artificial Intelligence and Natural Man* is a useful source on the research with learning programs.

6 The Golem has already risen against humanity, although in a way that has nothing to do with the legend. On 9 December 1981, the *Guardian* reported that an industrial robot had killed a worker at the Akashi plant in Japan. Kenii Urada had leaped over the safety fence surrounding the robot, at the same time accidentally brushing a switch that caused the work arm of the robot to trap him against a machine that was cutting gears. In general, industrial robot-related accidents have been many, without provoking any fears of a mechanoid uprising.

7 On the subject of volition in robots, a useful nontechnical article is Lem's "Smart Robots."

8 A good introduction may be Anderson's *Minds and Machines* which reprints Turing's original article together with a series of responses from the philosophical community.

9 It seems that questions of physiological and/or psychological (sexual?) nature could be profitable to pursue. Large parts of human brains are devoted to instinctively managing the body, and appropriate questions could perhaps bring out parts of that programming.

10 Moor's "Analysis of the Turing Test" also pokes holes in several standard objections to the TT, as presented in Anderson's *Minds and Machines.*

11 See Weizenbaum's *Computer Power and Human Reason.* In 1972 Colby, Hilf, Webev, and Kramer reported on PARRY, a computer simulation of a paranoid patient. The program was subjected to a kind of Turing test in which a group of psychiatrists were asked to assess the degree of paranoia of the subject on the basis of a teletyped interview.

12 Here I may sound like the butt of Larry Tesler's joke that AI is whatever has not been done yet. Still, if one is to believe Dale Jacquette, the "expectation among most philosophers today is that to pass the Turing test, a machine must be able to deceive any expert interrogator under limited time conditions with something approaching 100% success" (64).

13 This scenario is discussed by Lem in *Golem XIV,* also published in *Imaginary Magnitude.*

14 Dennett comments in "Fast Thinking," "No one complains that models only account for the 'behavior' of hurricanes or gall bladders or solar systems. What else is there about these phenomena for science to account for?" (334).

15 In "Troubles with Functionalism" Ned Block advanced essentially the same idea by describing a "propositional jukebox" machine, one that could pass the TT owing only to the brute power of its automated memory retrieval.

16 The standard answer to Searle may be Hofstadter and Dennett's in *The Mind's I.* See also Dennett's *Consciousness Explained* (438) and "Fast Thinking."

17 There seems little agreement on what the definition actually refers to. Computer thinking? Computer intelligence? The identity of computer and human thinking? Their equivalence? P.H. Millar leaves the matter open-ended, stating that the TT "constitutes an operational definition which ... can be used as a criterion" (595). The two recent writers on this subject differ as well; for Robert M. French the TT defines intelligence, and for Dale Jacquette, artificial intelligence.

18 We routinely and successfully attribute beliefs and desires to animals on the basis of their behaviour, mainly because, just like ours, it appears to be caused by information from the environment and the apparent desire to affect the environment in ways favourable to them.

CHAPTER SIX

1 This process has an analogue in humans: a special case of a different postnatal software from similar prenatal hardware may be the development of identical twins.

2 Such biological computers have been discussed by Lem in *Summa Technologiae.*

3 Perhaps fittingly, *Bagabone* was executed by a computer programmed by G.E. Hughes and his collaborators from the Jagiellonian University of Cracow, Poland – the city where Lem lives.

4 All citations in this and the next section refer to Iseminger's anthology, unless indicated otherwise.

5 In holding this view I am thus in complete disagreement with absolutists like P.D. Juhl, who in *Interpretation* claims that a "literary work has one and only one correct interpretation" (198).

6 Harey is the name in the Polish original, which, inexplicably, was changed to Rheya in the English translation.

7 In "Art, Intention, and Conversation" Nöel Carroll shows that if there is "thesis projection of nonfictional import – whereby actual authors express their views about life, society, morality, and so forth – and a great deal of literary (indeed artistic) interpretation concerns the identification of such theses, then intentionalist criticism has a wide arena of legitimate activity" (109). The unquestionable truth of the starting premise puts an end to the first of Beardsley's arguments.

8 See Levinson's *Music, Art, and Metaphysics* and Currie's *Ontology of Art.*

9 Wordsworth, "A Slumber Did My Spirit Seal" (1800). For a systematic critique of this outlandish claim, see Wilson's "Again, Theory."

10 Hirsh himself makes the same point: "the text ha[s] to represent *somebody's* meaning – if not the author's, then the critic's" (13).

11 Even Simons's conditional pronouncements reflect an unconditional faith of a proselyte. *Are Computers Alive?* opens with an avowal "that certain types of artificial systems may be alive" – this, let us not forget, already in 1983. The basic ambiguity of "may" again muddies the important distinction between "may" as in "may one day happen," or "may" as in "may already be the case."

12 As Simons describes it (71), this English professor made a computer randomly substitute words in a rigid framework, thus accidentally discovering first-order computhorship several decades after the first attempts of this kind.

13 This is, of course, not a comprehensive definition of life; all it is designed to do is to point out gaps in Simons's procomputer life rhetoric.

14 As a matter of fact, Simons himself cheerfully acknowledges that "Most robots have no survival instinct" (81); his arguments leave little doubt that "most" in the present industrial environment means simply "all."

15 One of the more lucid examples may be found in Dennet's *Consciousness Explained.*

16 A typical example may be Simon and Newall's "Heuristic Problem Solving" or "Report on a General Problem-Solving Program."

17 In fact, research investment continues to grow in most countries, including Japan and the United States. Lately the American Department of Defense has switched its endowments almost entirely to neural-network projects.

18 As reported in the *Guardian,* 5 January 1980 (18).

19 *Computer Weekly,* 17/24 December 1981; Briot "The Utilization of an 'Artificial Skin' Sensor."

20 Let us not forget, however, that massive parallel processing is not an automatic solution to all problems; recall the old army joke in which a captain

reasons that if one soldier can dig a foxhole in two hours, a hundred should do the job in a minute!

21 The reason for the quotes around "intelligence" is that Deep Blue's chess prowess reflects not so much its thinking power as brute computing capacity.

22 After Ochs et al., "The Effects of Exposure" and "Learning About Sex." I thank Eric Ochs for bringing these studies to my attention.

Bibliography

EDGAR ALLAN POE: GENERAL

Allen, Hervey. *Israfel: The Life and Times of Edgar Allan Poe*. 2 vols. New York: George H. Doran, 1926.

Allen, Michael. *Poe and the British Magazine Tradition*. London: Oxford University Press, 1969.

Allerton, Margaret. *Origins of Poe's Critical Theory*. New York: Russell & Russell, 1965.

Baldwin, Summerfield. "The Aesthetic Theory of Edgar Allan Poe." *Sewanee Review* 27 (1918): 210–21.

Baudelaire, Charles. *Fatal Destinies: the Edgar Poe Essays*. Trans. Joan Fiedler Mele. Woodhaven, N.Y.: Cross Country, 1981.

Beaver, Harold. *The Science Fiction of Edgar Allan Poe*. London: Penguin, 1987.

Bonaparte, Marie. *The Life and Works of Edgar Allan Poe: A Psycho-Analytic Interpretation*. Trans. John Rodker. London: Hogarth, 1949.

Broussard, Louis. *The Measure of Poe*. Norman, OK: University of Oklahoma Press, 1969.

Buranelli, Vincent. *Edgar Allan Poe*. Boston: Twayne, 1977.

Carlson, Eric W., ed. *The Recognition of Edgar Allan Poe: Selected Criticism since 1829*. Ann Arbor, MI: University of Michigan Press, 1966.

Carton, Evan. *The Rhetoric of American Romance: Dialectic and Identity in Emerson, Dickinson, Poe, and Hawthorne*. Baltimore, MD: Johns Hopkins University Press, 1985.

Dayan, Joan. *Fables of Mind: An Inquiry into Poe's Fiction*. New York: Oxford University Press, 1987.

Denuccio, J. D. "Fact, Fiction, Fatality: Poe's 'The Thousand-and-Second Tale of Scheherazade.'" *Studies in Short Fiction* 27 (1990): 365–70.

Fisher, Benjamin F. "That 'Daughter of Old Time': Science in the Writings of Edgar Allan Poe." *Publications of the Arkansas Philological Association* 9 (1983): 36–41.

Forest, William Mentzel. *Biblical Allusions in Poe.* New York: Macmillan, 1928.

Freundlieb, Dieter. "Understanding Poe's Tales: A Schema-Theoretic View." *Poetics* 11 (1982): 1–23.

Halliburton, David. *Edgar Allan Poe: A Phenomenological View.* Princeton, NJ: Princeton University Press, 1973.

Harrison, James A., ed. *The Complete Works of Edgar Allan Poe.* New York: Thomas Y. Crowell, 1902.

– *Life of Edgar Allan Poe.* New York: Haskell, 1903.

Hoffmann, David. *Poe Poe Poe Poe Poe Poe Poe.* New York: Doubleday, 1972.

Hough, Robert, ed. *Literary Criticism of Edgar Allan Poe.* Lincoln, NE: University of Nebraska Press, 1965.

Ketterer, David. *The Rationale of Deception in Poe.* Baton Rouge, LA: Lousiana State University Press, 1979.

Levine, Stuart, and Susan Levine, eds. *The Short Fiction of Edgar Allan Poe.* Indianapolis, IN: Bobbs-Merrill, 1976.

Mabbott, Thomas Olliver, ed. *Collected Works of Edgar Allan Poe.* 3 vols. Cambridge, MA: Harvard University Press, 1978.

Marion, Denis. "La Méthode intellectuelle de Poe." *Mesures* 6 (1940): 89–127.

Meyers, Jeffrey. *Edgar Allan Poe: His Life and Legacy.* New York: Scribner's, 1992.

Olney, Clarke. "Edgar Allan Poe: Science Fiction Pioneer." *Georgia Review* 12 (1958): 416–21.

Ostrom, John Ward. *The Letters of Edgar Allan Poe.* New York: Gordian Press, 1966.

Pollin, Burton R. *Discoveries in Poe.* Notre Dame, IN: Notre Dame University Press, 1970.

Quinn, Arthur Hobson. *Edgar Allan Poe: A Critical Biography.* New York: Appleton-Century, 1941.

Rans, Geoffrey. *Edgar Allan Poe.* Edinburgh: Oliver and Boyd, 1965.

Raynolds, David. *Beneath the American Renaissance: The Subversive Imagination in the Age of Emerson and Melville.* New York: Knopf, 1988.

Regan, Robert. *Poe: A Collection of Critical Essays.* Englewood Cliffs, NJ: Prentice Hall, 1967.

Silverman, Kenneth. *Edgar A. Poe: Mournful and Never-Ending Remembrance.* New York: Harper Collins, 1991.

Symons, Julian. *The Tell-Tale Heart: the Life and Works of Edgar Allan Poe.* London: Faber & Faber, 1978.

Tate, Allen. *The Man of Letters in the Modern World: Selected Essays: 1928-1955.* London: Meridian, 1955.

Thompson, G. R. *Essays and Reviews.* New York: Library of America, 1984.

Walker, I. M. *Edgar Allan Poe: The Critical Heritage.* London: Routledge, 1986.

Whalen, Terence. "The Code for Gold: Edgar Allan Poe and Cryptography." *Representations* 36 (1994): 35–58.

Wiener, Philip P. "Poe's Logic and Metaphysics." *The Personalist* 14 (1933): 268–74.

POE: "EUREKA"

Poe, Edgar Allan. "Eureka." *The Science Fiction of Edgar Allan Poe.* Ed. Harold Beaver. London: Penguin, 1987.

Benton, Richard P., ed. *Poe as Literary Cosmologer: Studies on "Eureka": A Symposium.* Hartford, CN: Transcendental, 1975.

Bond, Frederick Drew. "Poe As Evolutionist." *Popular Science Monthly* 71 (1907): 267–74.

Cantalupo, Barbara. "'Of or Pertaining to a Higher Power': Involution in *Eureka.*" *American Transcendental Quarterly* 4 (1990): 81–90.

Conner, Frederick William. "Poe's 'Eureka': The Problem of Mechanism." *Cosmic Optimism: A Study of the Interpretation of Evolution by American Poets from Emerson to Robinson.* Gainesville, FL: University of Florida Press, 1949.

Dayan, Joan. "The Analytic of the Dash: Poe's *Eureka.*" *Genre* 16 (1983): 437–66.

Hoagland, Clayton. "The Universe of *Eureka*: A Comparison of the Theories of Poe and Eddington." *Southern Literary Messenger* 1 (1939): 307–13.

Holman, Harriet R. "Hog, Bacon, Ram and Other 'Savants' in *Eureka*: Notes towards Decoding Poe's Encyclopedic Satire." *Poe Newsletter* 2 (1969): 49–55.

Ketterer, David. "Empedocles in *Eureka*: Addenda." *Poe Studies* 18 (1985): 24–5.

Kovalev, I. V. "Edgar Po i kosmologiia XX stoletiia." *Vestnik Leningradskogo Universiteta. Seriia Istorii, Iazyka i Literatury* 2 (1985): 21–30.

Manning, Susan. "'The Plots of God Are Perfect': Poe's *Eureka* and American Creative Nihilism." *Journal of American Studies* 23 (1989): 235–51.

McCaslin, Susan. "*Eureka*: Poe's Cosmogonic Poem." *Studies in Nineteenth Century Literature: Fourth Series.* Ed. James Hogg. Salzburg: Institut fur Anglistik & Amerikanistik, University of Salzburg, 1981.

Miecznikowski, Cynthia. "End(ings) and Mean(ing)s in *Pym* and *Eureka.*" *Studies in Short Fiction* 27 (1990): 55–64.

Nordstedt, George. "Poe and Einstein." *Open Court* 44 (1930): 173–80.

Thompson, G. R. "Unity, Death, and Nothingness – Poe's 'Romantic Skepticism.'" *PMLA* 85 (1970): 297–300.

Valéry, Paul. "Au sujet d'*Eureka.*" *Leonardo, Poe, Mallarmé.* Trans. Malcolm Cowley. Princeton, NJ: Princeton University Press, 1972.

Welsh, Susan. "The Value of Analogical Evidence: Poe's *Eureka* in the Context of a Scientific Debate." *Modern Language Studies* 21 (1991): 3–15.

Wylie, Clarence, R., Jr. "Mathematical Allusions in Poe." *Scientific Monthly* 63 (1946): 227–35.

POE: "THE PURLOINED LETTER"

Blythe, Hal, and Charlie Sweet. "The Reader as Poe's Ultimate Dupe in 'The Purloined Letter.'" *Studies in Short Fiction* 26 (1989): 311–15.

Dameron, J. Lasley. "Poe's Auguste Dupin." In *No Fairer Land: Studies in Southern Literature before 1900*, eds. J. Lasley Dameron, et al. Troy, NY: Whitston, 1986.

Dunn, Peter N. "Lazarillo de Tormes: The Case of the Purloined Letter." *Revista de Estudios Hispanicos* 22 (1988): 1–14.

Eddings, Dennis W. "Poe, Dupin, and the Reader." *University of Mississippi Studies in English* 3 (1982): 128–35.

Engel, Leonard W. "Truth and Detection: Poe's Tales of Ratiocination and His Use of the Enclosure." *Clues* 3 (1982): 83–6.

Irwin, John T. "Mysteries We Reread, Mysteries of Rereading: Poe, Borges, and the Analytic Detective Story." *Modern Language Notes* 101 (1986): 1168–1215.

– "A Clew to a Clue: Locked Rooms and Labyrinths in Poe and Borges." *Raritan: A Quarterly Review* 10 (1991): 40–57.

Kronick, Joseph G. "Edgar Allan Poe: the Error of Reading and the Reading of Error." In *Southern Literature and Literary Theory*, ed. Jefferson Humphries. Athens, GA: University of Georgia Press, 1990.

Major, René. "The Parable of the Purloined Letter: The Direction of the Cure and Its Telling." Tr. John Forrester. *Stanford Literature Review* 8 (1991): 67–102.

Muckley, Peter A. "The Radicalness of These Differences: Reading 'The Purloined Letter.'" *University of Mississippi Studies in English* 8 (1990): 227–42.

Muller, John P., and William J. Richardson, eds. *The Purloined Poe: Lacan, Derrida and Psychoanalytic Reading*. Baltimore, MD: Johns Hopkins University Press, 1988.

Rollason, Christopher. "The Detective Myth in Edgar Allan Poe's Dupin Trilogy." In *American Crime Fiction: Studies in the Genre*, ed. Brian Docherty. New York: St Martin's, 1988.

Swirski, Peter. "Literary Studies and Literary Pragmatics: The Case of 'The Purloined Letter.'" *SubStance* 81 (1996): 69–89.

Van Leer, David. "Detecting Truth: The World of the Dupin Tales." In *New Essays on Poe's Major Tales*, ed. Kenneth Silverman. Cambridge: Cambridge University Press, 1993.

STANISLAW LEM: GENERAL

Anninski, L.A. "On Lem's *The High Castle*." Trans. Nadia Peterson. *Science-Fiction Studies* 13 (November 1986): 345–51.

Astle, Richard. "Lem's Misreading of Todorov." *Science–Fiction Studies* 2 (1975): 167–9.

Balcerzan, Edward. "Language and Ethics in *Solaris*." Trans. Konrad Brodzinski. *Science–Fiction Studies* 2 (1975): 152–6.

Balcerzak, Ewa. *Lem*. Trans. Krystyna Cekalska. Warsaw: Author's Agency, 1973.

Barnouw, Dagmar. "Science Fiction as a Model for Probabilistic Worlds: Stanislaw Lem's Fantastic Empiricism." *Science–Fiction Studies* 6 (1979): 153–63.

Benford, Gregory. "On Lem on Cosmology and SF." *Science–Fiction Studies* 4 (1977): 316–17.

– Aliens and Knowability: A Scientist's Perspective." In *Bridges to Science Fiction*, ed. George Slusser et al. Carbondale, IL: Southern Illinois University Press, 1980.

Beres, Stanislaw. *Rozmowy ze Stanislawem Lemem* [Conversations with Stanislaw Lem]. Cracow: Wydawnictwo Literackie, 1987.

Blish, James. "Review of *Solaris.*" *Magazine of Fantasy and Science Fiction* 40 (May 1971): 42–3.

Brewster, Anne. "An Interview with Stanislaw Lem." *Science Fiction: A Review of Speculative Literature* 4 (1982): 6–8.

Caldwell, Patrice. "Earth Mothers or Male Memories: Wilhelm, Lem, and Future Women." In *Women Worldwalkers: New Dimensions of Science Fiction and Fantasy*, ed. Jane B. Weedman. Lubbock, TX: Texas Tech Press, 1985. 59–69.

Carter, Steven R. "The Science Fiction Mystery Novels of Asimov, Bester and Lem: Fusions and Foundations." *Clues* 1 (1980): 109–15.

Cheever, Leonard A. "Epistemological Chagrin: The Literary and Philosophical Antecedents of Stanislaw Lem's Romantic Misanthrope." *Science-Fiction Studies* 21 (July 1994): 212–24.

Csicsery–Ronay, Istvan, Jr. "Kafka and Science Fiction." *Newsletter of the Kafka Society of America* 7 (June 1983): 5–14.

– "The Book Is the Alien: On Certain and Uncertain Readings of Lem's *Solaris.*" *Science–Fiction Studies* 12 (1985): 6–21.

– "Editorial Introduction." *Science-Fiction Studies* 13 (November 1986): 235–41.

– "Twenty–Two Answers and Two Postscripts: An Interview with Stanislaw Lem." Trans. Marek Lugowski. *Science-Fiction Studies* 13 (November 1986): 242–60.

– "Modeling the Chaosphere: Stanislaw Lem's Alien Communications." In *Chaos and Order: Complex Dynamics in Literature and Science*, ed. N. Katherine Hayles. Chicago: University of Chicago Press, 1991.

Dann, Jack, and Gregory Benford. "Two Statements in Support of Sargent and Zebrowski." *Science–Fiction Studies* 4 (1977): 137–8.

Davis, J. Madison. "'Today's Exception Becomes Tomorrow's Rule': Stanislaw Lem's *The Chain of Chance.*" *Publications of the Mississippi Philological Association.* Jackson, MI: 1985.

– "Quirks, Quarks, and Fairy Tales." *Bloomsbury Review* 5 (1985): 19–20.

– "The Hydra of Science Fiction." *Bloomsbury Review* 7 (1987): 22, 30.

– "The Quest for Art: Lem's Analysis of Borges." *Extrapolation* 29 (1988): 53–64.

– *Stanislaw Lem.* Mercer Island, WA: Starmont, 1990.

Dick, Philip K., and Pamela Sargent. "The Lem Affair (Continued)." *Science–Fiction Studies* 5 (1978): 84.

Easterbrook, Neil. "The Sublime Simulacra: Repetition, Reversal, and Re–Covery in Lem's *Solaris.*" *Critique* 36 (Spring 1995): 177–94.

Engel, Peter. "An Interview with Stanislaw Lem." Trans. John Sigda. *The Missouri Review* 7 (1984): 218–37.

Everman, Welch D. "The Paper World: Science Fiction in the Postmodern Era." In *Postmodern Fiction: A Bio–Bibliographical Guide*, ed. Larry McCaffery. New York: Greenwood, 1986.

Farmer, Phillip Jose. "A Letter to Mr. Lem." *Science Fiction Commentary* 25 (1971): 19–26.

- "Pornograms and Supercomputers." *New York Times Book Review* (2 September 1984): 4.

Federman, Raymond. "An Interview with Stanislaw Lem." *Science-Fiction Studies* 29 (1983): 2–14.

Field, David. "Fluid Worlds: Lem's *Solaris* and Nabokov's *Ada*." *Science-Fiction Studies* 13 (November 1986): 329–44.

Fogel, Stanley. "*The Investigation*: Stanislaw Lem's Pynchonesque Novel." *Riverside Quarterly* 6 (1977): 286–9.

Foster, Thomas, and Luise H. Morton. "God or Game Players: The Cosmos, William Paley and Stanislaw Lem." *The Polish Review* 32 (1987): 203–9.

Geier, Manfred. "Stanislaw Lem's Fantastic Ocean: Toward a Semantic Interpretation of *Solaris*." Trans. Edith Welliver. *Science–Fiction Studies* 19 (July 1992): 192–218.

Gräfrath, Bernd. *Ketzer, Dilettanten und Genies: Grenzgaenger der Philosophie.* Hamburg: Junius, 1993.

- "Taking 'Science Fiction' Seriously: Stanislaw Lem's Philosophy of Technology." *Research in Philosophy and Technology* 15 (1995).

Grey, Paul. "Sci-Phi." *Time* (17 September 1984): 87–90.

Guffey, George R. "The Unconscious, Fantasy, and Science Fiction: Transformations in Bradbury's *Martian Chronicles* and Lem's *Solaris*." In *Bridges to Fantasy*, eds. George E. Slusser et al. Carbondale, IL: Southern Illinois University Press, 1982.

- "Noise, Information, and Statistics in Stanislaw Lem's *The Investigation*." In *Hard Science Fiction*, eds. George E. Slusser and Eric S. Rabkin. Carbondale, IL: Southern Illinois University Press, 1986.

Gunn, James. "On the Lem Affair." *Science–Fiction Studies* 4 (1977): 314–16.

Hayles, N. Katherine. "Space for Writing: Stanislaw Lem and the Dialectic 'That Guides My Pen.'" *Science-Fiction Studies* 13 (November 1986): 292–312.

- "Chaos and Dialectic: Stanislaw Lem and the Space of Writing." *Chaos Bound: Orderly Disorder in Contemporary Literature and Science.* Ithaca, NY: Cornell, 1990.

Helford, Elyce Rae. "'We Are Only Seeking Man': Gender, Psychoanalysis, and Stanislaw Lem's *Solaris*." *Science–Fiction Studies* 19 (July 1992): 167–77.

Hofstadter, Douglas R., and Daniel C. Dennett. "Reflections." *The Mind's I: Fantasies and Reflections on Self and Soul.* New York: Basic, 1981.

Jarzebski, Jerzy. "Stanislaw Lem, Rationalist and Visionary." Trans. Franz Rottensteiner. *Science–Fiction Studies* 4 (1977): 110–25.

- "Stanislaw Lem's Star Diaries." Trans. Franz Rottensteiner and Istvan Csicsery–Ronay, Jr. *Science–Fiction Studies* 13 (November 1986): 361–73.

- "The World as Code and Labyrinth: Stanislaw Lem's *Memoirs Found in a Bathtub*." Trans. Franz Rottensteiner. In *Science Fiction Roots and Branches: Contemporary Critical Approaches*, eds. Rhys Garnett and R. J. Ellis. New York: St Martin's, 1990.

Jonas, Gerald. "Looking for the Glitch." *New York Times Book Review* 17 (February 1980): 7, 33.

Kandel, Michael A. "Stanislaw Lem on Men and Robots." *Extrapolation* 14 (1972): 13–24.

- "On Translating the Grammatical Wit of S. Lem into English." Unpublished manuscript.
- "Lem in Review (June 2238)." *Science-Fiction Studies* 11 (1977): 65–8.
- "Introduction" to *Mortal Engines* by Stanislaw Lem. Trans. Michael Kandel. New York: Avon, 1982.
- "A Portrait of the Artist as a Thing Antedeluvian." *The Cosmic Carnival of Stanislaw Lem.* New York: Continuum, 1981.
- "Two Meditations on Stanislaw Lem." *Science–Fiction Studies* 13 (November 1986): 374–81.
Ketterer, David. "*Solaris* and the Illegitimate Suns of Science Fiction." *Extrapolation* 14 (1972): 73–89.
Kratz, Dennis. "Heroism in Science Fiction: Two Opposing Views." *Riverside Quarterly* 30 (1988): 81–8.
Lavery, David L. "'The Genius of the Sea': Wallace Stevens' 'The Idea of Order at Key West,' Stanislaw Lem's *Solaris,* and the Earth as a Muse." *Extrapolation* 21 (1980): 101–5.
Le Guin, Ursula K. "European SF: Rottensteiner's Anthology, and the Strugatskys, and Lem." *Science–Fiction Studies* 1 (1974): 181–5.
- "Science Fiction and Mrs Brown." In *Science Fiction at Large,* ed. Peter Nicholls. London: Gollancz, 1976.
- "Concerning the 'Lem Affair.'" *Science–Fiction Studies* 4 (1977): 100.
Lewis, Tom. "Review of *The Star Diaries.*" *World Literature Today* 51 (summer 1977): 464–5.
Liro, Joseph. "On Computers, Translation, and Stanislaw Lem." *Computers & Translation* 2 (April/June 1987): 89–104.
Livingston, Paisley. "Science, Reason, and Society." *Literature and Rationality: Ideas of Agency in Theory and Fiction.* Cambridge: Cambridge University Press, 1991.
- "From Virtual Reality to Phantomatics and Back." Unpublished manuscript.
Louis, Jean Paul. "Science–fiction et metaphysique de Stanislaw Lem." *Esprit* 150 (1989): 46–51.
Lyau, Bradford. "Knowing the Unknown: Heinlein, Lem, and the Future." In *Storm Warnings: Science Fiction Confronts the Future,* ed. Goerge E. Slusser et al. Carbondale, IL: Southern Illinois University Press, 1987.
Mabee, Barbara. "Astronauts, Angels, and Time Machines: The Fantastic in Recent German Democratic Republic Literature." In *The Celebration of the Fantastic: Selected Papers from the Tenth Anniversary International Conference on the Fantastic in the Arts,* eds. Donald E. Morse et al. Westport, CT: Greenwood, 1992. 221–35.
Malekin, Peter. "The Self, the Referent, and the Real in Science Fiction and the Fantastic: Lem, Pynchon, Kubin, and Delany." In *Contours of the Fantastic: Selected Essays from the Eighth International Conference on the Fantastic in the Arts,* ed. Michele K. Langford. New York: Greenwood, 1994. 29–36.
Malmgren, Carl D. "Towards a Definition of Science Fantasy." *Science–Fiction Studies* 15 (November 1988): 259–81.

– "Self and Other in SF: Alien Encounters." *Science–Fiction Studies* 20 (March 1993): 15–33.

Martin, George R. "Review of *Return from the Stars.*" *Book World* (22 June 1980): 7.

Meesdom, Tony. "The Gods Must Be Crazy: On the Utility of Playful Chaos in the Universe of Stanislaw Lem." In *Just the Other Day: Essays on the Future of the Future*, ed. Luk de Vos. Antwerp: EXA, 1985.

Miller, Edmund. "Stanislaw Lem and John Dickson Carr: Critics of the Scientific World–View." *Armchair Detective* 14 (1981): 341–43.

Mullen, R. D. "I Could Not Love Thee Dear, So Much." *Science–Fiction Studies* 4 (1977): 143–4.

Murphy, Patrick D. "The Realities of Unreal Worlds: King's *The Dead Zone*, Schmidt's *Kensho*, and Lem's *Solaris.*" In *Spectrum of the Fantastic*, ed. Donald Palumbo. Westport, CT: Greenwood, 1988.

Oates, Joyce Carol. "Post-Borgesian." *New York Times Book Review* 11 (February 1979): 7, 40.

Occiogrosso, Frank. "Threats of Rationalism: John Fowles, Stanislaw Lem, and the Detective Story." *Armchair Detective* 13 (1980): 4–7.

Offutt, Andrew. "How It Happened: One Bad Decision Leading to Another." *Science–Fiction Studies* 4 (1977): 138–43.

Parker, Jo Alyson. "Gendering the Robot: Stanislaw Lem's 'The Mask.'" *Science-Fiction Studies* 19 (July 1992): 178–91.

Philmus, Robert M. "The Cybernetic Paradigms of Stanislaw Lem." In *Hard Science-Fiction*, eds. George E. Slusser and Eric Rabkin. Carbondale, IL: Southern Illinois University Press, 1986.

– "*Futurological Congress* as Metageneric Text." *Science-Fiction Studies* 13 (November 1986): 313–28.

Potts, Stephen W. "Fiction: *A Perfect Vacuum.*" *Science Fiction & Fantasy Book Review* 1 (1979): 60.

– "Dialogues Concerning Human Understanding: Empirical Views of God from Locke to Lem." In *Bridges to Science Fiction*, eds. George E. Slusser et al. Carbondale: Southern Illinois University Press, 1980.

Purcell, Mark. "Lem in English and French. A Checklist." *Luna Monthly* (June 1972): 11.

– "Tarkovsky's Film *Solaris* (1972): A Freudian Slip?" *Extrapolation* 19 (1978): 126–31.

Rodnianskaia, Irina. "Two Faces of Stanislaw Lem: On *His Master's Voice.*" Trans. Nadia Peterson. *Science–Fiction Studies* 13 (November 1986): 352–60.

Rose, Mark. *Alien Encounters. Anatomy of Science Fiction.* Cambridge, MA: Harvard University Press, 1981.

– "Filling the Void: Verne, Wells, and Lem." *Science–Fiction Studies* 8 (1981): 121–42.

Rothfork, John. "Cybernetics and a Humanistic Fiction: Stanislaw Lem's *The Cyberiad.*" *Research Studies* 45 (1977): 123–33.

– "Having Everything Is Having Nothing: Stanislaw Lem vs. Utilitarianism." *Southwest Review* 66 (1981): 293–306.

- *"Memoirs Found in a Bathtub:* Stanislaw Lem's Critique of Cybernetics." *Mosaic* 17 (1984): 53–71.
- "The Ghost in the Machine: Stanislaw Lem's *Mortal Engines." Liberal and Fine Arts Review* 4 (1984): 1–18.

Rottensteiner, Franz. "Stanislaw Lem: A Profile." *Luna Monthly* (December 1971): 6.

Sargent, Pamela. "A Suggestion." *Science–Fiction Studies* 5 (1978): 84.

Sargent, Pamela, and George Zebrowski. "How It Happened: A Chronology of the 'Lem Affair.'" *Science–Fiction Studies* 4 (1977): 129–37.

Say, Donald. "An Interview with Stanislaw Lem." *Science Fiction Review* 3 (1974): 4–15.

Scarborough, John. "Stanislaw Lem." In *Science Fiction Writers*, ed. E. F. Bleiler. New York: Charles Scribner's Sons, 1982.

Scholes, Robert. "Lem's Fantastic Attack on Todorov." *Science–Fiction Studies* 2 (1975): 166–7.
- *Structural Fabulation: An Essay on Fiction of the Future.* Notre Dame, IN: Notre Dame University Press, 1975.

Scholes, Robert, and Eric S. Rabkin. *Science Fiction: History, Science, Vision.* London: Oxford, 1977.

Schwab, Gabriele. "Cyborgs and Cybernetic Intertexts: On Postmodern Phantasms of Body and Mind." In *Intertextuality and Contemporary American Fiction*, eds. Patrick O'Donnell and Robert Davis. Baltimore, MD: Johns Hopkins University Press, 1989.

Science-Fiction Studies 40 (1986). Special Lem issue.

Science–Fiction Studies 57 (1992). Special Lem issue.

Simonetta, Salvestroni. "The Science–Fiction Films of Andrei Tarkovsky." Trans. Robert M. Philmus. *Science–Fiction Studies* 14 (1987): 294–306.

Sire, James W. "Truths Too Bitter for This World." *Christianity Today* 20 (1978): 34–7.

Slusser, George E. "Structures of Apprehension: Lem, Heinlein and the Strugatskys." *Science–Fiction Studies* 16 (1989 March): 1–37.

Solotaroff, Theodore. *New York Times Book Review* (29 September 1976): 1.
- "Stanislaw Lem and the SFWA." *Science–Fiction Studies* 4 (1977): 126–44.
- "A History of Science Fiction and More." *New York Times Book Review* (29 August 1979): 1, 14–18.

Steiner, T. R. "Stanislaw Lem's Detective Stories: A Genre Extended." *Modern Fiction Studies* 29 (1983): 451–62.

Stoff, Andrzej. *Lem i inni: szkice o Polskiej science fiction* [Lem and Others: Sketches on Polish Science Fiction]. Bydgoszcz: Pomorze, 1990.

Suvin, Darko. "The Open–Ended Parables of Stanislaw Lem and *Solaris." Afterword. Solaris.* Trans. from the French by Joanna Kilmartin and Steve Cox. New York: Walker, 1970.
- "A First Comment on Ms. Le Guin's Note on the 'Lem Affair.'" *Science–Fiction Studies* 4 (1977): 100.
- "What Lem Actually Wrote: A Philologico–Ideological Note." *Science–Fiction Studies* 5 (1978): 85–7.

– "Three World Paradigms for sf: Asimov, Yefremov, Lem." *Pacific Quarterly* 4 (1979): 271–83.
– "The Social Consciousness of Science Fiction: Anglophone, Russian, and Mitteleuropean." *Proceedings of the Seventh Congress of the International Association of Comparative Literature*, ed. M. Dimic. Stuttgart: Bieber, 1979.

Swirski, Peter. "A Literary Monument Revisited: Davis' *Stanislaw Lem* and Seven Polish Books on Lem." *Science-Fiction Studies* 58 (1992): 411–17.
– "Playing a Game of Ontology: A Postmodern Reading of *The Futurological Congress*." *Extrapolation* 33 (1992): 32–41.
– "Of Games with the Universe: Preconceptions of Science in Stanislaw Lem's *The Invincible*." *Contemporary Literature* 35 (1994): 324–42.
– "Game Theory in the Third Pentagon: A Study in Strategy and Rationality." *Criticism* 38 (1996): 303–30.

A Stanislaw Lem Reader. Evanston, IL: Northwestern University Press, 1997.
– "Stanislaw Lem." *Science Fiction Writers*. Revised edition. New York: Scribner's, 1999.
– "Stanislaw Lem: *The Invincible*." *Encyclopedia of Popular Fiction*. Vol. 11. Ed. Kirk Beetz. Osprey, FL: Beacham Publishing, 1998. 5745–52.
– "Stanislaw Lem: *The Chain of Chance*." *Encyclopedia of Popular Fiction*. Vol. 11. Ed. Kirk Beetz. Osprey, FL: Beacham Publishing, 1998. 5267–76.
– "Stanislaw Lem: *Fiasco*." *Encyclopedia of Popular Fiction*. Vol. 12. Ed. Kirk Beetz. Osprey, FL: Beacham Publishing, 1998. 5491–5500.

Szpakowska, Malgorzata. "A Writer in No-Man's-Land." *Polish Perspectives* 10 (1971): 29–37

Theall, Donald F. "On sf as Symbolic Communication." *Science-Fiction Studies* 7 (1980): 253, 256–61.

Thomsen, Christian W. "Robot Ethics and Robot Parody: Remarks on Isaac Asimov's *I, Robot* and Some Critical Essays and Short Stories by Stanislaw Lem." In *The Mechanical God: Machines in Science Fiction*, eds. Thomas P. Dunn et al. Westport, CT: Greenwood, 1982.

Tierney, John. "A Mundane Master of Cosmic Visions." *Discover* (December 1986): 55–66.

Tighe, Carl. "Kozmik Kommie Konflikts: Stanislaw Lem's *Solaris*: An Eastern Block Parable." In *Science Fiction, Social Conflict and War*, ed. Philip John Davies. Manchester: Manchester University Press, 1990.

Updike, John. "Lem and Pym." *New Yorker* (26 February 1979): 115–21.
– "Review of *Return from the Stars*." *New Yorker* (8 September 1980): 106–11.

Vonnegut, Kurt. "Only Kidding, Folks?" *The Nation* (13 May 1978): 575.

Weinstone, Ann. "Resisting Monsters: Notes on *Solaris*." *Science–Fiction Studies* 21 (July 1994): 173–90.

Weissert, Thomas P. "Stanislaw Lem and a Topology of Mind." *Science–Fiction Studies* 19 (July 1992): 161–6.

Wilson, Reuel K. "Stanislaw Lem's Fiction and the Comic Absurd." *World Literature Today* 51 (1977): 549–53.

Wood, Michael. "Review of *Mortal Engines*." *New York Review of Books* (12 May 1977):
36–7.

Yossef, Abraham. "Understanding Lem: *Solaris* Revisited." *Foundation* 46 (1989): 51–8.

Ziegfeld, Richard E. *Stanislaw Lem*. New York: Ungar, 1985.

Ziembiecki, Andrzej. "' ... Knowing Is the Hero Of My Books ...'" *Polish Perspectives*
9 (1979): 64–9.

Zivkovic, Zoran. "The Future without a Future: An Interview with Stanislaw Lem."
Pacific Quarterly 4 (1979): 255–9.

SCIENCE, PHILOSOPHY OF SCIENCE

Barrow, John D. *The World within the World*. Oxford: Oxford University Press, 1990.

– *Theories of Everything*. New York: Fawcett Columbine, 1991.

Barrow, John D., and Frank J. Tipler. *The Anthropic Cosmological Principle*. Oxford:
Clarendon, 1986.

Boyd, Richard N. "On the Current Status of the Issue of Scientific Realism." *Erkentnis*
19 (1983): 45–90.

Bunge, Mario. *Causality and Modern Science*. Cambridge, MA: Harvard University
Press, 1959.

Caspar, Max. *Kepler*. London: Abelard-Schuman, 1959.

Chalmers, Alan. *Science and Its Fabrication*. Minneapolis, MN: University of Minnesota Press, 1991.

Chapelon, Jacques. "Mathematics and Social Change." In *Great Currents of Mathematical Thought*. Vol. 2, *Mathematics in the Arts and the Sciences*, ed. F. Le Lionnais.
Trans. Charles Pinter and Helen Kline. New York: Dover, 1971.

Cohen, Jack, and Ian Stewart. *The Collapse of Chaos*. New York: Viking, 1994.

Crews, Frederick. *Out of My System: Psychoanalysis, Ideology and Critical Method*.
New York: Oxford University Press, 1975.

Cunningham, Frank. *Objectivity in Social Science*. Toronto: University of Toronto
Press, 1973.

Daniels, George H. *American Science in the Age of Jackson*. New York: Columbia
University Press, 1968.

Davenport, Edward. "The Scientific Spirit." *Literary Theory's Future(s)*, ed. Joseph
Natoli. Urbana, IL: University of Illinois Press, 1989.

– "The Devils of Positivism." *Literature and Science: Theory and Practice*. Ed. Stewart
Peterfreund. Boston: Northeastern University Press, 1990.

Davies, Paul. *Superforce*. New York: Simon & Schuster, 1984.

Davies, Paul, and Julian Brown, eds. *Superstrings: A Theory of Everything?* Cambridge:
Cambridge University Press, 1988.

DeWitt, Bryce S, and Neill Graham, eds. *The Many-Worlds Interpretation of Quantum
Mechanics*. Princeton, NJ: Princeton University Press, 1973.

Eddington, Paul. *The Expanding Universe*. New York: Macmillan, 1933.

Edwards, Tony. "The Red Planet." In *Horizon: At the Edge of the Universe*, ed. Simon
Campbell-Jones. London: Ariel, 1983.

Einstein, Albert. *Ideas and Opinions by Albert Einstein.* New York: Bonanza, 1954.
- *The World As I See It.* New York: Covici Friede, 1934.
Esterson, Allen. *Seductive Mirage: An Exploration of the Work of Sigmund Freud.* Chicago: Open Court, 1993.
Gardner, Martin. *Fads and Fallacies in the Name of Science.* New York: Dover, 1957.
Grünbaum, Adolf. *Validation in the Clinical Theory of Psychoanalysis: a Study in the Philosophy of Psychoanalysis.* Madison, CN: International Universities Press, 1993.
Haack, Susan. *Evidence and Inquiry: Towards Reconstruction in Epistemology.* Oxford: Blackwell, 1993.
Hacking, Ian. *Representing and Intervening: Introductory Topics in the Philosophy of Science.* Cambridge: Cambridge University Press, 1983.
Hawking, Stephen W. *A Brief History of Time.* New York: Bantam, 1988.
Hempel, Carl. *Aspects of Scientific Explanation.* New York: Free Press, 1965.
- *Philosophy of Natural Science.* Englewood Cliffs, NJ: Prentice-Hall, 1966.
Hofstadter, Douglas R. *Gödel, Escher, Bach.* New York: Basic, 1979.
- *Metamagical Themas: Questing for the Essence of Mind and Pattern.* New York, Basic Books, 1985.
Horowitz, Tamara, and Gerald J. Massey. *Thought Experiments in Science and Philosophy.* Savage, MD: Rowman and Littlefield, 1991.
Jauch, Joseph M. *Are Quanta Real? A Galilean Dialogue.* Bloomington, IN: Indiana University Press, 1973.
Kemeny, John G. "Mathematics." *A Philosopher Looks at Science.* New York: Van Nostrand Reinhold, 1959.
Kerr, John. *A Most Dangerous Method: The Story of Jung, Freud, and Sabina Spielrein.* New York: Knopf, 1993.
Koestler, Arthur. *The Watershed: A Biography of Johannes Kepler.* New York: Anchor, 1960.
Kovalevsky, Jean. "Kepler's Laws and Modern Celestial Mechanics." *Kepler: Four Hundred Years,* eds. Arthur Beer and Peter Beer. Oxford: Pergamon, 1975.
Kuhn, Thomas. *The Structure of Scientific Revolutions.* Chicago: University of Chicago Press, 1970.
Lakoff, Robin Tolmach, and James C. Coyne. *Father Knows Best: the Use and Abuse of Power in Freud's Case of 'Dora.'* New York: Teachers College Press, 1993.
Le Lionnais, F. *Great Currents of Mathematical Thought.* Trans. Charles Pinter and Helen Kline. New York: Dover, 1971.
Levine, George. "What Might Scientists and Humanists Share?" *Decodings: The Newsletter of the Society for Literature and Science* 4 (spring 1995): 3–4.
Mill, John Stuart. *A System of Logic, Ratiocinative and Inductive: Being a Connected View of the Principles of Evidence and the Methods of Scienctific Investigation,* ed. J. M. Robson. Toronto: University of Toronto Press, 1978.
Miller, Richard W. *Fact and Method: Explanation, Confirmation and Reality in the Natural and the Social Sciences.* Princeton, NJ: Princeton University Press, 1987.
Pierssens, Michel. *Savoirs à l'œuvre: essais d'epistemocritique.* Lille: Presses Universitaires de Lille, 1990.

Popper, Karl. "Metaphysics and Criticizability." In *Popper: Selections*, ed. David Miller. Princeton, NJ: Princeton University Press, 1985.

Sagan, Carl. *Broca's Brain: Reflections on the Romance of Science.* New York: Ballentine, 1980.

– *Cosmos.* New York: Ballantine, 1980.

Shope, Robert K. *The Analysis of Knowing: A Decade of Research.* Princeton, NJ: Princeton University Press, 1983.

Sorensen, Roy A. *Thought Experiments.* New York: Oxford University Press, 1992.

Stockman, Norman. *Anti-Positivist Theories of the Sciences: Critical Rationalism, Critical Theory, and Scientific Realism.* Dordrecht: Reidel, 1983.

Sulloway, Frank J. *Freud, Biologist of the Mind: Beyond the Psychoanalytic Legend.* New York: Basic, 1979.

Wiener, Norbert. *The Human Use of Human Beings.* Boston: Houghton Mifflin, 1950.

Zemansky, Mark W., and Richard H. Dittman. *Heat and Thermodynamics.* New York: McGraw-Hill, 1981.

GAME THEORY

Balinski, M. L., and H. P. Young. "A New Method for Congressional Appointment." *American Mathematical Monthly* 82 (1975): 701–30.

Banzhaf, John F., III. "Weighted Voting Doesn't Work: A Mathematical Analysis." *Rutgers Law Review* 19 (1965): 317–43.

Bartoszynski, R., and M. Puri. "Some Remarks on Strategy in Playing Tennis." *Behavioral Science* 26 (1981): 379–87.

Bell, Robert I., and John Coplans. *Decisions, Decisions: Game Theory and You.* New York: Norton, 1976.

Brams, Steven, J. *Paradoxes in Politics.* New York: Free Press, 1976.

– *Rational Politics: Decisions, Games, and Strategy.* Boston: Academic, 1985.

– "Theory of Moves." *American Scientist* 81 (1993): 562–70.

Brams, Steven J., and Alan Taylor. *Fair Division: From Cake-Cutting to Dispute Resolution.* New York: Cambridge University Press, 1996.

Cassady, Ralph, Jr. "Taxicab Rate War: Counterpart of International Conflict." *Journal of Conflict Resolution* 1 (1957): 364–8.

Davis, Morton D. *Game Theory: A Nontechnical Introduction.* Revised edition. New York: Basic Books, 1983.

– *The Art of Decision-Making.* New York: Springer-Verlag, 1986.

Dixit, Avinash K., and Barry J. Nalebuff. *Thinking Strategically: The Competitive Edge in Business, Politics, and Everyday Life.* New York: Norton, 1991.

Geanakoplos, John, Dadid Pearce, and Ennio Stacchetti. "Psychological Games and Sequential Reality." *Games and Economic Behavior* 1 (1989): 60–79.

Gilboa, Ishak, and David Schmeidler. "Information Dependent Games: Can Common Sense Be Common Knowledge?" *Economics Letters* 4 (1988): 215–22.

Harsanyi, John C. "On the Rationality Postulates Underlying the Theory of Cooperative Games." *Journal of Conflict Resolution* 5 (1961): 179–96.

Harsanyi, John C., and Reinhard Selten. *A General Theory of Equilibrium Selection in Games.* Cambridge, MA: MIT Press, 1988.

– *Rational Behaviour and Bargaining Equilibrium in Games and Social Situations.* Cambridge: Cambridge University Press, 1977.

Heap, Shaun Hargreaves, et al. *The Theory of Choice: A Critical Guide.* Cambridge, MA: Blackwell, 1992.

"Logic and the Epistemic Foundations of Game Theory." Special issue of *Theory and Decision* 37 (1994).

Lucas, William F. "A Game with No Solution." *Bulletin of the American Mathematical Society* 74 (1968): 237–9.

Luce, R. Duncan, and Howard Raiffa. *Games and Decisions: Introduction and Critical Survey.* New York: Wiley, 1957.

Moglower, Sidney. "A Game Theory Model for Agricultural Crop Selection." *Econometrica* 30 (1962): 253–66.

Poundstone, William. *Prisoner's Dilemma.* New York: Anchor, 1992.

Ramamurthy, K. G. *Coherent Structures and Simple Games.* Dordrecht and Boston: Kluwer, 1990.

Rapoport, Amnon. *Experimental Studies of Interactive Decisions.* Dordrecht and Boston: Kluwer, 1990.

Rapoport, Anatol. *Fights, Games, and Debates.* Ann Arbor, MI: University of Michigan Press, 1960.

– "The Use and Misuse of Game Theory." *Scientific American* 207 (1962): 108–18.

– *Two Person Game Theory: The Essential Idea.* Ann Arbor: University of Michigan Press, 1964.

– *N-Person Game Theory: Concepts and Applications.* Ann Arbor, MI: University of Michigan Press, 1970.

– *The 2x2 Game.* Ann Arbor: University of Michigan Press, 1976.

–*Decision Theory and Decision Behaviour: Normative and Descriptive Approaches.* Dordrecht and Boston: Kluwer, 1989.

Rapoport, Anatol, and Albert M. Chammah. *Prisoner's Dilemma: A Study In Conflict and Cooperation.* Ann Arbor: University of Michigan Press, 1965.

Rasmusen Eric. *Games and Information: An Introduction to Game Theory.* Oxford: Blackwell, 1989.

Schellenberg, James A. *Primitive Games.* Boulder, CO: Westview, 1990.

Schelling, Thomas C. *The Strategy of Conflict.* Cambridge, MA: Harvard University Press, 1960.

Selten, Reinhard. *Models of Strategic Rationality.* Dordrecht and Boston: Kluwer, 1987.

Shubik, Martin. *Game Theory and Related Approaches to Social Behaviour: Selections.* New York: Wiley, 1964.

– *The Uses and Methods of Gaming.* New York: Elsevier, 1975.

– *Game Theory in the Social Sciences: Concepts and Solutions.* Cambridge, MA: MIT Press, 1982.

Singleton, Robert R., and William F. Tyndall. *Games and Programs: Mathematics for Modelling.* San Francisco: W.H. Freeman, 1974.

Smith, John Maynard. *Evolution and the Theory of Games.* Cambridge: Cambridge University Press, 1982.

Smith, John Maynard, and G.A. Parker. "The Logic of Assymetric Contests." *Animal Behavior* 24 (1976): 159–75.

Varoufakis, Yanis. *Rational Conflict.* Oxford: Blackwell, 1991.

Von Neumann, John, and Oskar Morgenstern. *Theory of Games and Economic Behavior.* Princeton, NJ: Princeton University Press, 1953.

Williams, J. D. *The Compleat Strategyst: Being a Primer on the Theory of Games and Strategy.* New York: McGraw, 1966.

Zagare, Frank. *Game Theory: Concepts and Applications.* Beverly Hills, CA: Sage, 1984.

GAMING AND GAME THEORY IN LITERATURE

Bayley, John. "Formalist Games and Real Life." *Essays in Criticism* 31 (1981): 271–81.

Bell, Pearl K. "Games Writers Play." *Commentary* 71 (1981): 69–73.

Bleich, David. "Intersubjective Reading." *New Literary History* 17 (1986): 401–21.

Brams, Steven J. *Biblical Games.* Cambridge: MIT Press, 1980.

– *Superior Beings: If They Exist, How Would We Know?* New York: Springer-Verlag, 1983.

– "Game Theory and Literature." *Games and Economic Behavior* 6 (1994): 32–54.

– *Theory of Moves.* Cambridge: Cambridge University Press, 1994.

Bruss, Elizabeth W. "The Game of Literature and Some Literary Games." *New Literary History* 9 (1977): 153–72.

Chambers, Ross. "Rules and Moves." *Canadian Review of Comparative Literature* 19 (1992): 95–100.

Davey, Lynda A. "Communication and the Game of Theatre." *Poetics* 13 (1984): 5–15.

De Ley, Herbert. "The Name of the Game: Applying Game Theory in Literature." *SubStance* 55 (1988): 33–46.

– "Montchretien's Aman and Racine's Esther: Toward a Game–Theory Definition of French Classicism." In *Rethinking Classicism: Overviews,* ed. David Lee Rubin. New York: AMS, 1989.

Dziechcinska, Hanna. "Les Mascarades dans la vie et dans la litterature." In *Les Jeux à la Renaissance,* eds. Philippe Aries and Jean Claude Margolin. Paris: Vrin, 1982.

Ehrman, Jacques, ed. *Game, Play, Literature.* New Haven, CT: Eastern, 1968.

Foust, R. E. "Poetics, Play, and Literary Fantasy." *New Orleans Review* 9 (1982): 40–4.

Hintikka, Jaakko. "Sherlock Holmes Formalized." In *The Sign of Three: Dupin, Holmes, Peirce,* eds. Umberto Eco and Thomas A. Sebeok. Bloomington, IN: Indiana University Press, 1983.

Hoeveler, Diane Long. "Game Theory and Ellison's *King of the Bingo Game.*" *Journal of American Culture* 15 (1992): 39–42.

Howard, Nigel. *Paradoxes of Rationality: Theory of Metagames and Political Behaviour.* Cambridge, MA: MIT Press, 1971.

– "The Plot of Dr Zhivago." *CONAN Newsletter* 2 (1988): 2–4.

Lanham, Richard A. "Games, Play, Seriousness." *Tristram Shandy and the Games of Pleasure.* Berkeley and Los Angeles: University of California Press, 1973.

Marcus, Solomon. "Editorial Note." *Poetics* 6 (1977): 203–7.

O'Neill, Barry. "The Strategy of Challenges: Two Beheading Games In Medieval Literature." In *Game Equilibrium Models*, ed. Reinhard Selten. Berlin: Springer-Verlag, 1991.

Pavel, Thomas. *The Poetics of Plot.* Minneapolis, MN: University of Minnesota Press, 1985.

Pedoto, Constance A. "Game Playing in the Fictions of Italo Calvino." *Italian Quarterly* 30 (1989): 43–53, 115–16.

Plimpton, George. "The Smaller the Ball, the Better the Book: A Game Theory of Literature." *New York Times Book Review* 31 May 1992: 16, 18.

Riker, William. *The Art of Political Manipulation.* New Haven, CT: Yale University Press, 1986.

Ross, Charles. *Richard III.* Berkeley: University of California Press, 1981.

Schelling, Thomas C. *Arms and Influence.* New Haven, CT: Yale University Press, 1966.

Steriadi-Bogdan, Mariana. "The Evolution of Plot and Problems of Strategy in a Detective Play." *Poetics* 6 (1977): 375–82.

Swirski, Peter. "The Role of Game Theory in Literary Studies." In *Empirical Approaches to Literature. Proceedings of the Fourth Biannual Conference of the International Society for the Empirical Study of Literature – IGEL*, ed. Gebhard Rusch. Siegen: LUMIS Publications, 1995. 37–43.

Vorob'ev, Nikolai. "Khydozhestvennoe Modelirovanie Konflikty i Teoria Igr" (Literary Conflict Modelling and the Theory of Games). In *Sodruzhestvo Nauk i Tainy Tvorchestva* (The Close Relationship of the Sciences and the Secrets of Artistic Creation). Moscow: Izkustvo, 1968.

Wilson, Robert Rawdon. "Godgames and Labyrinths: The Logic of Entrapment." *Mosaic* 15 (1982): 1–22.

–, ed. "Game and the Theories of Game." Special issue of *Canadian Review of Comparative Literature* 12 (1985).

PHILOSOPHY, LITERARY THEORY, LINGUISTICS, CRITICISM

Altieri, Charles. *Act and Quality: A Theory of Literary Meaning and Humanistic Understanding.* Brighton, England: Harvester, 1981.

Argyros, Alex. "Narrative and Chaos." *New Literary History* 23 (1992): 659–73.

Austin, J.L. *How to Do Things with Words.* 2d ed. New York: Oxford University Press, 1975.

Bach, Kent, and Robert M. Harnish. *Linguistic Communication and Speech Acts.* Cambridge, MA: MIT Press, 1979.

Barthes, Roland. "The Death of the Author." *Image/Music/Text.* New York: Hill and Wang, 1977.

– "De l'œuvre au texte." *La Revue d'esthétique* 3 (1971): 225–32. Trans. in *Textual Strategies: Perspectives in Post-Structuralist Criticism*, ed. Josué V. Harari. Ithaca, NY: Cornell University Press, 1979.

Baudrillard, Jean. *De la séduction.* Paris: Galilée, 1979.

- *Simulacres et simulation.* Paris: Galilée, 1981.

Beardsley, Monroe C. *Aesthetics: Problems in the Philosophy of Criticism.* New York: Harcourt, 1958.

Beaugrande, R. de, and W. Dressler. *Introduction to Text Linguistics.* London: Longman, 1981.

Bell, David F. *Models of Power: Politics and Economics in Zola's Rougon-Macquart.* Lincoln, NE: University of Nebraska Press, 1988.

- "Simulacra, or, Vicissitudes of the Imprecise." In *After Poststructuralism: Interdiscipinarity and Literary Theory,* ed. Nancy Easterlin and Barbara Riebling. Evanston, IL: Northwestern University Press, 1993.

Blanchot, Maurice. *L'Espace littéraire.* Paris: Gallimard, 1968.

Barradori, Giovanna, ed. *The American Philosopher: Conversations with Quine, Davidson, Putnam, Nozick, Danto, Rorty, Cavell, MacIntyre, and Kuhn.* Trans. Rosanna Crocitto. Chicago: University of Chicago Press, 1994.

Bratman, Michael E. *Intention, Plans, and Practical Reason.* Cambridge, MA: Harvard University Press, 1987.

- "What Is Intention?" In *Intentions in Communication,* ed. Philip R. Cohen et al. Cambridge, MA: MIT Press, 1990.

Brentano, Franz. *Psychology from an Empirical Standpoint,* ed. Linda L. Mcalister. New York: Humanities Press, 1973.

Brown, G., and G. Yule. *Discourse Analysis.* Cambridge: Cambridge University Press, 1983.

Bruce, Donald, and Anthony Purdy. *Literature and Science.* Atlanta, GA: Rodopi, 1994.

Carroll, Joseph. "Poststructuralism, Cultural Constructivism, and Evolutionary Biology." Unpublished manuscript.

Charolles, M., ed. *Research in Text Connexity and Text Coherence: A Survey.* Hamburg: Buske Verlag, 1986.

Cherniak, Christopher. *Minimal Rationality.* Cambridge, MA: MIT Press, 1986.

Chomsky, Noam. *Language and Politics.* Montreal: Black Rose, 1989.

Cohen, I.B. *Isaac Newton's Papers and Letters on Natural Philosophy and Related Topics.* Cambridge, MA: Harvard University Press, 1958.

Cole, Stephen. *Making Science: Between Nature and Society.* Cambridge: Harvard University Press, 1992.

Conte, M., J.S. Petöfi, and E. Sözer, eds. *Text and Discourse Connectedness.* Amsterdam: John Benjamins, 1989.

Crews, Frederick. "[ ]." In *After Poststructuralism: Interdiscipinarity and Literary Theory,* ed. Nancy Easterlin and Barbara Riebling. Evanston, IL: Nortwestern University Press, 1993.

Davidson, Donald. *Essays on Actions and Events.* Oxford: Clarendon, 1980.

Dijk, T. A. van. *Some Aspects of Text Grammars.* The Hague: Mouton, 1972.

Eisner, Will. *Comics and Sequential Art.* Tamarac, FLA: Poorhouse, 1985.

Elster, Jon. *Sour Grapes: Studies in the Subversion of Rationality.* Cambridge: Cambridge University Press, 1983.

- *Nuts and Bolts for the Social Sciences.* Cambridge, New York: Cambridge University Press.

Emerson, Ralph Waldo. *Essays and Lectures*, ed. Joel Porte. Literary Classics of the United States. New York: : Viking, 1983.

Feyerabend, Paul. "Atoms and Consciousness." *Common Knowledge* 1 (1992): 28–32.

Fish, Stanley. "Biography and Intention." In *Contesting the Subject: Essays in the Postmodern Theory and Practice of Biography and Biographical Criticism*, ed. William H. Epstein. West Lafayette, IN: Purdue University Press, 1991.

Foley, J. M. *Oral Traditional Literature: A Festschrift for Albert Bates Lord*. Columbus, OH: Slavica, 1981.

Foucault, Michel. "What Is an Author?" In *Textual Strategies: Perspectives in Post-Structuralist Criticism*, ed. Josué V. Harari. Ithaca, NY: Cornell University Press, 1979.

Fox, Robin. "Anthropology and the 'Teddy-Bear' Picnic." *Society* (November/December 1992): 47–55.

Gibbs, Nancy. "Can We Still Believe in Miracles?" *Time*. 10 April 1995.

Girard, René. *Deceit, Desire, and the Novel: Self and Other in Literary Structure*. Baltimore, MD: Johns Hopkins University Press, 1965.

Goodman, Nelson, and C. Elgin. "Interpretations and Identity: Can the Work Survive the World?" *Reconceptions in Philosophy*. Indianapolis, IN: Hackett, 1988.

Graesser, Arthur C. *Prose Comprehension beyond the Word*. New York: Springer, 1981.

Graff, Gerald. *Poetic Statement and Critical Dogma*. Chicago: University of Chicago Press, 1980.

Graves Barbara, and Carl H. Frederiksen. "Literary Expertise in the Description of a Fictional Narrative." *Poetics* 20 (1991): 1–26.

Grey, Paul. "The Assault on Freud." *Time*, 29 November 1993.

Grice, H. P. "Meaning." *Philosophical Review* 66 (1957): 377–88.

– "Utterer's Meaning, Sentence Meaning and Word Meaning." *Foundations of Language* 4 (1968): 225–42.

– "Utterer's Meaning and Intentions." *Philosophical Review* 78 (1969): 147–77.

– "Intention and Uncertainty." *Proceedings of the British Academy* 57 (1971): 263–79.

– "Meaning Revisited." In *Mutual Knowledge*, ed. N.V. Smith. New York: Academic, 1982.

Gross, Paul R., and Norman Levitt. *The Higher Superstition: The Academic Left and Its Quarrels with Science*. Baltimore, MD: Johns Hopkins University Press, 1994.

Harding, Sandra. *Sex and Scientific Inquiry*. Chicago: University of Chicago Press, 1987.

Hjort, Mette. *The Strategy of Letters*. Cambridge, MA: Harvard University Press, 1993.

– ed. Rules and Conventions: Literature, Philosophy, Social Theory. Baltimore, MD: Johns Hopkins University Press, 1992.

Hollis, Martin. *The Philosophy of Social Science*. Cambridge: Cambridge University Press, 1994.

Husserl, Edmund. *Ideas: General Introduction to Pure Phenomenology*. Trans. R. Boyce Gibson. London: Collier, 1975.

Ingarden, Roman. *The Cognition of the Literary Work of Art*. Trans. Crowley and Olson. Evanston, IL: Northwestern University Press, 1973.

Iser, Wolfgang. *The Act of Reading: A Theory of Aesthetic Response*. Baltimore, MD: Johns Hopkins University Press, 1978.

Jameson, Fredric. *The Prison-House of Language*. Princeton: Princeton University Press, 1972.

Johnson, Charles. *Philosophy in Literature*. San Francisco: EMText, 1992.

Kernan, Alvin. "Henry Rosovsky. The University: An Owner's Manual." *ADE Bulletin* 100 (winter 1991): 49–53.

Kolakowski, Leszek. *Religion*. New York: Oxford University Press, 1982.

Lang, Candace. "Aberrance in Criticism." *Substance* 12 (1983): 3–16.

Levin, Harry. *Why Literary Criticism Is Not an Exact Science*. Cambridge, MA: Harvard University Press, 1969.

Levin, Margarita. "Caring New World." *American Scholar* 57 (winter 1988): 100–6.

Levin, Richard. "The New Interdisciplinarity in Literary Criticism." In *After Poststructuralism: Interdiscipinarity and Literary Theory*, ed. Nancy Easterlin and Barbara Riebling. Evanston, IL: Nortwestern University Press, 1993.

– "Negative Evidence." *Studies in Philology* 42 (fall 1995): 383–410.

Lewis, David. *Convention: A Philosophical Study*. Cambridge, MA: Harvard University Press, 1969.

– "Truth In Fiction." In *Philosophical Papers*. Vol 1. Oxford: Oxford University Press, 1983.

– *Counterfactuals*. Oxford: Blackwell, 1986.

Limon, John. *The Place of Fiction in the Time of Science*. Cambridge: Cambridge University Press, 1990.

Livingston, Paisley. *Literary Knowledge: Humanistic Inquiry and the Philosophy of Science*. Ithaca, NY: Cornell University Press, 1988.

– "Literary Studies and the Sciences." *Modern Language Studies* 20 (1990): 15–31.

– *Literature and Rationality: Ideas of Agency in Theory and Fiction*. Cambridge: Cambridge University Press, 1991.

– "Literature and Knowledge." In *A Companion to Epistemology*, ed. Jonathan Dancey and Ernest Sosa. Blackwell, 1992.

– *Models of Desire: René Girard and the Psychology of Mimesis*. Baltimore, MD: Johns Hopkins University Press, 1992.

– "Convention and Literary Explanations." In *Rules and Conventions: Literature, Philosophy, Social Theory*, ed. Mette Hjort. Baltimore, MD: Johns Hopkins University Press, 1992.

Lord, A. B. *The Singer of Tales*. Cambridge, MA: Harvard University Press, 1960.

MacDonald, Heather. "The Ascendancy of Theor-ese." *Hudson Review* 45 (1992): 358–65.

Magliano, Joseph, and Arthur C. Braesser. "A Three-Pronged Method for Studying Inference Generation in Literary Text." *Poetics* 20 (1991): 193–232.

McColley, Grant. *Literature and Science: An Anthology from English and American Literature, 1600-1900*. Chicago: Packard, 1940.

Mele, Alfred R. *Springs of Action: Understanding Intentional Behaviour*. New York: Oxford University Press, 1992.

Millikan, Ruth Garrett. "Metaphysical Anti-Realism?" *Mind* 95 (1986): 417–31.

Minogue, Kenneth. "The Goddess That Failed." *National Review* (18 November 1991).

Moser, Paul. *Knowledge and Evidence*. Cambridge: Cambridge University Press, 1989.

Nozick, Robert. *Philosophical Explanations*. Cambridge, MA: Cambridge University Press, 1981.

O'Connor, D. J., ed. *A Critical History of Western Philosophy*. New York: Free Press, 1964.

O'Hear, Anthony. "Science and Art." In *A Companion to Aesthetics*, ed. David Cooper. Blackwell, 1992.

Okpewho, I. *The Epic in Africa: Toward a Poetics of the Oral Performance*. New York: Columbia University Press, 1979.

Ortiz de Montellano, Bernard. "Multicultural Pseudoscience: Spreading Scientific Illiteracy among Minorities: Part I." *Skeptical Inquirer* 16 (1991): 46–50.

– "Magic Melanin: Spreading Scientific Illiteracy among Minorities: Part II." *Skeptical Inquirer* 16 (1992): 163–6.

Parry, M. *The Making of Homeric Verse: The Collected Papers of Milman Parry*, ed. A. Parry. Oxford: Clarendon, 1971.

Peirce, Charles S. *Collected Papers*. Cambridge, MA: Harvard University Press, 1931–5.

Petöfi J., and H. Rieser. *Studies in Text Grammars*. Dordrecht: Reidel, 1973.

Polkinhorne, John. *The Faith of a Physicist*. Princeton, NJ: Princeton University Press, 1994.

Porush, David. *The Soft Machine: Cybernetic Fiction*. New York: Methuen, 1985.

– "Voyage to Eudoxia: The Emergence of a Post-Rational Epistemology in Literature and Science." *SubStance* 71/72 (1993): 38–49.

Rackin, Donald. *Alice's Adventures in Wonderland and Through the Looking Glass: Nonsense, Sense, and Meaning*. Boston: Twayne, 1991.

Rickert, Heinrich. *Kulturwissenschaft und Naturwissenschaft*. Freiburg: J. C. B. Mohr, 1899.

Rudner, Richard. "On Seeing What We Shall See." In *Logic and Art: Essays in Honor of Nelson Goodman*, ed. Richard Rudner and Israel Scheffler. Indianapolis, IN, and New York: Bobbs-Merrill, 1972.

Saul, John Ralston. *Voltaire's Bastards: The Dictatorship of Reason in the West*. Toronto: Penguin, 1992.

Schmidt, Siegfried. "Literary Science as a Science of Argument." *New Literary History* 7 (1975): 467–81.

Schnädelbach, Herbert. *Philosophy in Germany, 1831–1933*. Trans. Eric Matthews. Cambridge: Cambridge University Press, 1984.

Searle, John. *Speech Acts*. New York: Cambridge University Press, 1969.

– "The Logical Status of Fictional Discourse." *New Literary History* 6 (1974–75): 319–32.

– *Intentionality: An Essay in the Philosophy of Mind*. Cambridge: Cambridge University Press, 1983.

Siegel, Harvey. *Relativism Refuted: A Critique of Contemporary Epistemological Relativism*. Dordrecht: Reidel, 1987.

Simon, Herbert A. *Models of Man*. New York: John Wiley, 1957.
– *Reason in Human Affairs*. Stanford, CA: Stanford University Press, 1983.
Snow, C. P. *The Two Cultures and a Second Look*. Cambridge: Cambridge University Press, 1964.
Sorman, Guy. *Les vrais penseurs de notre temps*. Paris: Fayard, 1989.
Sperber, D., and D. Wilson. *Relevance: A Theory of Communication*. Cambridge, MA: Harvard University Press, 1986.
Spiegelman, Art. "A Problem of Taxonomy." Letter, *New York Times* 29 December 1991. In *The Complete Maus*. Computer software, Voyageur Company, 1994. Interactive CD-ROM.
Sprinker, Michael. "The Royal Road: Marxism and the Philosophy of Science." *New Left Review* 191 (1992): 122–44.
Stockman, Norman. *Anti-Positivist Theories of the Sciences: Critical Rationalism, Critical Theory, and Scientific Realism*. Dordrecht: Reidel, 1983.
Strawson, P. F. "Intention and Convention in Speech Acts." *Philosophical Review* 73 (1964): 439–60.
Sutherland, Robert Donald. *Language and Lewis Carroll*. The Hague: Mouton, 1970.
Swirski, Peter. "Playing a Game of Ontology: A Postmodern Reading of *The Futurological Congress*." *Extrapolation* 33 (1992): 32–41.
– "Critical Mass: Mass Literature and Generic Criticism." *Les Problèmes des genres littéraires/Zagadnienia rodzajów literackich* 37 (1994): 97–107.
– "Iser's Theory of Aesthetic Response: A Critique." *Reader* 32 (1994): 1–15.
– "Of Games with the Universe: Preconceptions of Science in Stanislaw Lem's *The Invincible*." *Contemporary Literature* 35 (1994): 325–42.
– "Genres in Action: The Pragmatics of Literary Interpretation." *Orbis Litterarum: International Review of Literary Studies* 52 (1997): 141–56.
– "Literature and Literary Knowledge." *Journal of the Midwest Modern Language Association* 31 (1998): 6–23.
– "The Nature of Literary Fiction: From Carter to Spiegelman." *M/MLA: Journal of the Midwest Modern Language Association*. Forthcoming.
Walsh, Dorothy. *Literature and Knowledge*. Middletown, CN: Wesleyan University Press, 1969.
Westfall, R. S. *Never at Rest: A Biography of Isaac Newton*. Cambridge: Cambridge University Press, 1980.
Wilder, Hugh. "Intentions and the Very Idea of Fiction." *Philosophy and Literature* 12 (1988): 70–9.
Wilson, George M. *The Intentionality of Human Action*. 2d ed., rev. Stanford, CA: Stanford University Press, 1989 (1980).
– "Again Theory: On Speaker's Meaning, Linguistic Meaning, and the Meaning of a Text." In *Rules and Conventions: Literature, Philosophy, Social Theory*, ed. Mette Hjort. Baltimore, MD: Johns Hopkins University Press, 1992.
Witek, Joseph. *Comic Books as History: The Narrative Art of Jack Jackson, Art Spiegelman, and Harvey Pekar*. Jackson, MS: University Press of Mississippi, 1989.

Wittgenstein, Ludwig. *Philosophical Investigations.* Oxford: Blackwell, 1953.
Wolf, Bryan Jay. *Romantic Re-Vision: Culture and Consciousness in Nineteenth Century Painting and Literature.* Chicago: University of Chicago Press, 1982.

AESTHETICS

Alter, Robert. "Mimesis and the Motive for Fiction." In *Motives for Fiction.* Cambridge, MA: Harvard University Press, 1984.
Altieri, Charles. "A Procedural Definition of Literature." In *What is Literature,* ed. Paul Hernadi. Bloomington, IN: Indiana University Press, 1978.
Anderson, James. "Musical Identity." *Journal of Aesthetics and Art Criticism* 40 (1982): 285–91.
Binkley, Timothy. "Piece: Contra-Aesthetics." *Journal of Aesthetics and Art Criticism* 35 (1977): 265–77.
Byrne, Alex. "Truth in Fiction: The Story Continued." *Australasian Journal of Philosophy* 71 (1993): 24–35.
Carroll, Noël. "Art, Intention, and Conversation." In *Interpretation and Intention,* ed. Gary Iseminger. Philadelphia, PA: Temple University Press, 1992.
Currie, Gregory. "Fictional Worlds." *Philosophy and Literature* 11 (1987): 351–2.
- *An Ontology of Art.* New York: St Martin's, 1989.
- *The Nature of Fiction.* Cambridge: Cambridge University Press, 1990.
- "Interpreting Fiction." In *Literary Theory and Philosophy,* eds. R. Freedman and L. Reinhardt. London: Macmillan, 1991.
- "Work and Text." *Mind* 100 (1991): 325–40.
- "Music, Art, and Metaphysics." *Philosophy and Phenomenological Research* 53 (1993): 471–5.
- "Interpretation and Objectivity." *Mind* 102 (1993): 413–28.
Daiches, David. "Literary Evaluation." In *Problems of Literary Evaluation,* ed. L.P. Strelka. *Yearbook of Comparative Criticism.* Vol. 2. University Park, PA, and London: Pennsylvania State University Press, 1969.
Davies, David. "Works, Texts, and Contexts: Goodman on the Literary Artwork." *Canadian Journal of Philosophy* 21 (1991): 331–45.
- "Fictional Truth and Fictional Authors." *British Journal of Aesthetics* 36 (1996): 43–55.
Davies, Stephen. "The Aesthetic Relevance of Authors' and Painters' Intentions." *Journal of Aesthetics and Art Criticism* 41 (1982): 65–76.
- *Definitions of Art.* Ithaca, NY: Cornell University Press, 1991.
Eagleton, Terry. *Literary Theory: an Introduction.* Minneapolis, MI: University of Minnesota Press, 1983.
Feagin, Susan. "Incompatible Interpretations of Art." *Philosophy and Literature* 6 (1982): 133–46.
Goldman, Alvin I. "Interpretation Psychologized." *Mind and Language* 4 (1989): 161–85.
Goodman, Nelson. *Languages of Art: An Approach to a Theory of Symbols.* Indianapolis, IN: Bobbs-Merrill, 1968.
Hamilton, Andy. "An Ontology of Art." *Philosophical Quarterly* 40 (1990): 538–41.

Hernadi, Paul, ed. *What Is Literature*. Bloomington, IN: Indiana University Press, 1978.

Hirsh, E. D. "What Isn't Literature." In *What Is Literature*, ed. Paul Hernadi. Bloomington, IN: Indiana University Press, 1978.

Iseminger, Gary, ed. *Intention and Interpretation*. Philadelphia, PA: Temple University Press, 1992.

Juhl, P. D. *Interpretation*. Princeton, NJ: Princeton University Press, 1980.

Levinson, Jerrold. "What a Musical Work Is." *Journal of Philosophy* 77 (1980): 5–28.

– "Autographic and Allographic Art Revisited." *Philosophical Studies* 38 (1980): 367–83.

– *Music, Art, and Metaphysics: Essays in Philosophical Aesthetics*. Ithaca, NY: Cornell University Press, 1990.

– "Intention and Interpretation: A Last Look." In *Interpretation and Intention*, ed. G. Iseminger. Philadelphia, PA: Temple University Press, 1992.

– "An Ontology of Art." *Philosophy and Phenomenological Research* 52 (1992): 215–21.

Lévi-Strauss, Claude. "Les limites de la notion de structure en ethnologie." In *Sens et usages du terme structure dans les sciences humaines et sociales*, ed. R. Bastide. The Hague, 1962.

Livingston, Paisley. "The Wolves and the Manger: Analytic Aesthetics and the Dogmas of Poststructuralism." *Poetics Today* 13 (1991): 369–86.

– "Texts, Works, and Literature." *Spiel* 11 (1992): 197–210.

– "Characterization and Fictional Truth in the Cinema." In *Post-theory: Reconstructing Film Studies*, ed. David Bordwell and Nöel Carroll. Madison, WI: University of Wisconsin Press, 1995.

Livingston, Paisley, and Alfred Mele. "Intention and Literature." *Stanford French Review* 16 (1992): 173–96.

Morawski, Stefan. *Inquiries into the Fundamentals of Aesthetics*. Cambridge, MA: Cambridge, MIT Press, 1974.

– "What's Wrong with Aesthetics". In *Die Ästhetik, das tägliche Leben und die Künste*. 8. Internationale Kongress für Ästhetik. Bonn: Bouvier, 1984.

Nehamas, Alexander. "What an Author Is." *Journal of Philosophy* 83 (1986): 685–91.

Pavel, Thomas. *Fictional Worlds*. Cambridge, MA: Harvard University Press, 1986.

Peer, Willie van. "But What Is Literature? Toward a Descriptive Definition of Literature." In *Literary Pragmatics*, ed. Roger D. Sell. London: Routledge, 1991.

– "Text." In *The Encyclopedia of Language and Linguistics*. Pergamon, 1993.

Prado, C. G. *Making Believe: Philosophical Reflections on Fiction*. London: Greenwood, 1984.

Pratt, Mary Louise. *Towards a Speech-Act Theory of Literary Discourse*. Bloomington, IN: Indiana University Press, 1977.

Schmidt, Siegfried J. "Conventions and Literary Systems". In *Rules and Conventions: Literature, Philosophy, Social Theory*, ed. Mette Hjort. Baltimore, MD: Johns Hopkins University Press, 1992.

Scholes, Robert. "Towards a Semiotics of Literature." In *What is Literature*, ed. Paul Hernadi. Bloomington, IN: Indiana University Press, 1978.

Schusterman, Richard. "Interpreting with Pragmatist Intentions." In *Interpretation and Intention*, ed. Gary Iseminger. Philadelphia, PA: Temple University Press, 1992.

Sibley, Frank. "Aesthetic Concepts." *Philosophical Review* 68 (1959): 421–50.
– "Aesthetic and Non-Aesthetic." *Philosophical Review* 74 (1965): 135–59.
Slote, Michael A. "The Objectivity of Aesthetic Value Judgements." *Journal of Philosophy* 68 (1971): 821–39.
Stecker, Robert. "Fish's Argument for the Relativity of Interpretive Truth." *The Journal of Aesthetics and Art Criticism* 48 (1990): 223–30.
– "Incompatible Interpretations." *The Journal of Aesthetics and Art Criticism* 50 (1992): 291–8.
– "Pragmatism and Interpretation." *Poetics Today* 14 (1993): 181–91.
– "The Role of Intention and Convention in Interpreting Artworks." *The Southern Journal of Philosophy* 31 (1993): 471–89.
– "Art Interpretation." *The Journal of Aesthetics and Art Criticism* 52 (1994): 193–206.
– "A Definition of Literature." Unpublished manuscript.
Stevenson, C. "Interpretation and Evaluation in Aesthetics." In *Art and Philosophy*, ed. W.E. Kennick. New York: St Martin's, 1964.
Swirski, Peter. "Interpreting Art, Interpreting Literature." *Orbis Litterarum: International Review of Literary Studies.* Forthcoming.
Taine, Hippolyte. *Philosophie de l'art.* Paris: Herman, 1964.
Tolhurst, William E. "On What a Text Is and How It Means." *The British Journal of Aesthetics* 19 (1979): 1–14.
Tolhurst, William E., and Samuel C. Wheeler III. "On Textual Individuation." *Philosophical Studies* 35 (1979): 187–97.
Walton, Kendall. "Categories of Art." *Philosophical Review* 66 (1970): 334–67.
– "Pictures and Make-Believe." *Philosophical Review* 82 (1973): 283–319.
– "How Remote Are Fictional Worlds from the Real World?" *Journal of Aesthetics and Art Criticism* 37 (1978): 11–24.
– "Fiction, Fiction-Making, and Styles of Fictionality." *Philosophy and Literature* 7 (1983): 78–88.
– *Mimesis as Make-Believe: On the Foundations of the Representational Arts.* Cambridge, MA: Harvard University Press, 1990.
Wellek, René. "What is Literature." In *What Is Literature*, ed. Paul Hernadi. Bloomington, IN: Indiana University Press, 1978.
Wimsatt, W., and Monroe Beardsley. "The Intentional Fallacy." *Sewanee Review* 45 (1946): 469–88. Reprinted in W. Wimsatt, *The Verbal Icon.* Lexington, KY: University of Kentucky Press, 1954.
Wollheim, Richard. *Art and Its Objects.* New York: Harper & Row, 1968.
Wolterstorff, Nicholas. "Towards an Ontology of Artworks." *Nous* 9 (1975): 115–42.
– *Works and Worlds of Art.* Oxford: Clarendon, 1980.
Wreen, M. "Once Is Not Enough." *British Journal of Aesthetics* 30 (1990): 149–58.

COMPUTERS

Allen, Robert F. "The Stylo–Statistical Method of Literary Analysis." *Computers and the Humanities* 22 (1988): 1–10.

Anderson, Alan Ross, ed. *Minds and Machines.* Englewood Cliffs, NJ: Prentice-Hall, 1964.

Bernal, J. D. *The Origins of Life.* London: Weidenfeld and Nicholson, 1967.

Berrill, N. J. *Biology in Action.* London: Heinemann, 1967.

Block, Ned. "Troubles with Functionalism." *In Perception and Cognition: Issues in the Foundations of Psychology,* ed. C.W. Savage. Vol. 9. Minneapolis, MN: University of Minnesota Press: 1978. 261–325.

Boden, Margaret. *Artificial Intelligence and Natural Man.* Brighton, England: Harvester, 1977.

Bolton, W. F. "A Poetic Formula in Beowulf and Seven Other Old English Poems: A Computer Study." *Computers and the Humanities* 19 (1985): 167–73.

Bradham, Jo Allen. "Baleful Greetings from Morgan's 'Christmas Card.'" *College Literature* 14 (1987): 49–53.

Briot, M. "The Utilization of an 'Artificial Skin' Sensor for the Identification of Solid Objects." In *Proceedings of the Ninth International Symposium on Industrial Robots.* 1979.

Burrows, John F. "Computers and the Study of Literature." In *Computers and Written Texts,* ed. Christopher Butler. Oxford: Blackwell, 1992.

Caras, Pauline. "Literature and Computers: A Short Bibliography, 1980–1987." *College Literature* 15 (1988): 69–82.

Cohen, Gillian. *The Psychology of Cognition.* London: Academic, 1977.

Colby, K.M., et al. "Turing-Like Indistinguishability Tests for the Validation of Computer Simulation of Paranoid Processes." *Artificial Intelligence* 3 (1972): 199–221.

Corns, Thomas N., and Margarette E. Smith. "Literature." In *Information Technology in the Humanities: Tools, Techniques, and Applications,* ed. Sebastian Rahtz. Chichester and New York: Horwood and Wiley, 1987.

– "Computers in the Humanities: Methods and Applications in the Study of English Literature." *Literary and Linguistic Computing* 6 (1991): 127–30.

Dennett, C. Daniel. "Fast Thinking." *The Intentional Stance.* Cambridge, MA: MIT Press, 1987.

– *Consciousness Explained.* Boston: Little, Brown, 1991.

Dreyfus, Hubert. *What Computers Can't Do: A Critique of Artificial Reason.* New York: Harper & Row, 1972.

Fortier, Paul A. "Theory and Practice in the Use of Computers for the Study of Literature." In *Actes du VIIIe Congres de l'Association Internationale de Litterature Comparee/Proceedings of the 8th Congress of the International Comparative Literature Association,* eds. Bela Kopeczi and Gyorgy M. Vajda. Stuttgart: Bieber, 1980.

French, Robert M. "Sumcognition and the Limits of the Turing Test." *Mind* 99 (1990): 53–65.

Gregory, Richard, and Pauline K. Marstrand, eds. *Creative Intelligence.* Norwood, NJ: Ablex, 1987.

Gurewich, David. "Games Computers Play." *New Criterion* 7 (1989): 81–4.

Haugeland, John, ed. *Mind Design.* Cambridge, MA: MIT Press, 1981.

Hofstadter, Douglas R., and Daniel C. Dennett, eds. *The Mind's I: Fantasies and Reflections on Self and Soul.* New York: Basic, 1981.

Horn, William Dennis. "The Effect of the Computer on the Written Word." In *Sixth International Conference on Computers and the Humanities*, eds. Sarah K. Burton and Douglas D. Short. Rockville, MD: Computer Science Press, 1983.

Horowitz, Irving Louis. "Printed Words, Computers and Democratic Societies." *Virginia Quarterly Review* 59 (1983): 620–36.

Ide, Nancy M. "A Statistical Measure of Theme and Structure." *Computers and the Humanities* 23 (1989): 277–83.

Jacquette, Dale. "Who's Afraid of the Turing Test?" *Behavior and Philosophy* 20/21 (1993): 63–74.

Kasparov, Gary. "The Day That I Sensed a New Kind of Intelligence." *Time* (1 April 1996): 57.

Kern, Alfred, and James F. Sheridan. "BASIC Poetry: The Computer as Poet." In *Sixth International Conference on Computers and the Humanities*, eds. Sarah K. Burton and Douglas D. Short. Rockville, MD: Computer Science Press, 1983.

Lacey, K. "Factory Where Man Is a Mere Observer." *Machinery and Production Engineering*, 3 March 1982.

Leebaert, Derek, ed. *Technology 2001: The Future of Computing and Communications.* Cambridge, MA: MIT Press, 1991.

Lem, Stanislaw. "Smart Robots." Trans. Peter Swirski. *SPECTRUM*. Forthcoming.

Lenat, Douglas. "Eurisco: A Program That Learns New Heuristics and Domain Concepts." *Artificial Intelligence* 21 (March 1983): 61–98.

Liro, Joseph. "On Computers, Translation, and Stanislaw Lem." *Computers and Translation* 2 (1987): 89–104.

Marcus, Stephen. "Computers and the Poetic Muse." In *Sixth International Conference on Computers and the Humanities*, eds. Sarah K. Burton and Douglas D. Short. Rockville, MD: Computer Science Press, 1983.

Meehan, James R. "Tale-Spin, an Interactive Program That Writes Stories." In *Proceedings of the Fifth International Conference on Artificial Intelligence.* Vol. 1. Pittsburg, PA: Carnegie-Mellon University Department of Science, 1977.

MELPOMENE. *Bagabone, Hem 'I Die Now.* New York: Vantage, 1984.

Michie, Donald. *On Machine Intelligence.* 2d ed. Chichester, England: Ellis Horwood, 1986.

Michie, Donald, and Rory Johnston. *The Creative Computer: Machine Intelligence and Human Knowledge.* Harmondsworth, England: Viking, 1984.

Minsky, Marvin. "Why People Think Computers Can't." *AI Magazine* (fall 1982): 3–15.

Moor, James H. "An Analysis of the Turing Test." *Philosophical Studies* 30 (1976): 249–57.

Moto–oka, T., ed. "Fifth Generation Computer Systems." *Proceedings of the Conference in Tokyo, October 1981.* Amsterdam: JLPDEC/North Holland, 1982.

Myrsiades, Kostas, ed. "Literature and Computers." *College Literature* 15 (1988).

Negroponte, Nicholas. "The Return of the Sunday Painter." In *The Computer Age: A Twenty–Year View*, eds. Michael Dertouzos and Joel Moses. Cambridge, MA: MIT Press, 1979.

Niesz, Anthony J, and Normal N. Holland. "Interactive Fiction." *Critical Inquiry* 11 (1984): 110–29.

Ochs, Eric P, et al. "The Effects of Exposure to Different Sources of Sexual Information on Sexual Behaviour: Comparing a 'Sex-Expert System' to Other Educational Material." *Behavioural Research Methods, Instruments, & Computers* 25 (1993): 189–94.

– "Learning about Sex outside the Gutter: Attitudes towards a Computer Sex-Expert System." *Journal of Sex and Marital Therapy* 20 (summer 1994): 86–102.

Peat, F. David. *Artificial Intelligence: How Machines Think.* New York: Bean, 1988.

Peer, Willie van. "Quantitative Studies of Literature: A Critique and an Outlook." *Computers and the Humanities* 23 (1989): 301–7.

Potter, Rosanne G. "Statistical Analysis of Literature: A Retrospective on Computers and the Humanities, 1966–1990." *Computers and the Humanities* 25 (1991): 401–29.

RACTER [William Chamberlain, and Thomas Etter]. *The Policeman's Beard is Half Constructed.* New York: Warner, 1984.

Roberts, S. K. "Artificial Intelligence." *Byte* (September 1981): 164–78.

Robinson, William S. *Computers, Minds and Robots.* Philadelphia, PA: Temple University Press, 1992.

Roper, John P.G., ed. *Computers in Literary and Linguistic Research.* Paris: Champion, 1988.

Saxby, Steven. *The Age of Information.* New York: New York University Press, 1990.

Schank, Roger C. *Dynamic Memory: A Theory of Reminding and Learning in Computers and People.* Cambridge: Cambridge University Press, 1982.

Schwartz, Richard Alan. "New Possibilities for Computer Literature." In *Sixth International Conference on Computers and the Humanities,* eds. Sarah K. Burton and Douglas D. Short. Rockville, MD: Computer Science Press, 1983.

Searle, John. "Minds, Brains, and Programs." *The Behavioral and Brain Sciences* 3 (1980): 417–57.

– *Minds, Brains, and Science.* Cambridge, MA: Harvard University Press, 1984.

– "The Mystery of Consciousness." *New York Times Book Review,* 2 November 1965, 60–6.

Shurkin, Joel. *Engines of the Mind: A History of the Computer.* New York: Norton, 1984.

Simon, Herbert A., and Allen Newall. "Heuristic Problem Solving: The Next Advance in Operations Research." *Operations Research* 6 (1958): 1–10.

Simons, Geoff. *Are Computers Alive: Evolution and New Life Forms.* Boston: Birkhäuser, 1983.

Smith, Paul. "The Joke Machine: Communicating Traditional Humour Using Computers." In *Spoken in Jest,* ed. Gillian Bennett. Sheffield, England: Sheffield Academic Press, 1991.

"Software für die Seele." (Software for the Soul). *Der Spiegel,* 5 September 1994, 116–18.

Stine, G. Harry. *The Untold Story of the Computer Revolution.* New York: Arbour, 1985.

Swirski, Peter. "Computhors and Biterature: Machine-Written Fiction?" *SubStance* 70 (1993): 81–90.

Turing, Alan. "Computing Machinery and Intelligence." Reprinted in *Minds and Machines*, ed. Alan Ross Anderson. Englewood Cliffs, NJ: Prentice-Hall, 1964.

Weizenbaum, Joseph. *Computer Power and Human Reason.* San Francisco: W.H. Freeman.

Wiener, Norbert. *God and Golem Inc.* Cambridge, MA: MIT Press, 1964.

Index